Content Licensing

CHANDOS
PUBLISHING SERIES

Chandos' new series of books are aimed at all those individuals interested in publishing. They have been specially commissioned to provide the reader with an authoritative view of current thinking. If you would like a full listing of current and forthcoming titles, please visit our website www.chandospublishing.com or email info@chandospublishing.com or telephone +44 (0) 1223 891358.

New authors: we are always pleased to receive ideas for new titles. If you would like to write a book for Chandos, please contact Dr Glyn Jones on e-mail gjones@chandospublishing.com or telephone number +44 (0) 1993 848726.

Bulk orders: some organisations buy a number of copies of our books. If you are interested in doing this, we would be pleased to discuss a discount. Please email info@chandospublishing.com or telephone +44(0) 1223 891358.

Content Licensing

Buying and Selling Digital Resources

MICHAEL UPSHALL

Chandos Publishing
Oxford • Cambridge • New Delhi

Chandos Publishing
TBAC Business Centre
Avenue 4
Station Lane
Witney
Oxford OX28 4BN
UK
Tel: +44 (0) 1993 848726
Email: info@chandospublishing.com
www.chandospublishing.com

Chandos Publishing is an imprint of Woodhead Publishing Limited

Woodhead Publishing Limited
Abington Hall
Granta Park
Great Abington
Cambridge CB21 6AH
UK
www.woodheadpublishing.com

First published in 2009

ISBN:
978 1 84334 333 2

Typeset by Domex e-Data Pvt. Ltd.
Printed in the UK and USA.

Contents

List of figures and tables

Figures

Tables

About the author

Michael Upshall is a content licensing and information strategy consultant. A co-founder of Helicon Publishing, the UK reference publisher, he was publisher of *The Hutchinson Encyclopedia*, the UK's first online encyclopedia, and set up a successful licensing programme with over 20 regular feeds both to the UK and to the US. He has worked with several major publishers, including Pearson, Dorling Kindersley and Random House. His content licensing experience includes managing projects for JISC Collections, and advising publishers such as Continuum and The Stationery Office (TSO), and information-rich organisations such as Building Research Establishment (BRE). He has also managed digital media projects at web design agencies such as Abacus eMedia and Reading Room. As a content management consultant his clients include Henley Management College and the Royal Botanic Gardens, Kew. He is a regular contributor to *InPublishing* Magazine. In his spare time he edits *Elucidate*, the journal for information professionals belonging to the UK Electronic Information Group (UKeiG).

The author can be contacted at michael@consultmu.co.uk

Foreword

Today's publishers, as content creators or purchasers, are equipped with the notion that digital content is the centre of any new product discussion and strategy. Yet they still might prefer to live by the perhaps less complicated business models around the development and distribution of a printed book. Times have changed. Content still remains a core asset for any publisher, but one now needs to look at what happens once content is digitised: there are now many more paths available for distribution, purchase and access. One of the most common paths for distribution of digital content is to host your content on your own platform. A reasonable venture, but one that comes at a large initial cost and potentially mandates that the only place a consumer can access *your* content is on *your* platform. One can probably argue that publishers could make a sustainable business from self-hosting, but there is also another path available, a very wide one, which can provide new revenue streams that are certainly welcomed during these difficult economic times.

I am speaking of content licensing. Whether you are producing your own content digitally, or are in the market to purchase the same, the business of buying and selling digital resources through licensing models should be at the forefront of any discussions of how your firm will survive moving forward. Licensing content is by no means a new concept. But add in the 'digital' to the process, and many new challenges, and perhaps hurdles, find their way to your legal, editorial, marketing and sales teams' everyday planning. The concept of digital rights management alone is a scary one. But, as mentioned, this is a very wide territory, which means there are many different paths you can take. Knowing which paths to take will allow you to maximise your content's potential.

Content Licensing: Buying and Selling Digital Content is an excellent map that goes into great detail on how to navigate down these paths successfully. The mass of perfectly illustrated industry examples alone will give you an excellent start in understanding all the many models and best practices that have been in the forefront of this new era of licensing. As a publisher who has embarked on many digital licensing adventures over the last five years, I was humbled by how much more there is to learn after reading this book. Whether you are a publisher using the most sophisticated licensing models, or one just starting out with licensing, this is a must read, and don't be shy with it, your entire team should read it as well.

Rolf A. Janke
Vice President, Publisher
SAGE Reference
May 2009

Preface

Buying and selling digital resources seems at first sight a straightforward activity. Yet in practice it raises several issues, given that it is placed at the intersection of publishing and information technology, cutting across several self-contained sectors: although content licensing is easy to get involved with, it can lead to a transformation of existing business models for the organisation. It includes contract issues (exclusive or non-exclusive? What kind of subscription?), technical questions (selecting formats and standards, deciding how to store and to deliver the content) and business models (just because content is licensed, there is no guarantee it will be accessed – you cannot assume that if you build it they will come), all in an industry that at times appears to be wavering with uncertainty about fundamental principles, such as whether content should be free or paid. All these topics are inter-related: decisions about storage formats affect how and where the content can be delivered; contract issues can prevent content licensing taking place at all. Although there have been books about negotiating rights, and about content management, there is a dearth of books devoted to content licensing covering all the above topics, so I hope this title meets a need.

A book of this kind will include a fair number of technical terms; a glossary is provided at the back of the book, in addition to terms being explained at their first use.

I would like to thank many people for their help in answering questions and reading early drafts of this book. Thanks to Patrick Gibbins, for answering questions on map licensing; to Dr David Penfold, whose detailed assessment of the text improved it dramatically; to Oxford Brookes University Library, for allowing me access to their rich collection of information titles; and to Logos Bible Software, for providing screenshots. I would like to thank Dr Glyn Jones of Chandos Publishing for his patience and advice, and Jane Anson for reading the text. Of course, despite all the helpful suggestions I have received, I accept responsibility for remaining errors.

Finally, I should add a disclaimer: I am a member (unpaid) of the Credo Reference advisory board.

Oxford, May 2009.

Introduction

Providing digital content has been a major agent of change in education, in business and in libraries over the last 30 or so years. Whereas much content was available only at specific times and on specific days of the week in libraries, it can today be available online 24 hours a day and seven days a week. In addition, the quantity of content available online has grown out of all proportion. Who provides all this content, and how does it appear on licensed sites? And how can anyone be making money out of it, when so much of it seems to be available free of charge to the end user? How is its usage tracked?

The opportunities for content owners, creators and institutions from licensing content are substantial, quite apart from the benefit to the end user. This book examines whether there is a business case for content licensing, and examines the practical and technical issues involved in selecting, capturing and organising that content for licensing. By its nature, content licensing cuts across traditional publishing boundaries such as production and editing. In addition, content licensing often straddles several areas that were formerly kept separate, between books and magazines, between journals and articles, and between published content of any kind and databases.

This book provides an overview of content licensing, with practical recommendations for those involved in licensing, including publishers, aggregators and institution managers, as well as recommendations for best practice in specific markets, and with specific media. Some parts of the book may only be relevant in particular markets or particular situations, but my experience makes me believe it is worth understanding the whole gamut of content licensing, because what has been learnt in one market (for example, journals) can prove to be highly applicable in another (such as books). By examining the licensing opportunities, benefits and drawbacks of each sector, readers should get an overview of the entire market and how their part of the licensing world compares with the rest of it. In addition, the checklists of points to consider at each stage of licensing content may prove cost- and time-effective to those involved.

1.1 Why license content?

Because this is a vital question for content owners, perhaps the most important question of all, it is touched on several times in this book (see also section 5.15). The case for digital delivery of content is well established, comprising four main areas: availability, cost of production, geographical reach and new market opportunity.

1. Availability: a book has to be bought, or borrowed, before it is read, and this requires travelling to a library or bookshop. Digital content, by comparison, is available at the desktop immediately.
2. Cost of production: the cost of creating additional copies for online content is zero; even the cost of producing physical media such as CD-ROMs is low, compared with print.
3. Geographical reach: there is no intrinsic geographical limitation on electronic sales. Content, particularly in online form, is available anywhere via the Web. There may be limitations on bandwidth in some regions, but it is increasingly the case that worldwide availability of online content is the norm. The logistical problems of moving printed copies of stock from one continent to another disappear at a stroke.
4. No alternative: the stark reality facing many content owners is that content is being accessed in digital form. Unless they move their content to where the users are, they face a shrinking market.

The market for digital content is expanding steadily, whether in business and professional publishing, in STM, or most recently in trade books. Reed Elsevier has ruthlessly sold off print-based divisions of its organisation to concentrate on digital publishing.[1] Sales of books via smartphones and mobiles, as well as e-book readers, are showing a dramatic increase (see section 4.11).

Quite apart from the case for providing content digitally, there are some specific advantages to be gained by licensing content:

- Extending market reach. Licensed content is typically available as part of a paid service. However, paid services are only used by a small proportion of the total number of possible users. The total number of paid services that any user will access is limited, and a case can be made for providing content via a number of collections.

- Content licensing facilitates market segmentation. The same content can be licensed at different prices to specific segments, such as higher education, commercial purchasers and government. Segmentation of markets is also possible by providing alternative access routes to different groups in the community, for example as a member benefit to organisations (see section 5.14). Segmentation need not only be by price. Some aggregated music sites, for example, provide higher quality recorded music to individual subscribers than via delivery to institutions.

- Speed to market. By licensing content, a publisher can reach a market more rapidly than would be possible by setting up a dedicated content platform. Speed to market can be vital when new markets are created, for example by taking advantage of a new technology such as the e-book reader (see section 4.12).

- For the publisher, licensing content provides an excellent opportunity for testing a market with little capital outlay, and minimal business risk (see section 6.8.1 for more on this).

- Moreover, content licensing enables market extension: the creation of new markets that could not be reached using existing channels. For example, several picture agencies created an additional market for licensed images by providing specific metadata linked to UK curriculum requirements and then licensing the images to aggregators (see the case study in section 4.5.1). It is often the case that domain-specific metadata enable new sales to be made.

For a print-based publisher, adding a digital content licensing sale may complement or substitute for sales in other media. Of course, some see content licensing as an opportunity, whereas others see it as a threat. But there is little doubt that revenue from digital sales comprises a steadily increasing proportion of total revenue to content owners, although industry-wide sales figures across various media are difficult to obtain. Content licensing enables the mix between digital delivery and traditional media to be managed most effectively. There is no guarantee that revenue from licensing can fully compensate for the decline that many publishers experience in the print market, but this is not an argument for not licensing content – far from it. Content licensing together with digital publishing may well provide a higher total revenue than print sales alone.

Perhaps the most convincing argument in favour of content licensing is its effect on the market. It is well known that external changes in a market can cause a major redistribution of market share, and this redrawing of the boundaries between the market players may be more powerful and more dramatic than any advertising and marketing budget could achieve. There are plenty of examples of seemingly stable markets where the established market leader has struggled once the market has experienced a substantial technological change. Kodak, for so many years the dominant player in the traditional film-processing market, has found it difficult to achieve a similar position in the digital photography market: the existing market looks likely to disappear entirely within a few years, and the new market currently sees Kodak at a much smaller market share. Other companies have moved more quickly to take advantage of the profound change in technology to grab market share in the digital photography and related markets.

Through content licensing, a number of new aggregators such as NetLibrary and ebrary have become established as major sources of content. These are not companies that attract headlines as dotcom pioneers; nonetheless, their confirmed position in the digital content delivery market is clear. This book contains several examples of successful aggregators of this kind.

Perhaps because their rise has been less noticeable than that of companies such as Google or Amazon, content licensing companies have received less attention. This is true both from outside and within publishing. Electronic rights, which includes content licensing, takes up only two (albeit lengthy) chapters in Lynette Owen's book *Selling Rights* (fifth edition, 2006) (a list of further reading is given at the back of this book). Yet for many publishers, one of the few markets that display opportunities for substantial growth is the digital publishing area. For some years this was more the case for professional (business-to-business) publishers, with the content licensing opportunities being lower for fiction and mass-market publishers. But the situation has changed with the rapidly changing technology on which content licensing is based. The first e-book readers, for example, were cumbersome and not easy to use. Today, now that better-functioning readers are available, the e-book market looks likely to transform digital sales of fiction at a stroke. For more about e-book readers, see section 4.12.

For many publishers, content licensing marks the transition of content into digital published form, which can have the following benefits:

- Full-text searching for words anywhere in the content provides an immediate benefit for users.

- Individual titles can be made available as part of a larger collection, the whole being more valuable than the sum of the parts. For example, a website with 15 different translations of the Bible has value as a convenient single source for comparing Bible translations.

- A major work or a collection of thematically related works, such as the *Nature Encyclopedia of Life Sciences*, or the *Routledge Encyclopedia of Philosophy*, or *The New Grove Dictionary of Music*, can become a major subject portal in its own right, with a dedicated sales staff selling subscriptions to the resource.

Although these developments may seem incidental to content licensing, they provide excellent examples of the benefits to the user from the licensing process.

1.2 Who is this book for?

A book that attempts to explain content licensing from only the licensor's or the licensee's point of view is doomed to failure. If it is considered only from the point of view of the publisher or the aggregator, the whole process is impossible to understand. Moreover, content licensing usually represents an ongoing relationship between parties. Reaching a harmonious meeting point of interests between the partners enables all involved to benefit, and hence increases the likelihood of them working together again. Therefore, this book considers content licensing from several standpoints:

1. Authors or content creators: without them, none of the rest is possible, although paradoxically the creator may be at some distance from the point of sale in a content-licensing relationship.

2. The owner of rights to the intellectual property (who may not be the same as the content creator).

3. The vendor of the content: this may be the rights owner, or may be employed by the rights owner to act on their behalf.

4. The aggregator, or the owner of the channel by which that content is transmitted.

5. The buyer – typically an information manager.

6. Software solutions providers, who build the software systems for delivering content, and for content retrieval.

Of course, the most important role in the whole process is the end user, who may gain access to the content in a wide variety of ways: direct from the publisher, or via the aggregator or a library, or by a combination of these. By being in this way at some distance from the content creator, it is all too easy to lose sight of the effect of content licensing on the end user and how it benefits him or her.

Most readers will have experience of one or more of the roles described above. It may seem that any book about publishing must cover most of these roles, yet such is the segmented nature of the information industry that it is relatively rare for one title to consider both book and serial publishing, or both academic and professional publishing, or both content creation and content licensing. Considering distinct areas of the information world or simply of the publishing industry may be more innovative than might at first be thought. The story of the journal publisher from one of the larger academic publishers is not entirely apocryphal: he was attending a conference about XML standards, and when asked about the XML standards used by the book division of his own company, he answered that he had no idea – he was attending the conference to find that out himself. It should not be necessary to attend a conference to find out what is happening inside your own publishing company, but perhaps this book can help by revealing some of the similarities and differences.

Much of current practice in content licensing is informed not by detailed formal knowledge, but by knowledge that has been gained by experience and by word of mouth. Increasingly, there is a body of formal knowledge, but this book describes a mixture of formal and informal knowledge, of current practice, and some pointers to where more formal knowledge may be gained.

1.3 What this book includes

This study of content licensing begins with a brief historical overview. The way content licensing works today is based on decisions and changes that are perhaps unconnected today to digital licensing, but which were of significance at the time. Frequently, an understanding of these origins can help explain the current situation with licensing.

Following on, the book describes the main areas that need to be understood by anyone involved in the content-licensing business: the process, the current business models, contracts and terminology, and technical details. The book is written from a neutral standpoint, i.e. not favouring the author, publisher, aggregator or library. Some space is devoted to how content is searched and retrieved, because this is a fundamental part of the new value proposition that electronic content provides. As a how-to guide, this book contains recommendations in each section, but the last chapter summarises those suggestions into lists for authors, libraries, publishers and aggregators.

At various points the book includes case studies, which exemplify an interesting development in content licensing, or which show an aspect of content licensing that might be relevant in other areas. The term 'content licensing' is interpreted broadly here to include portals set up by publishers to provide digital editions of their own works, which of course is not technically licensing. This is because the boundary between providing third-party content and publishers' own content is a fine one, and the business and strategic thinking that has to take place for the first to happen is largely the same as for the second; and for librarians and for end users, there is no difference. Several of the case studies show publishers moving from one to the other, for example, taking advantage of digital publishing to create a themed collection of articles.

1.4 What this book does not include

This book is a general overview of content licensing, attempting to compare how licensing takes place with different media, such as text, and still and moving images. The field is already too wide to cover each of these licensing areas in exhaustive detail, covering, for example, all the many codecs (decoding software) used by audio and video. The aim is simply to provide anyone involved in the licensing chain with enough background to be aware that several different business and technical models can be used, from publishing via an aggregator, to publishing direct to end users.

By its very nature, content licensing is an interdisciplinary activity, covering several different domains with more or less detail. Thus, for example, more detailed information about serials licensing is available elsewhere, just as more detail on what constitutes copyright can be found in more specialised resources. The lack of detailed guidance in these areas is compensated for at least partially by revealing details from other areas of content licensing that may be less familiar to the reader.

The content licensing market is a young and rapidly developing business, straddling several different media industries, and no single book can hope to keep entirely up to date in all these areas. However, most of the business cases, as well as details of contracts and details of what kind of content service to provide for end users, will have similar features and similar issues.

1.5 Why is content licensing so important?

The growing importance of content licensing as a discipline leads to the risk of the establishment of a discipline called 'content licensing': there is the danger that as soon as someone in an organisation has 'content licensing' in their job title, everyone else in the process abandons responsibility and knowledge of the subject, delegating it to the designated expert. This would be a shame, because content licensing is in many ways a microcosm of the entire information-delivery process; it is successful only when the right content is made available in the right format, is easily retrieved, and put to effective use that meets the user's needs: this is essentially a collaborative process. It requires the input and understanding of several people in a number of organisations.

A recent French report into the future of licensing summarised the subject quite neatly:[2] 'By becoming digital, the printed book becomes a book right.' The best way to think about printed books, in other words, is as just one more expression of the many licensing opportunities for content. This book is all about how such licensing works.

Notes

1. For example, 'Reed Elsevier to sell education unit', *International Herald Tribune* 16 February 2007.
2. «Rapport sur le livre numérique», Ministère de la culture et de la communication, June 2008, by Bruno Patino, *http://www.culture.gouv.fr/culture/actualites/index-rapports.htm*

2

Brief history of content licensing

Content licensing has been taking place for longer than might be imagined; it certainly pre-dates digital content delivery. Probably newspapers were the first content licensors, with their practice of syndicating content, reselling articles from one newspaper to another, from the mid-nineteenth century. Another claim to the earliest content-licensing activity is held by picture libraries, the oldest of which, Alinari of Florence, was founded in 1852. Picture agencies hold content authored by third parties and license the images on their behalf. Radio and TV syndication flourished before the PC had even been thought of. After an interlude with CD-ROMs, the Internet has delivered the most powerful content delivery service. Earlier examples could probably be found.

Each of these examples showed one principle clearly: due to the economies of scale from reuse of content, licensing content can be far more profitable than using content once only. That much is obvious, but content licensing in all its forms has also shown what is perhaps slightly less intuitive: that large collections of content tend to be disproportionately more popular than small ones – what those in the trade call the bucket principle. Libraries want, within reason, the largest possible collection within their means. Intermediaries want to process the largest possible quantity of data. Users want to go to the smallest number of sources. It is usually no more difficult to set up, digitise and license a hundred titles than to do the same with a single title. In other words, the licensing process tends to be associated with large-scale collections, as seen with some of the most familiar photo agencies, such as Corbis and Getty with their vast collections.

However, the tendency towards single collections of content has always been paralleled by thematic groups – smaller collections of content around a common theme. This has been true of online journal collections for years, and is increasing in the world of licensed books.

Because the cost of replication for digital content is negligible, digital content licensing has spread in a way never thought possible for earlier forms of licensing. As we shall see later, an image can be selected from hundreds and then downloaded in high-resolution form within seconds via the Internet; a huge difference from 20 years ago, when sample images were sent for selection by post.

2.1 Syndication and news agencies

Syndication was a precursor of the modern content-licensing business. The reuse of content has been practised successfully for many years in print by the syndication of newspaper articles, both news and opinion columns. The first news agency was Agence France-Presse (AFP), founded in 1835, although it was known as Agence Havas until 1945. Other news agencies, such as Reuters, Associated Press and (in the UK) the Press Association follow similar principles: they create news stories and then license the content for use by a specific newspaper or magazine. The practice of columnists syndicating articles dates back to the same period – one of the first was 'Jenny June' (Jane Cunningham Croly), who was writing syndicated articles from the 1850s.[1] Cartoon strips are another well-known example of syndicated content; one of the earliest is *The Yellow Kid*, which appeared in the *New York World* in 1895.[2] In the case of cartoons, several companies appeared (and some still exist) specialising in nothing but syndicated content. Universal Press Syndicate (*Doonesbury*, *Garfield*) is one of the largest and best-known.

Syndication also takes place with sound and TV broadcasts, not only with comedy and drama series, but also news and chat shows; the '100 episode' mark is widely thought to be the number of episodes a TV series has to create to be considered worth selling on for syndication rights. Today, syndication lives on in a rather different form as Web syndication (see section 5.4).

2.2 Licensed images

Almost as soon as photography was invented, the advantages of holding a library of images for licensing purposes became apparent. For a publisher, instead of acquiring a new photo by commissioning a photographer to travel to take it – a slow and expensive business – a representative image (of a building, a place, a job, an item of clothing, etc.), if it were available, could be provided for use at a lower price. In this way the stock photography library was born. Alinari, in 1852, was probably the first;

other pioneers include Keystone (today American Stock Photography), founded in the 1920s, and Hulton (today part of Getty), founded in 1938.

In a similar way, stock file and video footage have been available since the earliest days of the movies. The longest-established stock film footage company in the US is Producers Library, founded in 1957, although of course footage was being reused from the earliest days of the cinema.

Both syndicated news companies and picture agencies established the principle well before 1900 that a content-based company could thrive without being a publisher in its own right, simply by licensing the content to third parties. Content licensing, therefore, is not such a new idea.

2.3 Abstracting services

Abstracts have a far older history than syndication and picture licensing. The first is thought to be the *Journal des scavans* (the 'Journal of the Learned') founded in Paris in 1665.[3] Not only was it the first abstracting journal, it also provided a cumulative index after ten years of publication. But the main growth of abstracting services came with the foundation of the professional societies in the late nineteenth and early twentieth centuries. *Engineering Index*, for example, was founded in 1884, *Chemical Abstracts* in 1907.

Chemical Abstracts, the most important abstracting journal in chemistry, was a pioneer in online databases. Three-dimensional representations of chemical structures were being captured as long ago as 1965. An online version was launched in 1980, using a proprietary graphics terminal. A search for a chemical structure could therefore be carried out and the results viewed more than 25 years ago. However, this service was for specialist information professionals only.[4] Like most of the abstracting publications, *Chemical Abstracts* was at first compiled entirely by volunteers; exceptionally, in the case of *Chemical Abstracts*, the volunteer involvement continued until the 1960s (and it was the increasingly sophisticated metadata coding requirements, not a lack of volunteers, that made *Chemical Abstracts* switch to paid compilers). One of the first fully online services was MEDLINE, launched in 1970 (see section 2.4.3).

2.4 The early commercial databases

Online databases came into being as a result of the explosive growth in science literature. The first of these databases were in medicine, education and space research.

Note that, from their introduction, commercial databases were (and still are) sold on a subscription basis – there is no ongoing right to access the material. Once the subscription has expired, the purchaser has nothing to show for their money, unlike the owner of a printed book.

The online content services described in this section were mainly based around licensed content. They are considered in this book quite simply because content cannot be licensed unless it has some location where it can be bought, sold and retrieved. Without the early online databases, content licensing as we know it would probably not have appeared. Even today they still represent a large proportion by value of all content licensing activity. It is difficult, in other words, to consider the goods, without also discussing the shop, and the shop window.

2.4.1 Dialog

Dialog was the leading provider of online resources in the 1980s and 1990s. Although Dialog as a company only existed from 1972, the first Dialog service began in 1966, by a team of Lockheed staff at Lockheed's Palo Alto Research Laboratory. Dialog was therefore the world's first large-scale online information-retrieval system. It is interesting to see how several of the features present at its launch do not appear in current search engines such as Google:

- Command-line searching (rather than a Windows-style search box)
- Interactive, so searchers can amend searches
- Index display
- Payment based on number of hours used.

This indicates how business information systems were (and to some extent still are) geared towards professional researchers with considerable information skills. Google, of course, in its basic interface, lacks any kind of search refinement capability. Dialog's first customers were in space research: first NASA, then the European Space Research Organization, and the US Atomic Energy Commission (AEC). These organisations had (for the time) unparalleled quantities of information and a need to access this information rapidly and intelligently. Initially, the Dialog system accessed NASA's own content. It was only later that Dialog had the idea of holding third-party content, and providing a simplified search interface so that the client needed no computing skills, simply a terminal providing access. The first customer to have content hosted by Dialog was ERIC (the US Educational Resources Information Center).

Dialog was sold to Knight Ridder in 1988, and was acquired by Thomson Corporation in 2000. It was sold again to ProQuest in 2008 (see ProQuest in section 7.4.2).

2.4.2 ORBIT

Like Dialog, SDC ORBIT was created out of a large-scale commercial environment, in this case, RAND Corporation. SDC's first customers were the US Air Force, and the National Library of Medicine; they demonstrated the use of a teletype terminal (a primitive device resembling a typewriter providing access to a remote mainframe computer) for searching the ERIC database in 1971. The first release of ORBIT software was the same year. Astonishingly, ORBIT carried out a survey of 7000 would-be users in 1972 and found that only 1% of those surveyed were interested in a commercial information-retrieval service. Commented Carlos Cuadra of SDC:[5] 'I was a Ph.D. psychologist and I thought I knew how to do surveys. But I finally decided that my survey was wrong, or the respondents were wrong.' They proceeded to build the service anyway, running ERIC, the best-known US bibliography of educational articles, and then *Chemical Abstracts*, and the service was a commercial success. Subsequently, ORBIT was sold to Pergamon Press, and in 1994 sold to Questel.

2.4.3 BRS/Search

BRS, short for Bibliographic Retrieval Services, had its origins in the provision of MEDLINE,[6] one of the leading indexing services for biological and medical sciences, to universities, dating back to 1968. It began commercial operation in 1976, and continued under various changes of ownership until it was bought by Open Text Corporation in 2001. After using third-party search software initially (STAIRS), BRS developed its own database and retrieval software.

Why was BRS so successful in medical searching? Jan Egeland of BRS explains:[7]

> This was a library-based service. Getting medical information out faster was becoming critical. In the medical library environment, people struggled through Index Medicus — it was an indexed

system, not full-text — and they had to go to the reference librarian for help. There was an 8,000-term vocabulary. If people didn't know the vocabulary, they couldn't find anything.

A full-text indexing service clearly provided an enormous step forward; in fact, the librarians were astonished even to find that BRS could index every word in a document title (quite apart from the full text):

> You could sit down and plunk in 'Ritalin' and everything with 'Ritalin' in the title came up. The librarians were beside themselves. Probably the single biggest event that I remember is the looks on their faces at the meeting when we said, 'OK, you asked for it; you got it.'

Why were the pioneers of information retrieval like Dialog, ORBIT and BRS so important for content licensing? Because they established one of the first principles of content licensing, that by providing a full-text index to a very large quantity of text, a new market could be created, as access to that information was now quicker and therefore more cost-effective.

2.5 The age of CD-ROMs

CD-ROM technology was invented by Philips and Sony Corporation in 1982, and started to be widely used towards 1990. Because of its vast capacity, some 660 MB per disk, it was first used as a competitor to existing online products; this was the basis of SilverPlatter's growth, by taking sales away from Dialog, since CD-ROM usage incurred no hourly fees, unlike online subscription services.

CD-ROMs are still used today to provide content in some contexts, such as educational publishing. But there are substantial problems with CD-ROMs (and with their successor, DVD-ROMs), which make them less than ideal for content licensing:

- Once manufactured, there is no effective way of updating the content on a CD-ROM. Some content providers managed to create a hybrid CD-ROM with online updates, but the result tended to have all the problems of both formats without the advantages of either.
- CD-ROMs often require retrieval and display software to be loaded to the user's PC to access the content, and it is cumbersome to update that software without an online connection.

- Although CD-ROMs can be networked, there are performance problems in providing simultaneous access to a single CD.
- Early CD-ROMs had little standardisation; different products often made use of different DLLs (dynamic-link libraries), which conflicted when more than one CD-ROM was installed on a PC.
- Despite the capacity of a CD-ROM, if the information does not fit on one disk, it is cumbersome to spread the content across several disks.
- CD-ROMs have very slow access time compared with searching for content from a hard drive or from a modern online connection.
- There was little standardisation of user interfaces on CD-ROMs. Each CD-ROM required a new learning process for the user to become familiar with navigation and with searching.
- Despite claims that CD-ROMs were indestructible, many of them stopped working after being frequently handled and reloaded.

Nonetheless, CD-ROMs provided a dramatic explosion to the content licensing business. There were clear reasons for this:

- CD-ROMs are a physical asset that can be bought and sold like books (although some were sold with licence conditions that prevented their being resold).
- CD-ROMs are read-only, so the integrity of the published information remains intact. This is similar to the reassurance provided by PDF for publishers.
- Every CD-ROM can have a unique customised interface that is designed specifically for that product. The requirement for a unique interface may have been less common than most publishers believed, yet for some products it enabled highly effective searching and retrieval.
- The faults that made CDs difficult to update made them more attractive to publishers. They are simple to sell, and the updated content can then be sold again, on a new CD-ROM. This meant either a subscription sale or a completely new transaction, both of these options being welcome to the publisher.

2.5.1 SilverPlatter

SilverPlatter was, as might be imagined from the name suggests, a CD-ROM publisher, one of the first companies to produce CD-ROMs commercially, mostly for the library and academic market.[8] It was founded in 1983 by Bela Hatvany, with Ron Reitdyk as the first CEO of the US company, and concentrated on medical, scientific and business subjects, including the MEDLINE database. In fact, SilverPlatter was about as pioneering in this area as it is possible to be: it was involved in the initial High Sierra meeting in 1985 that determined the format for CD-ROM to incorporate text, audio and multimedia content on a single disk; this format was subsequently adopted as ISO-9660. SilverPlatter was one of the first companies to create CD-ROMs for both PCs and Macintosh computers. It also created its own retrieval software, SPIRS (SilverPlatter Information Retrieval Software). SilverPlatter's best-known product was an edition of ERIC (see section 2.4.2). A further reason for SilverPlatter's dramatic growth was that its prices for accessing content via CD-ROM undercut rival online services, for example MEDLINE via Dialog – an example of new technology overturning a market equilibrium.

The company created methods for networking CD-ROMs (in 1988), and then introduced ERL, the Electronic Reference Library, which enabled searching across several databases, regardless of location. Online versions followed soon after, together with more innovation in the provision of pay-as-you-go access in 1997. However, SilverPlatter's link with a specific technology was also its limitation; it remained in most users' perceptions a CD-ROM publisher, and other companies that were focused more exclusively on online developments took advantage of this view. The company was bought by Wolters Kluwer in 2001.

2.5.2 Case study: Microsoft Bookshelf

Microsoft has been the source of many technical innovations, and some have been unfairly overshadowed by parts of the company with a higher profile in different markets. In the content-licensing world, Microsoft Bookshelf (Figure 2.1) can claim to be a true pioneer. Bookshelf was perhaps not the very first ready-built collection of reference titles, but it was undoubtedly the slickest, and as a result largely created the reference compilation product. Although it was created for the end-user market, Bookshelf has subsequently influenced the content-licensing industry in several other areas. The idea of Bookshelf was simple: if an encyclopedia and dictionary are useful, how much more useful could they be in a digital product linked by a single search interface? Still more useful would be a collection including a dictionary of quotations, a chronology of history and an atlas. This was the composition of the first edition of

Figure 2.1   Microsoft Bookshelf, 1992 edition

Microsoft Bookshelf in 1987. It is indicative of how fast the market was moving that Microsoft had only created a CD-ROM division in 1986.[9] Based on a proprietary search engine, the first edition of Bookshelf pre-dated MS Windows. Bookshelf was therefore innovative both as a business initiative and from a technical point of view, being considerably slicker in performance than most other online products of its time, proving that old adage that the whole can be greater than the sum of its parts. It was the inspiration for subsequent online collections such as KnowUK and KnowEurope (see Chadwyck-Healey below), which followed the same model of licensing the entire content, but creating added value by providing the titles together. Bookshelf itself was published annually until 2000, by which time it was being superseded by online collections.

2.5.3 Chadwyck-Healey

This pioneer licensing company was founded in 1973 and sold to ProQuest in 1999. In its 26-year history, it was a remarkable innovator in academic content licensing. Chadwyck's goal was to create collections so vast that they became a required resource for academic study. So, for example, large-scale or complete editions of Goethe, English Poetry (including some 160,000 poems), Early English Prose Fiction and English Verse Drama were all initially created as collections on CD-ROMs, and only later provided as an online database. Academics loved it because of its power as a research tool: this was the first time they had been provided the opportunity to search for terms across a whole genre. Other major collections that were digitised included Migne's *Patrologia Latina* (all 221 volumes of it, originally published 1844–1855), a collection of the writings of the Christian Fathers from AD 200 to 1216. The *Patrologia* was initially sold at a price of £4,293, for an annual subscription for two to four simultaneous users, or £32,550 for an outright purchase on CD-ROM.

Subsequently, the three English literature collections were grouped together in one larger online resource called LION (Literature Online). It is difficult to imagine with what a sense of astonishment and wonder these collections were greeted when they first appeared. For example, here is Catherine Alexander, of the University of Birmingham, in 1999, reviewing the Chadwyck-Healey titles:[10]

> I return the review material and my LION password with great reluctance and make a strong recommendation to all lecturers, students and researchers to use this fine resource. It's a healthy reminder of one's own ignorance and an exciting opportunity to remedy the situation.

This was despite the reviewer having to search across multiple CD-ROMs, or to use a dial-up modem for an Internet connection.

Paradoxically, Chadwyck-Healey encountered difficulties with the arrival of online publishing. Libraries were happy to buy outright, even at a site licence price of £26,500, a copy of *English Poetry*, since they then owned it and felt free to make what use of it they wished. The same libraries were far less willing to pay a smaller amount for an annual subscription to the same resource, with nothing to show at the end of the subscription period for their outlay. That discussion still exists today, with many aggregators offering two models of content licensing: either a subscription or a 'perpetual access' model (see section 9.13).

Later major collections were developed exclusively for online use, including KnowUK and KnowEurope. These titles aimed to replicate the collection any user would have from a small public reference library collection, and again demonstrated the 'whole greater than the sum of the parts' technique. By combining standard reference titles such as *Who's Who*, *Whitaker's Almanack* and *Social Trends*, Chadwyck-Healey (by now part of ProQuest) created a powerful reference collection, and ultimately one that became a brand name in its own right.

For the subsequent history of Chadwyck-Healey as part of ProQuest, see section 7.4.2.

2.6 AOL and CompuServe

These two companies were responsible for much of the dramatic development of the Web. The content model they provided was that of the 'walled garden', content that was available only to subscribers (although this model was later expanded to offer subscribers additional content in return for further payment). The 'holiday camp' model, where everything was free once you were inside the gate, gave a powerful demonstration of the appeal of online content, particularly when combined with interactive features. AOL had begun as a provider of games to desktop PCs, and from 1991 provided a pioneering graphical user interface and interactive features such as chatrooms; it was the chatrooms that were the basis of its success. Following its merger in 2000 with Time Warner, AOL has had a steady decline in subscribers, as the Web moved increasingly towards the advertising-driven model of many of today's sites. Nonetheless, at its peak it was described as 'the most successful Internet-based company'.[11] AOL showed what can be achieved with the walled-garden model, with many managed discussion groups led by enthusiastic volunteers, and was not afraid to be innovative. For example, it hosted regular 'talk to the expert' sessions to promote its online encyclopedia content.

CompuServe was founded in 1969 in Columbus, Ohio, but only began providing online services in 1977. Whereas AOL was aimed at the average user, CompuServe was always pitched at more technically adept and business-orientated users. It provided financial and business information, but its most successful areas were based around interactive forums. CompuServe was partially merged with AOL in 1988.[12]

Both AOL and CompuServe were initially based around time-based access, with payments per minute. Although both companies moved to a subscription-based model, providing unlimited access to counter the growing popularity of the World Wide Web, they did not respond sufficiently during the 1990s to counter the growth of free (and wider-ranging) content from public sites.

2.6.1 Case study: Helicon Publishing

The pioneer database companies described above were creators of technology and creators of markets, out of which was created an industry of buying and selling content licensing. One of many companies that was caught up in this new world was Helicon Publishing. Helicon's immediate origin was a management buy-out of the reference list at Random House UK, in 1992. Random House was (and is) a general trade publisher, and did not see reference publishing as core to its activities. So the reference list, comprising initially little more than one single-volume encyclopedia, *The Hutchinson Encyclopedia*, a venerable title first published around 1944, was allowed to become independent. Helicon created a database of reference text and images, and soon discovered its opportunity. Of all the types of publishing, dictionaries and encyclopedias forced publishers into electronic publishing faster than any other (except perhaps directories). What was grandiosely termed 'electronic publishing' was primitive indeed: at the beginning 'digital' simply meant digital storage for print publication. The first database systems for publishers were for compilation and storage rather than for electronic publication – to hold content in digital form did not imply digital dissemination, even if it facilitated the process. Because an encyclopedia, like a directory, comprises tens of thousands of short, self-contained entries that are at the same time interlinked, it makes sense to use an automated system to compile, edit, update and output this content, and to hold the associated media alongside it (initially photos and diagrams, but later audio and video clips, animations, and many other types of links) in digital form.

The *Hutchinson Encyclopedia* content was stored in a BRS/Search database, which today would be called a content-management system, but which in those days was simply a full-text database – not even a relational database. At that time relational databases did not typically include full-text indexing, and it was not felt necessary to use a relational structure for encyclopedia content. Despite many textbooks warning of the dangers of technology preceding the market, of companies developing a technology and then waiting in vain for customers, in this case, the technology enabled the content licensing; certainly the licensing would not have been possible without the technology. Although the database format itself was proprietary, it proved simple to output the content in SGML, the precursor of XML. SGML and XML are similar in that both are platform-independent formats, specifically designed for simple transformation and exchange of content.

The *Hutchinson Encyclopedia* became the UK's first CD-ROM encyclopedia in 1993, and the UK's first online encyclopedia in 1995. By this time the database had grown from 750,000 words to over four million words.

Within five years, Helicon Publishing had increased its staff from two to over 25, and was delivering regularly updated content on both sides of the Atlantic to meet varied customer requirements in terms of age and ability range, with an updated delivery of encyclopedic content to one of Helicon's content partners every two weeks or so. The revenue from content licensing was by now starting to approach the revenue from the print publishing programme. Subsequently, Microsoft acquired a 40% stake in the company, and Helicon (based in Oxford) found itself creating content for the new Microsoft Encyclopedia, *Encarta* (first published 1993).

Helicon, then, was a model of creating a content-licensing operation out of a content-based company. The key principles that enabled this transformation to happen were:

1. The creation of platform-independent standards for content, such as SGML and XML.

2. Helicon typically acquired content outright or cleared rights to publish the content on all platforms and in all territories. Clearing content rights at acquisition in this way is far simpler than trying to negotiate additional rights for content acquired solely for print publication.

3. A database structure was set up facilitating a wide range of content licences; for example, a single source was used to output encyclopedias of different sizes from a pocket edition up to the equivalent of a 12-volume edition. Once content has been captured in a platform-independent and flexible form, it is a simple matter to license that content in a variety of ways into markets that could never have been anticipated when the content system was created.

4. The drive to make the content completely platform-independent meant that all illustrations were designed to be optional; illustrated editions would include them, while text editions did not. Picture captions therefore made no reference to the surrounding text.

5. There were no references anywhere to page numbers (unlike most print books, where cross-references are shown by page); all cross-references were compiled for machine-based checking and maintenance, and could all be output as hyperlinks.

6. All weights and measurements were held both in imperial and metric form, and could be output in either.

Using these tools, Helicon created a kind of content-licensing machine, which could provide customers with an entry for Shakespeare that was 75 words long, or 250 words, or 2,500 words, in either British English or in American English, with or without illustrations, with or without a table of Shakespeare's plays, with or without spoken-word extracts from the sonnets, and with or without well-known quotations. At output, the extracted content could be automatically checked for consistency, for linking and for cross-references, in addition to the parsing check provided as part of the SGML/XML output.

Like several other reference publishers, Helicon focused increasingly on publishing through licensed content. Publishing encyclopedia content may seem today a risky model for adding value, but remarkably, although less extensively than before, Helicon continues to create and to license content profitably today.

Notes

1. See Morse, Caroline (ed.), *Memories of Jane Cunningham Croly, 'Jenny June'*, 1904 (available on Project Gutenberg at *http://www.gutenberg.org/etext/12099*)
2. Source: Ohio State University Cartoon Research Library, *http://cartoons.osu.edu/yellowkid/index.htm*
3. See the *Encyclopedia of Library History*, 1994 'Abstracting and Indexing Services'.
4. See Flaxbert, David (2007). The Chemical Abstracts Centennial: Whither CAS? Issues in Science and Technology Librarianship, Winter 2007. *http://www.istl.org/07-winter/viewpoints.html*
5. Interview with Susanne Bjorner, *Searcher*, June 2003, *http://www.infotoday.com/searcher/jun03/ardito_bjorner.shtml*
6. Produced by the US National Library of Medicine, a Federal-funded library.

7. Interview with Jan Egeland, *Searcher*, July/August 2004, *http://www. infotoday.com/SEARCHER/jul04/ardito_bjorner.shtml*

8. For a background to SilverPlatter, see Rayport, J.F. and Bower, W. 'Information on a *SilverPlatter.' Journal of Interactive Marketing* 13, no. 2 (Spring 1999): 29–48.

9. Allan, Roy. *A History of the Personal Computer: The People and the Technology*. London, Canada: Allan Publishing, 2001, Chapter 12.

10. Alexander, Catherine. 'Review of Chadwyck-Healey *English Poetry, Early English Prose Fiction, and English Verse Drama* CD-ROM databases.' Interactive Early Modern Literary Studies (October, 1999) 1–16: *http://purl.oclc.org/emls/iemls/reviews/alexlion.htm*

11. McAfee, R. Preston: *Competitive Solutions: The Strategist's Toolkit*. Princeton: Princeton University Press, 2002.

12. For more about CompuServe see *The International Directory of Company Histories*. Gale, 1999, vol. 27.

3

The licensing process, from start to finish

Of course, there is no such thing as a typical content-licensing process. Nonetheless, there are several steps that need to be taken for content to be licensed. They may not take place in the order described here, but by reading through this list, anyone anticipating getting involved in content licensing will be able to think about some of the issues before, rather than after, they hold everything else up, or cause a dramatic increase in the cost of the whole exercise, or result in an unnecessarily small market for the resulting content.

The act of content licensing is only the last link in the chain of information creation and dissemination:

1. The information owner creates content.
2. A market is identified for that content.
3. The content owner licenses the content.
4. The content is converted to a format that enables it to be disseminated.
5. Any relevant permissions are cleared.
6. The content is delivered, either once (as with a book or CD-ROM), or many times (as when the content is hosted for repeated online access).
7. The customer access and uses the content.

As described here, nothing could be simpler, yet there are pitfalls at each stage. Sharp-minded readers will notice immediately the use of the passive voice in several of the statements above: 'the content is converted' (who does the conversion?), 'the content is delivered' (who does this delivery?) and so on. Any successful business process should have clearly defined responsibilities for each stage in the value chain, so some careful thinking is required before being able to recommend a definitive process to manage the seven stages listed above.

3.1 Create content

This seems the most obvious thing in the world. Authors are creating content all the time, so what is the issue? Unfortunately, many of the problems in the licensing process arise because the creation of the content takes place before any licensing is considered, which then means that expensive retrospective conversion needs to take place.

The content frequently contains format-dependent features. Consider, for example, the humble 'op. cit.' in a print publication, which refers to a preceding citation for which details have already been given. However, the term 'op. cit.' is only intelligible for readers who start at the beginning of an article or book and who proceed in a linear fashion until they reach the end. It is likely that only a small part of anyone's reading is ever done in that fashion, and for licensed content, it is even less likely. More probable is that the reader will dip into the book, discover an 'op. cit.' reference and then spend many minutes trying to find the first reference to the item they want to know about.

So one maxim to think about when creating content for licensing is: does that content include elements that are format-dependent? Is it possible to create the content not just for one output, but for all?

Another example of content becoming unintelligible out of context when print content is repurposed for the Web happens especially with newspaper and magazine headlines. When the content is transferred to a website, content that makes perfect sense in the context of a print page becomes unusable outside of its original context. A headline 'Q3 Profits Up' may make sense in the context of a financial page of a trade magazine, where the page as a whole provides the context in which understanding is possible – for example, the print page might have a running heading that says 'financial news'. However, when the same article, without the context, and without the heading, then appears on a web page that uses the same content, the stark headline 'Q3 Profits Up' makes little sense without the context – which company are we talking about? Which quarter? In cases such as this, either the title needs to be rewritten, which may be a major task, or an intelligent use of metadata may be possible, for example to tag every story from the financial pages as a finance story.

Another example, from reference publishing, involves indexing to the page. Some dictionaries of quotations continue to be indexed by page number, e.g. '31:2' refers to the second quotation on page 31 of the book. Such a system is of course useless for digital publishing.

If licensing is seen as something that comes at the end of the publishing process, then inevitably the process will be more difficult and will lose some of the benefits that a publisher can bring to it. Instead of treating licensing as an add-on to the process, the publisher can be more fundamentally involved with the process. As Y. S. Chi of Elsevier put it, 'publishers are putting on a new face by adopting, adapting, transforming, and inventing'.[1] Which, of course, is what they have always done, although it is better that the adopting, adapting and transforming are done at the beginning of the process rather than at the end.

3.2 Identify a market

Again, this seems simple. Content is offered at a price, and some users will be prepared to pay that price. But the reality is rather more complex. Usually, there is a mixture of substitution and an element of complementarity: to some extent licensing content creates a new market, and to some extent it takes sales away from an existing market.

Notice also that the rich segmentation capability of digital publishing (it is possible to target specific groups precisely, at different prices or via different channels) means that the situation is only rarely a binary opposition: that either all the content is available to the end user, or no content at all. Traditionally, the situation was very simple: if your 'content', for example, was a major sports event, then you might think you could charge spectators to see the match, and if they did not pay the money, then they would see nothing. Of course, the reality is today very different. There can be several markets coexisting simultaneously; some consumers will pay a high price to see the event at the ground; another market is prepared to pay a lower price to watch the match live on TV, others may follow the action by listening to the radio, yet another group will see the highlights on TV and others may purchase a collection of highlights from the season. Most of these rights can also be sold in other territories; for example, there will be a number of users interested in Premier League football around the world. In other words, there are many market segments, and content licensing at its best is providing intellectual property to satisfy multiple markets. Yet many content owners do not see any way of presenting the content except via a single payment option: the user has all the content delivered, or none at all.

Another aspect of markets that often surprises those discovering content licensing for the first time is just how much content is suitable for licensing. It is easy to underestimate the potential of content for licensing; again and again stories appear of content being licensed where formerly it was not available at all, simply because the opportunity for buying and selling had not been recognised. For example, the *London Gazette*, the oldest English daily newspaper, contains regular announcements of UK government notices, including the official notification of individual bankruptcies or companies going into liquidation. These notices are used by financial information companies to compile registers of liquidations and insolvencies. TSO (The Stationery Office), modern-day publisher of the *Gazette*, created an online resource but also discovered a licensing opportunity by providing the insolvency information as a regular data feed to several companies selling financial information.

So the lesson here is, never ignore the possibility that content may have value in a specific (and clearly differentiated) market that may not have been noticed before; this book aims to reveal some of the possibilities for content that owners might not have thought possible.

3.3 The licensing deal is made

Once the content is complete and published, either the publisher or the licensing agent will see the benefit and the established market, and will propose an electronic sale. Often, publishers are approached by an aggregator who has identified a possible sales opportunity. Alternatively, the publisher can employ an agent to identify possible sales channels for the content. Equally, an institution can identify information needs, or an end user can sign up directly for a service.

3.4 The data are captured or converted

If content is created with reuse in mind, then little or no data conversion is required. However, pre-existing content will typically be licensed before it is captured or converted. Data capture and conversion are discussed in detail in Chapter 6.

One reason why data conversion and capture are typically handled by specialist companies is simply one of volume. To convert a small file for digital use is not too much of a problem; but typically, content owners have a large repository of content that needs to be converted. Hence, while the conversion may be done by the content owners themselves, more frequently a specialised data conversion company does the conversion (or capture). Before that capture is carried out, the publisher should think carefully about the intended use of the content and should load a sample to the intended platform.

3.5 Any permissions are cleared

Payments for copyright clearance can be made directly to the copyright owner, although in practice most payments are made to a collecting society, an organisation that collects payments on behalf of owners and then redistributes them to the intellectual property (IP) owners or to their publishers. Collecting societies provide an efficient way of clearing rights, because a single collecting society may handle clearances for thousands of IP owners in a particular medium. There is no need for the copyright owner to send a bill to the radio station that broadcasts his or her song, for example; this is done by the collecting society.

For more about collecting societies, see section 9.12.

The principle of clearing permissions is straightforward, although the practical aspects can become complex. Content in copyright (i.e. content owned by a third party) can only be published (replicated) if permission has been granted. This is true whether the copyright work in question forms the entire work or simply a small part of another work, as, for example, the use of copyright photos in a textual work. Permissions usually have to be cleared for use in different formats. This means in practice that licensing a print book with photos can become complicated. Not only does the author have to grant rights to the text, but rights have also to be cleared for the copyright photos and illustrations contained within the work. It is not usually sufficient that rights have been cleared for use in the original format, typically for print; unless the licensing agreement explicitly states rights in other formats have been cleared, it is unwise to assume the content can be used. This applies to photographs, videos, lengthy quotations from other works and so on.[2]

Hence the difficulty of clearing permissions. Frequently it consists of many small transactions with many different rights owners. It is not only that the details are complicated – the duration of copyright varies widely depending on the type of work, the territory, and so on. A further difficulty is the logistical problem of how long it takes to obtain the agreement of the rights owners when several are involved. For many content owners, the situation is remarkably complicated, and the time involved should not be underestimated. In a recent case study, The American Association of Law Libraries estimated it took on average 12 hours to clear a single permission.[3] This might seem excessive, but when a variety of media and rights are involved, the time to clear rights can be substantial. When the British Library attempted to digitise a collection of digital music and sound recordings by multiple performers that took place in St Mary-le-Bow Church, London, it took 302 hours of research time to identify, contact and request permission from the 299 rights holders – and the result was the clearance of only eight clips. That represents a rate for the successful clearances of almost 38 hours per clip.[4] Given such lengthy timescales, it is not surprising that many publishers look for ways to speed up the process, for example using a standard letter and tacit agreement process (see section 9.1).

A further problem is caused by contributions to a work by freelancers, as there are different legal opinions, at least in US law, on what constitutes a re-publication and what is a new work. Thus, in 2001 the US Supreme Court ruled that re-publication of freelance writers' articles in Lexis/Nexis was an infringement of the freelancers' copyright;[5] but a separate ruling in 2008 by a New York circuit judge ruled that the reuse of freelance photographs in a CD or DVD from *National Geographic*, in an archive collection of many issues of the magazine in a collection, did not amount to re-publication, and hence did not infringe the freelancers' copyright.[6] There will be circumstances where it is difficult to make the distinction.

A further complication is what is known as 'orphan works' – material that may be in copyright, but whose author cannot be identified or located. One method for dealing with this is for the publisher to create a large advertisement, explaining that the works of XYZ are being digitised, and that anyone with a reasonable claim to ownership of rights should contact the licensor. In the event of a failure to agree terms, the publisher (or library) will then remove the relevant content from the published collection. Often it is felt that such a procedure constitutes a reasonable attempt to identify the copyright owner, and so lessens the risk of the publisher being sued for breach of copyright. Of course, there is considerable discussion about what constitutes a 'reasonable attempt'.[7]

3.6 Deliver the content

The content has to reach the end user in some way. Information owners can disseminate their own content, but typically do not have skills of information dissemination, sales, authentication and so on. It is more usual for the dissemination to be done by intermediaries: publishers, aggregators and libraries. Content delivery involves the use of software to hold, navigate and retrieve the content. This involves skills such as interface design, usability and accessibility, all of which require specific subject knowledge that is more likely to be held in specialist companies.

3.7 The content is accessed and used

For the end user to access the content, one or two requirements must typically be satisfied. First, the user has to find the content: this can be as simple as knowing where to look, or locating the content via a search engine. Secondly, there will often be some kind of authentication process, by providing a password, or more securely based on a check of the machine location where the access is coming from.

Many delivery mechanisms include some means of tracking how and where the content is being used. The content might, for example, be used to write a student essay. In this case, it is helpful for the system to provide citation details for the content in the major citation styles (Figure 3.1).

Figure 3.1   Showing citation details

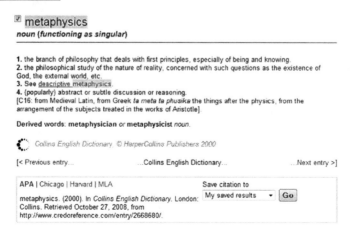

☑ metaphysics
noun (functioning as singular)

1. the branch of philosophy that deals with first principles, especially of being and knowing.
2. the philosophical study of the nature of reality, concerned with such questions as the existence of God, the external world, etc.
3. See descriptive metaphysics.
4. (popularly) abstract or subtle discussion or reasoning.
[C16: from Medieval Latin, from Greek *ta meta ta phusika* the things after the physics, from the arrangement of the subjects treated in the works of Aristotle].

Derived words: **metaphysician** *or* **metaphysicist** *noun.*

Collins English Dictionary. © HarperCollins Publishers 2000

[< Previous entry...   ...Collins English Dictionary...   ...Next entry >]

APA | Chicago | Harvard | MLA   Save citation to
metaphysics. (2000). In *Collins English Dictionary*. London: My saved results ▾ [Go]
Collins. Retrieved October 27, 2008, from
http://www.credoreference.com/entry/2668680/.

Thus, the content-licensing process should include an awareness of how the content is found, and for what purpose the content is being used, and ideally providing that management information to all the preceding links in the chain – the library, the aggregator, the publisher and even the author – to ensure the content-licensing process can be fine-tuned to provide maximum benefit to the users. Quite separately from the delivery of existing content, for example, there should be some method by which end users can make suggestions for additional content or for improvements to the user interface and functionality.

3.8 Implications for content licensing

The above description represents only a quick overview of the licensing process, which will be considered in more detail below. Even at this stage, however, some recommendations have become clear:

3.8.1 Consider the entire licensing process

If each stage in the licensing process is managed as an independent operation, then the licensing process will be at best a limited success. The entire licensing process implies carrying out not just one stage of the licensing operation, but several, understanding the entire chain.

3.8.2 Think of the licensing before creating the content

This may of course not be possible in many cases, but it is generally far more cost-effective to license content that was created with licensing in mind than to adapt or to convert existing context. In this way, the licensing process can be managed far more effectively. For example, if permissions are cleared at the outset for digital as well as for print editions of a title, the total cost of those permissions is likely to be far less than clearing the rights in two separate operations.

3.8.3 Make your content context- and format-independent

Remove context-dependent features; do not use 'op. cit.' and similar references, which require text to be in the correct position in the original published work to make sense. A better system is to use Harvard-style references (e.g. 'Smith (1994)'), which are intelligible from any point at which the content is accessed. Try not to create cross-referencing by page number. This problem is familiar to creators of books, because all index links and cross references in a print book are typically typeset in a separate pass once the page proofs have been created, a labour-intensive process that has a high error rate – and which then has to be done again if the print book is repaginated, as on most current e-book readers (see below).

3.8.4 Don't leave content out

Much about content licensing seems simple, even trivial, but it is worth mentioning at this point that if you propose to digitise a resource, then it makes sense to digitise all of it. In the case of journals, that includes material that appears on the covers, as this often includes details of the editorial board and the editorial policy of the journal. In the case of books, a surprising amount is left out when the book is digitised. This may include glossaries of terms, chronologies, brief introductions to the contents of the book and even (as issued by one of the UK's largest university publishers) the preface containing the editor's unapologetic explanation of why a book was not the comprehensive collection of essays that its title claimed. Without this explanation, the digital version gave a far less comprehensive coverage of its subject than had been claimed.

Notes

1. Y. S. Chi, presentation to BSEC 2008 conference, 'Taking on our new identity', *http://www.buy-sell-econtent.com/2008/DayTwo.shtml#Session215*
2. See Pedley (2007) for more about copyright clearance for digital use.
3. 'Scan and Deliver', *Information World Review*, July 2008.
4. *Information World Review*, July 2008.
5. *New York Times* v Tasini.
6. US 11th Circuit Court of Appeals, 2008.
7. See, for example, US Copyright Office January 2006 'Report on Orphan Works', p. 96 (*http://www.copyright.gov/orphan/orphan-report.pdf*)

Media for licensing

This chapter looks at the various media that can be licensed (such as print, audio and video), as well as some of the major forms that content appears in (such as journals, books and databases) and examines some similarities and differences between them. It soon becomes clear there are major differences in licensing via these different media or channels: for example, a scholarly article is licensed in different ways and through different channels from a video clip. Some of these differences are inherent to the medium, but some interesting findings emerge from this comparison that show how licensing in different media sometimes develops in a curiously independent way, as if each medium was unaware of any other. For a further discussion on the legal aspects of what rights can be licensed in each medium, see Chapter 9, 'Copyright, royalties and contracts'.

4.1 Journal licensing

The number of peer-reviewed scholarly journals is disputed, but some clear trends are visible. Their number is steadily increasing, but the number of digitised journals is increasing faster than print journals. In 2003 around one-third of journals were available in digital form.[1] Five years later, in 2008, there were around 25,000 peer-reviewed journals, and the number available in digital form had doubled. Moreover, over a thousand refereed journals are now (2009) available only in online format.[2] The trend towards digital delivery has happened sooner and more extensively in journal delivery than with books. In 2006, journal delivery to US academic libraries was split approximately equally between print only (30%), electronic only (37%), and both print and electronic (33%). In other words, 70% of all journals in US academic libraries were available in electronic form.[3]

Here are some points about the journal business and how it affects, or is affected by, content licensing:

- There is a steadily increasing concentration of journal publishing by the largest publishers. A small number of publishers, mainly Elsevier, Informa and Blackwell/Wiley, either publish or manage the bulk of academic journals on behalf of smaller organisations. In other words, many smaller IP owners license their publishing rights to larger publishers who have a greater ability to sell the journal to academic markets, notably in digital form.

- Journals are today mostly licensed via volume agreements (see discussion of consortia in section 5.2). It is not substantially more difficult to create a delivery platform to provide a hundred journals than it is to deliver one journal. By the same token, it is little more work to license a hundred journals than to license one. Hence, journals tend to be licensed in large-scale collections, typically from one of the largest journal publishers (nicknamed 'the big deal'), although there are some interesting examples of collections of journals from independent publishers, such as the ALPSP Learned Journals Collection (see section 5.2).

- The problem of perpetual access (the problem of how to continue to access content after a publisher ceases to provide the online journal) was debated first with reference to journal licensing, and solutions to it appeared here first also. There is more about this in section 9.6.3.

- Academic libraries are stating increasingly that they prefer online-only delivery of journals, and ask publishers to justify the existence of both print and electronic versions of a title – this has not yet happened for books. Libraries prefer digital journals because they are more widely accessed, and because life-cycle costs for holding a digital resource (the comparison between renting the shelf space and a few gigabytes of hard drive space) are much lower.

- Journal prices are increasing more rapidly than book prices, and by more than the rate of inflation: between 2004 and 2008, journal-published prices for academic licensing increased by some 38%, or 7.5% per year.[4] As a result, institutions are keen to explore ways in which they can maximise value to the institution, for example by negotiating perpetual licences (see section 9.13).

One aspect of digital content delivery is not required by journal publishers. Digital publishing can provide rapid updating of content, but the current practice of journal publishing requires that the content does not change. The journal article records formally what was researched by whom over what period of time. While the advancement of knowledge is a process of constant interaction, the journal article represents a milestone that cannot be changed. The act of publication of a journal article forms a public record of research carried out, an essential part of the process, rather similar to what linguists term a performative act: when a grandee breaks a bottle of champagne against the hull of a boat and says, 'I name this ship ...' we all of us already know what the name is. Paradoxically, the public record role of a journal publisher is increasingly at odds with researchers' need to publish the work as quickly as possible. If a journal article appears as a matter of record only, it is not very important that it is published immediately. Increasingly, scholarly articles are published first in a pre-publication repository, whether maintained by the journal publisher, by a professional association or by the scholar's own institution (an institutional repository). In other words, it is increasingly recognised that the act of scholarly publication is in a sense a licence of the content to a journal publisher, and there are several other ways in which the same article can be licensed.

The recent development of institutional repositories in universities and higher-education institutions is particularly interesting. An institutional repository can be an aggregated collection of content in its own right, published with the agreement of the copyright owners in the interests of education – that is, with free access to the content. An institutional repository typically holds published and unpublished content, drafts of papers, reading lists, and so on; by managing a repository, information professionals become more involved with the publishing process itself. Typically, these repositories are freely accessible, although restrictions are placed on commercial use of the content. An example of an institutional repository is St Andrews University, using the open-source software (Figure 4.1). This repository currently contains theses and research articles from the University.

Institutional Repositories are typically used to hold open-access content (see section 5.11). Many paid journal publishers have attempted to mirror institutional repositories by providing 'fast-track' services, by which research can be published faster than the standard process.[5]

When journals were first licensed, the instinct of aggregators and publishers was to add as many journals as possible into the largest package. Frequently, libraries would not have the choice of which journals could be taken – it was a question of take it or leave it. Hence, the famous 'big deal' produced by Elsevier and other major publishers,

Figure 4.1 St Andrews University Institutional Repository

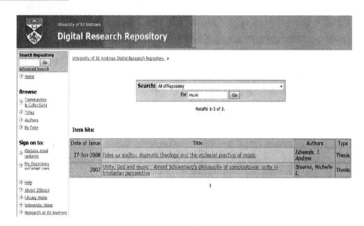

which were sold to libraries in a single deal with little alternative, even though many of the titles were of little interest to the relevant subject teams. After considerable protest, publishers have tended to retract from that inflexible viewpoint and have offered purchasers more flexibility by providing a wider choice of journals to subscribe to. This requires accurate usage records to be kept (see section 10.26).

4.2 Database licensing

Databases, structured collections of content, were created to facilitate content retrieval and manipulation, so content licensing is an obvious way to derive maximum value from database repositories. A database can comprise full text, for example the collections of UK and US statute law from LexisNexis and Westlaw, or may comprise only citations, such as collections of abstracts and bibliographic information. These include Scopus (an abstract and citation database from Elsevier), Web of Science (a collection from Thomson Reuters that includes the Science Citation Index) and Cambridge Scientific Abstracts (from ProQuest). The distinction between abstract and full-text collections is becoming less clear as more and more abstract collections add the full-text of the articles they are abstracting.

Databases for licensing may simply comprise collections of records, and some of the most interesting innovations in content licensing are taking place in this area. For example, the UK site *http://www. athleticsdata.com* provides a collection of athletics results from across the UK, available free for non-commercial use. It is searchable by event, by athlete and by rankings. Here is an example of a copyright database built out of publicly available data; the information from which it has been derived is probably retrievable elsewhere and could therefore be replicated, but only with great difficulty. In this case, the database creates value first by creating a unique aggregation of data (Figure 4.2), and then by providing easily accessible reports from that collection.

Databases raise an interesting issue of copyright. First, the creative aspect of a database is recognised under copyright law:[6] even where the information contained in the database may be compiled from the public domain, the database itself can be copyright because of the creative work that went into designing and creating it.

In addition, under a 1996 directive the European Union provides a 'sui generis' right, which offers legal protection of the time and money spent to create a database, regardless of whether or not the database design itself was innovative.[7] By this principle, the results of athletics events, even if not the copyright of Athletics Data, can become part of a new copyright collection of data.

It is important to note that some widely available database content is copyright and a licence payable if it is reused. For example, UK postcodes are the copyright of Royal Mail, and a fee is payable for reproducing them. In the US, by contrast, zip codes can be freely copied. Nonetheless, some commercial organisations sell collections of zip code data by adding value, for example by having a more up-to-date collection than the US Postal Service.[8]

Figure 4.2 *www.athleticsdata.com*: Example of individual athletes' performances

What kind of database content is most suitable for licensing? It is difficult to give general guidance, but some criteria appear frequently when databases are being sold, including the following:

1. The information is presented in a format that facilitates retrieval.
2. There is no direct competition.
3. The content is up to date.

Even where one or more of these criteria are not satisfied, a licensing opportunity may still exist. Of course, if the second criterion is true, then being up to date is far less important. Many information owners are reluctant to make their database information available because they believe that all online information is updated constantly. The reality, of course, is that only a small proportion of information available online is genuinely up to date; most of it is out-of-date information that is simply retrieved more quickly. For most collections, convenience and uniqueness are the qualities that should determine whether to publish or not. Equally important to the above criteria is the underlying principle for online access that because content is available somewhere on the Web, it does not mean that all potential users can find it. There is often a case for licensing content that is already available in one location on the Web, simply so that it can be retrieved at a different location where many potential users are looking for it. If this were not the case, why would the replication of newspaper headlines from other sites be such a common practice?

The separate problem of how to bring the content up to date and to keep it that way is discussed later (see section 11.9).

4.3 Magazine licensing

Individual stories from magazines are frequently licensed, but magazines are not typically licensed in their entirety. Some companies have created a business providing an aggregated site where digital editions of the print magazine can be downloaded, for a fee. An example is Exact Editions (*http://www.exacteditions.com/*) (see Figure 4.3). This company operates by licensing the content from the publisher and creating an aggregated service. This creates an additional market for print magazines; for the digital edition provider, their site becomes the online equivalent of a newsagent.

Figure 4.3 Exact Editions

Currently, these sites provide PDFs, with a few additional components such as contents lists and indexes with hyperlinks added. Sales are by subscription or by individual issue. There are several ways in which this basic model can be extended; for example, Exact Editions now offers institutional access, so everyone in a company can have access to a magazine (unlike the typical company situation where a single print edition slowly circulates from one in-tray to another). Library-wide access is also offered. A marginal benefit is single-click internet dialling for many of the phone numbers contained in the magazines, by converting phone numbers in the text to hyperlinks.

In the future, such sites might add advertising or value-added services around the magazine collection. As portability is a major feature for many print magazines, it is likely that e-book readers will provide further opportunities for magazine licensing of this kind.

4.4 Map licensing

Map data are copyright like any other information. For technical reasons, as well as the cost and strategic importance of having reliable and up-to-date geographical survey data, it is an area of content where governments have a vested interest.

In the UK, the Ordnance Survey is the UK Government agency that controls copyright in the official map data. Licences must be purchased from the Ordnance Survey for any map use that is based in whole or part on Ordnance Survey mapping. The situation in the US is very different. There is a central portal, *http://www.geodata.gov*, which provides access to digital map data as part of a federal initiative. The US National Map (*http://nationalmap.usgs.gov/*) is based on data from a number of federal agencies, including NASA and the US Geological Survey. The conclusion reached by US agencies was that charging for federal information was counter-productive; for example, from a 2004 report:

> During the 1990s, many jurisdictions experimented with cost-recovery fees for geographic data. Ten years later, many of these entities have concluded that fee programs:
>
> - Cannot recover a worthwhile fraction of government data budgets,
> - Seldom cover operating expenses, and
> - Act as a drag on private-sector investments that otherwise would add to the tax base and grow the economy.[9]

In the UK, there is a long-standing view that because the Ordnance Survey receives funding from the Government, its data should be provided at low or zero cost: that is the argument of the Campaign for Freedom of Information (since 1984).[10] The UK *Guardian* newspaper has for some time been running a campaign with a similar goal. To counter this, it could be argued that the Ordnance Survey is only partly funded by public money; it also receives revenue from sale of its maps, which enables it to provide more detailed mapping. If the Ordnance Survey were to give away its mapping data free, why should a small number of commercial organisations benefit as a result from an investment in mapping data they did not fund?

The problem is that the market is not truly competitive: the Ordnance Survey is a monopoly supplier, being funded both by the Government and by revenue from licensing its data, and acts like any other revenue-generating company to maximise its income. Nonetheless, this does not justify any misuse of its position. For example, one complaint about the Ordnance Survey, noted by the Office of Fair Trading (OFT) in 2006, was that, as a Public Sector Information Host (PSIH), the Ordnance Survey did not provide access to that data on an equal basis for all its licensing partners. Some licensees would appear to receive more favourable treatment than others.[11] In fact, the OFT concluded that if all the UK PSIHs made raw information more easily available, the UK economy would benefit by £1 billion each year.

However, this recommendation is of little use for any organisation wishing to license data from the Ordnance Survey. Before licensing, it is a good idea to consult other licensees in a similar situation, to compare details on the type of licence being offered, and the cost of the licence. It is sensible to expect that the agency will offer equivalent terms for all licensees of the content.

For more about public information and its availability, see section 5.5.

4.5 Image licensing

Traditionally, images were not sold or licensed direct to end users, but to publishers, who then add value to the images by putting text around them, in the form of books, magazines or newspapers. Picture agencies and organisations that hold collections of images were therefore not well placed to deal with providing electronic versions of images to end users, and certainly not familiar with the idea of licensing access to images via an aggregator. The situation has changed substantially with digital licensing; today there is a flourishing market for providing individual images or collections of images for websites, self-publishing and so on.

Some image libraries have become their own publishers, providing collections of images with captions and metadata not only to publishers but direct to authors (an example of disintermediation – see section 11.3). However, this requires additional skills that an agency may not possess: the agency must develop a customer-orientated service for selecting and providing images, and the images themselves need to be retrievable – that is, they need to have good metadata. Unfortunately it remains the case that image libraries do not typically have the publishing skills that enable them to write good, authoritative descriptions of the images in their collection. Images licensed for use in a digital publication need to have good metadata to ensure that appropriate and accurate title and caption information are present for the use made of them in publications. Many image agencies are responding only slowly to the importance of metadata in content licensing – it is more than just the picture.

A recent development is the creation of royalty-free image collections, which can be purchased by a single fee for unlimited use. Many of the major picture agencies now provide such a collection, for example Getty Images (*http://www.gettyimages.com/*), where the price to the user is based on the resolution of the image.

Image agencies also provide other more innovative licences than the traditional 'rights-managed' licence. One model is the 'rights-ready' licence, where the publisher agrees in advance the rights for which the image will be used without the need to draw up a custom contract.

Other innovative services include websites that provide access not only to photos but also to royalty-free drawings and diagrams, for example Clipart.com (Figure 4.4; *http://www.clipart.com/*), which provides a powerful search capability, and several different digital formats for downloading, all for a monthly subscription – this is a long way from the traditional picture agency.

It is important to note that terms such as 'royalty-free' do not mean that the user does not have to read the licence. Different agencies have different interpretations of what 'royalty-free' might mean, and each of the image licensing sites offers slightly different terms, so it is important to read the terms of use before proceeding; there are often limitations on image file

Figure 4.4   Image licensing

Clipart   < Return to search results

Keywords: banana, food

Format	Size	Dimensions	Resolution	Color Info
non-interlaced GIF	17.7K	750 x 806 pixels	72 pixels/inch	24-bit RGB color
EPS	178.6K	N/A	N/A	24-bit RGB color
PNG with transparent background	129.8K	698 x 750 pixels	72 pixels/inch	24-bit RGB color
JPEG	127.2K	750 x 806 pixels	72 pixels/inch	24-bit RGB color
WMF	4.4K	N/A	N/A	24-bit RGB color

Item: #21557415   Subscribe | Sign In

Group Browse images in this collection

size, reselling of the images and the use made of the image. A similar situation applies in the area of video and audio licensing (see below).

4.5.1 Case study: Bridgeman Education extending the licensing market

Simply adding appropriate tags to an existing collection can create an additional market. Bridgeman Art Library is a London-based photo agency specialising in fine art, which created a business by licensing content from major public and private collections. Why should users go to Bridgeman rather than directly to the collections themselves? Mainly because it is more convenient. A famous painting may be held in one of thousands of major art galleries, and it is easier to search one large collection of images than first having to find out where the painting is held, and then to deal with the licensing practice of what may be an unfamiliar institution based in a foreign location. Many institutions that license their own content directly to third parties also make their images available to aggregators such as Bridgeman, and are happy to do so, because it provides additional revenue for the institution that would otherwise be lost. The lesson here is that providing a single source for content may not be the most effective solution for content owners.

In an imaginative extension to their core business, Bridgeman recognised an opportunity for content licensing to a new market, which had not before been directly accessible: the education market. Bridgeman licenses images to schools and colleges, which access the content via appropriate (education-relevant) metadata. Bridgeman Education (*http://www.bridgemaneducation.com/*), launched in April 2008, provides images tagged by curriculum areas such as 'Citizenship', as well as more obvious topics such as 'English' or 'History'. It is provided on a subscription basis, and the images can then be used in the organisation's virtual learning environment (VLE).

4.6. Video and audio licensing

The aim of this brief section on audio and video licensing is not to provide a detailed account of this area, but simply to point out some features of these markets that are relevant to the wider world of content licensing.

The publication of video and audio involves multiple rights. Thus, music tracks, for example, have a composer (or music publisher acting on behalf of the composer), plus a performer; both rights have to be cleared when an audio clip is licensed. Performance rights are when the song is performed, whether live in a concert, or broadcast on the TV or radio. Mechanical rights are paid whenever a song is recorded and then sold or licensed. Synchronisation rights are payable when a song is used alongside other media, for example as background music in a feature film. Typically, the publisher is paid 50% of the total mechanical royalties, and 25% of the performance royalties, although of course these figures vary from contract to contract.

Collecting societies (discussed in section 9.12) collect rights payments for video and audio. Performance and synchronisation rights are payable to performance societies, such as ASCAP (The American Society of Composers, Authors and Publishers) or PRS (The Performing Rights Society).

Video and audio are delivered to the end user in a variety of ways. Online content can be delivered either by downloading an entire file, which is then played in its entirety on the user's PC, or by streaming. Streamed media are delivered to the PC in small chunks and played before the file has completed downloading. Streaming enables users to begin watching large video files sooner.

For the content owner of audio and video, the option chosen has a bearing on the licensing. Downloaded content, once copied to the user's PC, usually remains in their possession indefinitely; unless some copy protection technique is applied (as, for example, in the case of Audible, see section 10.21), the content can be copied at will. Streamed media, on the other hand, are published to the user without any long-term storage of the content on the end user's PC (any temporary files created during the process are deleted later). Hence for the content owner, streaming is usually a better protection against piracy – even though there are several software tools available on the Internet that can capture streamed video and audio.

4.7 Audio licensing

Not all music licensing follows the above standard pattern requiring rights to be cleared with two or three different agencies. In the case of production music, also known as library music, the rights for reuse are somewhat simpler, typically with one agency (in the UK the Mechanical Copyright Protection Society, MCPS) managing all these rights together.

The cost varies depending on the rights and territories required. This is because the agency has acquired the copyright of the music from the composer (that is, the composer provided the music under a 'work-for-hire' arrangement). Production music is easier (and usually cheaper) to license.

Audio content is also available royalty-free from various stock libraries, but this does not necessarily mean that the tracks can be performed in public without further payment. For example, Stockmusic.net (*http://www.stockmusic.net/*), a royalty-free music provider, charges a one-time additional fee for performance rights; this is split 50:50 with the composer. Usually, but not always, the performance fee is collected by the performance rights organisation.

To give an idea of the importance of licensing in the audio world, Table 4.1 shows revenue for the UK MCPS–PRS Alliance (the collecting society for UK audio providers). For some years, the proportion of total revenue from licensed audio content via audio CDs has been decreasing, and in 2007, for the first time, online and broadcast revenue exceeded revenue from sales of the physical product, mainly CDs.

The history of digital audio is a salutary one for print publishers. The audio industry was transformed through technical developments, first by the invention of devices that enabled content to be copied, such as tape and cassette recorders, and then by the innovation of compression software that enabled high-quality audio files to be dramatically reduced in file size, notably the MP3 format. When low-quality cassette recorders were superseded by cheap copying devices that enabled CDs and DVDs to be replicated cheaply and quickly, copying of audio became very appealing. The last link in the chain was the capability to download audio (and video) files using peer-to-peer technology (for example, following the launch in 1999 of Napster, the best-known of the peer-to-peer sharing services). All these innovations enabled media to be shared, regardless of intellectual property rights. Soon, more music was being

Table 4.1   Audio revenue in the UK by revenue stream

Revenue stream	2007 (£m)	2006 (£m)	Percentage change
Broadcasting and Online	155.5	144.4	8
Physical products (e.g. CD)	151.8	170.7	−11
Public performance	133.6	121.8	10
International	121.2	109.9	10

Source: MCPS-PRS-Alliance 2007.

downloaded free of charge than was being sold. One of the reasons for this was the audio industry's reluctance to provide paid downloads to end users. Napster was sued by the US recording industry in 2000, and closed down in 2001, although by that time the principle of peer-sharing technology was widely established, and continues today; despite repeated lawsuits, new sharing services continue to appear. However, the audio industry is slowly recapturing some of its market by providing more easily accessible paid downloads, most notably with one of the most successful initiatives in content licensing, the launch of iTunes from Apple in 2001 (see section 10.19.1). Moreover, the industry has started to target users who provide copyrighted content via their ISPs, via a voluntary agreement (set up in the UK in July 2008); regaining a lost market is, however, far more difficult than maintaining a market by keeping up with technical changes. The audio industry's current woes are due at least in part to its lack of response to technical developments that bypassed it, and to its failure to recognise a major shift in the way users wanted to access and to play recorded music.

4.7.1 Case study: Why an orchestra might eventually pay you to record them

As with every other area of content licensing, the buying and selling of audio and performance rights have changed substantially during the last 20 years or so. Twenty years ago, the performance rights for a work by a major orchestra were high enough to deter any but the largest record labels from buying them. Today, with developments in technology making it possible to create professional sound recordings at a fraction of the cost of a few years ago, there has been a mushrooming of recording companies. Interestingly, however, rather than all these record labels chasing the same few elite performers, the number of artists whose recordings are appearing is increasing. Hence there are more opportunities for performers to be recorded, but at a lower average price for the performance right.

Instead of attempting (at great cost) to license the top-name orchestras from their existing contracts, Naxos was a pioneer in selecting less well-established orchestras or orchestras without a major recording contract. The orchestras were happy to negotiate low royalties, or, increasingly, a fee, for the recording. Why do the orchestras agree? For the orchestra, the recording provides a marketing (if not monetary) benefit to its reputation, which may be of more long-term value than the recording fee, because any orchestra that has recordings to its name is considered more prestigious. Furthermore, many orchestras are funded by the city or region in which they are based, and by making recordings, they can reach a wider proportion of their audience base than the small proportion who attend the live concerts.

The conclusion of this trend is to move beyond licensing completely and to create a label for each orchestra or performing group. For many orchestras, rather than wait for an elusive recording contract, creating their own site and providing recordings direct to the public from a website, is increasingly the best strategy. For example, the Milwaukee Symphony Orchestra site offers downloads of both its commercially released recordings and additional content (*http://download.mso.org/*). Beyond even this, the Berlin Philharmonic Orchestra has offered (since January 2009) a 'digital concert hall',[12] where home-based concert-goers can view a lived streamed performance of an individual concert or a season of concerts. This is a further example of disintermediation (see section 11.3).

4.8 Video licensing

As with audio licensing, video licensing involves multiple rights – for authors, for performers and potentially for syndication. The licensing of feature films and major television programmes is a highly specialised market that, because of its scale and complexity, differs in many ways from other areas of content licensing.

Licensing of film clips themselves is typically managed by direct negotiation with the major studios, such as Sony or Paramount. Stock film and video footage, on the other hand, are sold by a number of agencies who operate in a similar way to stock photo agencies: they typically provide a low-resolution version of the clip for sampling, and then once the license is purchased, provide a higher-quality version of the same clip.

As with still-image licensing, there are many collections of stock video footage. Major libraries for licensing video are maintained by organisations such as the BBC Motion Gallery,[12] which also sells third-party content, and which provides a number of royalty-free collections; Corbis Motion[13] has a similar service. The BBC Motion site (Figure 4.5) has an impressive search capability, which includes search not only by decade when the shot was taken, but also by the type of camera shot, weather and time of day, in addition to either royalty-based or royalty-free

Figure 4.5 BBC Motion Gallery advanced search screen

Source: http://www.bbcmotiongallery.com/Customer/AdvancedSearch.aspx?searchValue=fulani.

licensing. In addition, the clips have an extensive number of searchable keywords such as 'romantic' or 'sad'. This makes the process of locating relevant video content straightforward, as long as the metadata chosen by the agency correspond with the requirements of the licensee. There is even a 'concept randomiser', which displays clips for a vast range of concept terms such as 'enlightenment' or 'energy'.

Taking full advantage of the Web, the site iStockphoto (Figure 4.6; *http://www.istockphoto.com/*) provides the opportunity both to buy and to sell stock video footage, audio tracks and photos from the same site. After compulsory registration and a quality check, users can upload video clips or photos and receive a 20% royalty on all sales (the royalty rate increases as more files are downloaded from one user). The impressive site also includes lists of the most popular downloads, and the highest rated clips by users. However, the iStockphoto business model, by which users tag their own content, may result in a service that is not as powerfully searchable as the BBC Motion Gallery; the model is undoubtedly cheaper to administer, but may result in less reliable metadata.

Figure 4.6 iStockphoto: image selection

Source: *http://www.istockphoto.com/file_closeup.php?id=2040026.*

Most of the stock video libraries have tags designed for retrieval by commercial users such as advertisers; hence licensees can search for terms such as 'adventure', 'happy' or 'thoughtful'. These tags would not be very helpful in other contexts, such as education.

4.9 Brand licensing

In the trade market, major video, audio programmes, feature films and computer games provide opportunities for related products, for example, the *Star Wars* series of films has created hundreds of licensed brands, logos, toys and other spin-offs based on characters in the films. This kind of licence opportunity, known as brand extension, is restricted to content that has a major consumer market. These licence deals are typically based on a royalty on sales. The major US show where such licences are bought and sold is the annual Licensing International Expo (*http://www. licensingexpo.com/*); the equivalent in Europe is Brand Licensing Europe. The International Licensing Industry Merchandisers' Association (LIMA) is a major trade association. Although figures for the size of the worldwide brand licensing market vary, it is probably far greater than the stock photo, video and audio licensing market put together.

4.10 Licensing on mobile phones

Despite the near ubiquity of the mobile phone, content licensing for mobiles has not been a huge success (apart from an exception discussed below). There could be various reasons for this. One issue has been the high charges for accessing content to mobile users; a further problem is the difficulty of adapting online content to a very small screen. Moreover, the advertising model that funds much of Web content delivery is difficult to replicate on a mobile.

Provision of licensed book content for mobiles was slow in starting. The most successful content delivery to mobiles has been from companies such as Mobipocket. Freely available e-books, such as Project Gutenberg titles, can be displayed on mobile phones using software such as Stanza and Feedbooks. All these companies are discussed in more detail in section 10.18.

One independent company active in this area in the UK is ICUE (*http://www.i-cue.co.uk/*). In 2004 eBooks.com signed an agreement to provide books for Nokia phones, but the company has since concentrated more on providing marketing tools for publishers via mobiles.

The one great success in mobile-phone licensing has been ringtones, a market that took everyone by surprise. Users could customise their ringtones by downloading a tune from a website; from nowhere, a market developed that was worth £100m per year in the UK alone[14] in 2007. That market, however, looks sure to decline as the technology for users to create their own ringtones from downloaded tracks evolves.

4.11 Book licensing

The licensing of books in their entirety has been a relatively recent part of the content licensing industry, a situation that may change with the arrival of the e-book reader (see below). The term e-book simply means a book, fiction or non-fiction, which is available in digital form; an e-book does not require an e-book reader. Although since the earliest days of computing many texts have been captured digitally for small-scale circulation, mainly science fiction and IT titles, reflecting the community that was capturing them, the earliest published e-books appear to be those created by Project Gutenberg from 1971 (see section 5.9). Since then, large-scale digital book delivery began with the earliest aggregators, from around 2000; they are discussed in detail in Chapter 6. There were a handful of highly publicised e-book initiatives, such as Stephen King's novella *Riding the Bullet*, published in electronic form only, in 2000, and it is revealing how far digital delivery has progressed, for some librarians asked at the time just where they would store such a digital-only title in their collection – a question that would not be asked today.

One difference between books and journals is the lack of a standard directory of which books are available in digital form. For journals, the standard list is *Ulrich's Periodicals Directory* (see *http://www.ulrichsweb .com/*). Even though this list may not be comprehensive, it is at least better than nothing; and as there are many more books than there are journal titles, it is more difficult to keep track of which books are available in digital form, and which ones any one institution has purchased. Thus, it is difficult for institutions to find out if a book title is available in digital form, and also difficult to keep a single aggregated list of titles licensed. As with journals, it is simpler for aggregators, publishers and libraries to make a few licensing deals comprising lots of titles than to make many deals with only one or two titles each. The present situation in which each aggregator has an overlapping but incomplete collection is not very helpful for institutions, and does not facilitate market growth.

4.12 The BBC iPlayer

The BBC iPlayer is a software service, not a device. It enables audio and TV programmes to be replayed for a short period after the original broadcast. It was launched in 2007 after extensive trials. The iPlayer includes both downloading and streaming of content. The iPlayer runs on PCs, but also on some cable TV services, providing additional options from the BBC service on cable. The service has been remarkably successful.

4.13 The e-book reader

The trade book market has resisted moves towards digital publishing for several years, until the paradoxical situation developed by which books are written digitally, typeset and printed digitally, but distributed and sold on paper. While music and video download sites are widespread, for example using the iTunes one-off purchase model, there have been few large-scale text-based initiatives to date. Some aggregators provide end-user pay-per-view services, but the real development in the market (compared, as are too many developments in digital publishing, with Gutenberg's invention of printing) is the e-book reader. The best-known readers currently are the iRex Technologies Iliad E-reader, the first on the UK market, launched in 2006, the Sony Reader Digital Book, launched in the same year, and the Amazon Kindle E-Reader, released in 2007 (with an updated version, the Kindle 2, launched in the USA in 2009). The Kindle has not been released in Europe, but US sales of the first model of the Kindle were estimated at 500,000.[15]

E-book readers continue to improve in terms of functionality and usability. Manufacturers are still experimenting to find the best combination of features for end users, but the business model for all the devices seems clear: it is the twenty-first-century equivalent of the lending library or bookshop. Users will buy or rent titles that can be accessed on a time-limited basis, perhaps with an expiry date after which the content is deleted, or stored on an external device such as a PC. Content has been available for downloading to a desktop PC for several years, but few people are interested in reading lengthy texts at their computer screen. E-book readers are, of course, not the only hand-held devices that can display content: the smartphone is another one, although it appears in practice that most smartphone users do not find it easy to read lengthy textual content on a very small screen. The convenience of the e-book reader seems certain to create a new market for licensed content, once a device simple and suitably well-designed for using on the bus or train has been developed; for most content-licensing purposes, it is irrelevant which device becomes the most popular e-book reader – more important is that there is a new channel by which content can be licensed. This became all the more true when Amazon released in March 2009 a free 'Kindle App' reader for iPhones, so users of these smartphones can download digital books to their smartphone without having to buy a Kindle at all: Amazon is developing a channel rather than a product.

It is difficult to determine precisely the size of the e-book market, because it covers both titles read on e-book readers, and titles read on PCs and laptops via aggregators' and publishers' online sites. However, some idea of the potential of this area can be seen by year-on-year comparisons. Wholesale e-book sales in the US increased by over 38% in the first half of 2008 compared with the first half of 2007,[16] although e-book sales were thought to comprise less than 1% of total US publishing sales.

The effect of the impending e-book business has had a dramatic effect on trade publishers. Whereas directory and professional publishers had been steadily moving towards digital publishing for several years, the arrival of the e-book reader impacted on a sector of the media business that had until then largely resisted attempts to change its business processes. The effect was well described by Michael Healy in a presentation at the London Book Fair in April 2008. Rather than frantically trying to convert their content to this or that e-book format, publishers were at last beginning to realise, rather belatedly, that the most appropriate response was to manage the creation and delivery of their intellectual property in a more structured way. In this way, the advent of the e-book reader is transforming the content-creation business, as well as the book retail business, and publishers now realise the need for organised repositories of digital content, to enable them to provide content in multiple formats to different markets. For more on publishers' responses to e-books, see section 10.18.

4.14 What content can be accessed on e-book readers

The Amazon Kindle would appear to have the widest access to content, because its built-in wireless link enables magazines and newspapers to be downloaded automatically, without any transactions taking place on the device (this is all handled separately). In fact, delays in launching the Kindle in Europe were caused more by delays in agreeing licenses with broadband providers than in ensuring that sufficient content was available. In addition, Amazon has ensured that the Kindle has a bigger catalogue of e-book titles available than any other device, in addition to newspaper and magazine content. As a further convenience, the Kindle has a licensed dictionary included with it. In other words, the entire development of this channel is based around the development of a new content-licensing market.

The downside of current book readers is that both the Kindle and the Sony Reader Digital Book were at the time of launch enabled only for downloads of content from an exclusive source, the repository of the company owning the player, and with content in a proprietary format. Proprietary collections of content favour the repository owner, but not the end user. Currently, the Iliad has the most open architecture, supporting PDF, XHTML and txt formats. For more about e-book formats, see section 10.18.

Notes

1. Carol Tenopir, 'Online databases – online scholarly journals: How Many?' *Library Journal* 2, January 2004.
2. Source: *Ulrich's Periodicals Directory, www.ulrichsweb.com.* See also Sally Morris, 'Mapping the journal publishing landscape: how much do we know?'. *Learned Publishing*, 20/4, October 2007, pp299–310.
3. Chandra Prabha, 'Shifting from Print to Electronic Journals in ARL University Libraries'. *Serials Review* 33:1, March 2007.
4. Information from EBSCO at *http://www2.ebsco.com/en-us/Documents/customer/OVERVIEW-2008.pdf*
5. See, for example, the Institute of Physics site *http://www.iop.org/EJ/journal/-page=extra.ftc/0022-3727*
6. In the UK, under the Copyright, Designs and Patents Act 1988.
7. See *http://ec.europa.eu/internal_market/copyright/prot-databases/prot-databases_en.htm*
8. See, for example, GreatData.com *http://www.emory.com/progress/prozip.htm*
9. *Licensing Geographic Data and Services*, US National Research Council, 2004.
10. *http://www.cfoi.org.uk/*
11. OFT Press Release, 2 December 2006 *http://www.oft.gov.uk/news/press/2006/171-06*
12. *http://dch.berliner-philharmoniker.de/*
13. *www.bbcmotiongallery.com*
14. *www.corbismotion.com*
15. 'Hanging up on ringtones', *Guardian*, 28 June 2007.
16. 'Amazon unveils updated electronic book reader', *Financial Times,* 10 February 2009.
17. Source: IDPF, *http://www.openebook.org/doc_library/industrystats.htm*

5

Business models for content licensing

In its short history, digital content licensing has seen dramatic changes in business models for selling and buying. This can be seen, for example, in the long-running debate over providing free or paid access to content. There have been well-known examples of content that has moved from one to the other model, and there is regular discussion about the merits of free (that is, advertising-supported) compared with paid (typically subscription or pay-per-view) access. In discussing the possibility of the *Wall Street Journal* moving from its current paid subscription model to a free model, one analyst estimated that it would require 12 times as much traffic to support an advertising-based model than a subscription-based one.[1] However, such statistics are disputed, and it is rare in this debate to have access to figures that allow a comparative analysis: in the fast-changing world of web-based publishing, it is difficult to set up a controlled experiment in which the only variation is the cost of accessing the content.

Changes in technology can have an unexpected effect on the market. As described earlier (section 2.5), the lingering perception that CD-ROM was a 'permanent' medium made many libraries reluctant to move to online delivery, although it is clearly a better means for delivering information. One outcome of concerns about 'losing' content has been the creation of perpetual licences; for more about how they seek to resolve this problem, see section 9.13.

Deals for selling content come in a bewildering variety, from a one-off flat fee to an annual licence, or a royalty based on usage. One of the first decisions the information owner has to choose is whether to license content via an aggregator, or to sell content direct to end users. There is no single answer; either of these might be appropriate, depending on the circumstances. The advantages of selling via aggregators are:

- It is simple to implement – these deals require little in-house resource or technical expertise.

- The deals require no capital investment, and so are good for the publisher's cash-flow.

- Hence such deals present little risk for the publisher, especially if the deal is non-exclusive (see section 9.6.1).

- Because the content owner is not creating a new market but accessing a pre-existing one, via the aggregator, content will start to produce a return sooner than creating a market from scratch.

But deals with an aggregator have disadvantages as well:

- The aggregator takes a substantial part of the revenue.

- The aggregator's service will usually serve the best interests of the aggregator, not the interests of the publisher – for example, the aggregator aims to promote their own brand before that of the publisher's.

- The content owner has little control over the interface; it may not be possible to differentiate one publisher's product through an aggregator.

- Working with an aggregator leaves the publisher with little control over sales and marketing, and little opportunity for publishers to learn about the digital market, that is, where customers' needs and preferences lie.

- Currently, many aggregators do not offer a wide range of access options. By selling direct, the publisher can sell by chapter, by section or even by page if appropriate; the publisher has complete control of what and how content is sold, and the offering may well be different for selling (say) student textbooks than for fiction. For example, the publisher can provide a wide range of time-based access, for example access for 24 hours, access for a year, or one-time download.

- Providing content via aggregators often involves a lock-in period: the publisher may have to commit to a number of years with an aggregator, which may cause problems if the publisher subsequently decides to host material directly.

- Decisions may be taken on publishers' behalf that are not in the best interests of the publisher or content owner (e.g. format for capture, sales methods, selling to markets or territories where the publisher already has strong sales channels).

Content owners and publishers should also consider some other implications of hosting and selling content directly:

- Creating a direct sales website requires a compelling collection of content. Only a few publishers have a sufficiently powerful collection of content to consider a single-publisher portal.

- To host content requires set-up time, some software for hosting and retrieving content, and skills in interface design and website management. Unless the organisation already has this capability, there should be a budget to implement all of these, as well as ongoing maintenance costs.

- In addition, if content is being sold from the site, the site owner needs to deploy and manage e-commerce and online marketing skills. Most publishers traditionally outsource such skills; for example, trade publishers typically hand retail sales to bookshops, in recognition of the specialised nature of bookselling.

5.1 Where buying and selling take place

Content licensing tends to be bought and sold at industry events organised by channel. Thus, for example, TV, film, and interactive media rights are sold at MIPTV-Milia (Cannes, spring of each year).[2] Rights for such content-related topics as cartoon characters and branding are handled in separate shows such as the Seoul Character Fair,[3] the largest show of its kind in Asia.

Text licensing deals take place in major library and information exhibitions, notably the ALA (American Library Association) Annual Conference and Exhibition (actually twice a year, the summer conference being the most important). This has always been the most important US show for content licensing to academic libraries; there is no UK equivalent. However, traditional book fairs such as the London Book Fair (annually in the spring, London) and Book Expo America – the major US trade book fair, which takes place annually in June – now have a substantial digital component for buying and selling content. The largest book fair is the Frankfurt Book Fair, which was slow to develop a substantial electronic licensing market, focusing instead on print publishing rights, but which has become progressively more important for content licensing. An indication of the scale of the Frankfurt rights market can be seen from the EFRIS (Extended Frankfurt Rights Information system, an online system for buying and selling rights remotely; Figure 5.1). This system was developed

Figure 5.1 The Frankfurt Book Fair rights database

in 1999 and launched in 2000. It was a development by a consortium including PIRA International, the Frankfurt Book Fair and the Federation of European Publishers (FEP).[4]

Finally, there are exhibitions that focus primarily on digital content, such as Online Information (December, London), where large-scale content aggregators such as LexisNexis and Dow Jones Factiva have prominent stands.

Given the vast subject range of digital content, it is not surprising that generic shows with 'online' in the title are increasingly supplemented by smaller, subject-based events; for example, in theology, the American Theological Library Association (ATLA) has a major annual conference where deals are done to buy and sell digital content in theology, and in addition there is an annual BibleTech conference (*http://www.bibletech. com*) where Bible-related content is licensed.

5.2 Consortia

Consortia are groups of buyers or sellers, typically libraries, which take advantage of their collective bargaining power to negotiate bulk deals, whether for buying or selling, and to ensure that the best possible terms are achieved, or (in the case of sellers) enabling their content to be sold at all – given the limited time available to most libraries, it is not cost-effective to do individual deals with many small publishers. Consortia have advantages both for content owners and for libraries. One of the oldest-established purchasing consortia is OhioLINK (Ohio Library and Information Network, *http://www.ohiolink.edu*), founded in 1987, a cooperative of some 90 libraries in the state of Ohio, which created models that have subsequently been followed by many later consortia. While OhioLINK covers both public and academic libraries, some consortia concentrate on one or other sector only. The NERL (NorthEast Research Libraries Consortium) produces some excellent guidelines for licensing content.[5]

In the UK, notable consortia include the Southern Universities Purchasing Consortium,[6] comprising some 80 higher-education institutions. It was founded in 1974, but only later began negotiating the licensing of e-content. It concluded a major deal with ProQuest in August 2005, and with Ebrary in 2007. All UK Higher Education institutions are part of the JISC Collections consortium (see section 7.4.5), a government-funded collective initiative. JISC Collections also manages the National Electronic Site Licence (NESLi, now called NESLi2[7]), which provides a collective agreement that operates between journal publishers selling content via a standard licence, and with UK higher education institutions, who buy this content collectively.

Similarly, publishers may act as a consortium to sell content, unless they are one of the largest three or four, such as Elsevier or Oxford University Press (OUP), in which case they usually sell their own collection direct. An example of a sales consortium for journals is the Association of Learned and Professional Society Publishers (ALPSP) Learned Journals Collection (a partnership between ALPSP and Swets, launched in 2003),[8] which provides content mainly from smaller publishers. By creating a single packaged collection, this initiative enables smaller publishers to compete in the market with larger single-publisher collections from Elsevier and Informa. The ALPSP Learned Journals collection has grown steadily since its first introduction, and in 2008 comprised several hundred journals.

Although buying in bulk can be very cost-effective, it is important for libraries to retain some choice over which journals are included in the deal. There is little point in licensing thousands of journals if many of them are never accessed by library users. To ascertain which journals are accessed, usage figures need to be compiled: for more about monitoring usage, see section 10.26.

5.3 Slicing and dicing content

Content can be licensed as a unit or as a collection, but it can also be licensed as a subunit. The model for this came from journal publishers who realised that they could provide, in addition to a subscription for the entire journal, access to a single paper, for a one-off fee. This model produces a growing revenue stream that undoubtedly creates an additional market for the content, an example of market extension. Most journal hosts now provide single-article access; pioneers were Elsevier (all articles in Science Direct are available through their pay-per-view service) and IngentaConnect (see section 6.11.2). Articles may be provided as a one-time PDF download, or alternatively an article can be provided for on-screen access only, for a limited time. The period may vary from a day to a month or more. An interesting study published in 2007 compared various business models for delivering individual journal articles to institutions, both pay-per-view and subscription-based access for the entire journal.[9] Perhaps not surprisingly, the study found that for institutions, subscriptions were a better model, but for most publishers the opportunities from pay-per-view are most likely to come from non-academic markets such as commercial researchers and pharmaceutical companies, for whom a full subscription might not be convenient.

Journal articles lend themselves to stand-alone delivery because it is rare for an issue of a journal to have any kind of thematic link from one article to another. For most purposes, users have no interest whatever in the other articles that comprise one issue of a journal.

One rights issue that should be considered when splitting an original work into constituent parts is any possible change to the rights as a result of the split. A single image provided as part of a book or article will have very different rights if it is extracted from the work and reused elsewhere.

In cases where part of the entire work is sold, content owners attempt to prevent cannibalisation of sales of the entire content by pricing sections from the content higher than pro-rata (Table 5.1).

Many academic courses make use of extracts from a range of sources, when a lecturer uses a chapter from one book, an extract from another and so on. This model is becoming increasingly common, corresponding

Table 5.1 Typical pricing scale for content segments

Proportion of the entire content bought (%)	Percentage of total price charged
10	20
15	25
20	30
30	40
40	50

to the Web 2.0 idea of a mash-up of various content sources to produce a customised product. There are now tools available to facilitate such content selection and combination (see section 5.7.1).

5.4 Web syndication

Much content is disseminated by replicating content that has already appeared on other websites. A news-based website can greatly enhance the reach of its content by making that content available to third-party sites, either the headlines only or a summary of the articles, using automatic tools (see below). At first glance it might seem that Web-based syndication, the act of copying content from one website to appear on another, is a singularly pointless activity, since what can be seen on one website is only a hyperlink away from any other page. Yet given the number of websites in existence, over 182 million in October 2008,[10] and despite the best efforts of search engines, the chances of finding relevant content diminishes daily. As the Web continues to grow in size, findability becomes more of an issue. Hence the advantage for most content providers to add signposts to their content.

Content is typically provided to third parties using a technology such as RSS feeds or Atom (see section 10.15). It is an indication of the immediacy of the Web that news can be copied very rapidly in this way. It might take two days to write an article for a newspaper, but only a fraction of a second for that story to appear on news aggregator sites around the world. An example of a Web syndication company is Yellowbrix (*www.yellowbrix.com*), which provides business and news content; it acquired iSyndicate in 2001. However, syndication is simple to do directly, using RSS and similar technologies.

Having a clear idea of the business model almost certainly takes more time than implementing the RSS feeds. If it is simple to let others know when sections of a website have changed, it is also simple technically to extract changed content from a website without permission, a technique known as 'scraping' or 'harvesting'. It is one thing to disseminate content, and quite another to find content being disseminated without permission and without payment. The fact that the original content is provided free of charge does not mean it can be republished. There has been much discussion about protection of intellectual property with regard to scraper sites – the development of Automated Content Access Protocol (ACAP) was intended to allow publishers to have more control over this process (see section 10.22).

Google itself is, of course, nothing but a scraper site, comprising almost nothing but snippets of other sites that it is republishing, along with adverts, in response to a search. Most Web users probably regard this activity of search engines such as Google to be acceptable (apart from some news and print publishers – see section 8.2.1). The technology is not the problem, in other words, but the use made of it. Publishers' objections are typically based around content where even a few words or figures are sufficient to threaten the publisher's market. If the scraper site comprises (for example) stock market prices, or other valuable content, it is easy to see the issue.

5.5 Monopoly and competition issues

Can content licensing facilitate a freer market by providing competition? In economic terms, the products of academic publishing – monographs and textbooks – are not substitutable. If a library does not have a copy of a specific monograph or textbook, it would be unacceptable for the user to accept an alternative title. Once a book or article is on a reading list, or deemed to be a standard work, students and libraries have no choice but to access it in some way. Hence by implication there will be little price competition between academic titles. Unsurprisingly, as a result of the increase in price for academic monographs, end-user purchase of monographs has almost disappeared. The only purchasers of print copies of monographs are libraries.

With the arrival of content licensing, the situation has changed somewhat. Whereas initially there was no market for purchase of, or access to, digital versions of monographs, the creation of digital collections such as Oxford Scholarship Online has changed matters – although unless the same content is available from two or more sources, there is unlikely to be any price competition.

Textbook publishing is similar to monograph publishing in this respect; there are no obvious substitutes to a textbook once it is placed on a course reading list, even though publishers make every effort to compete with established adopted textbooks by producing rival titles to a standard work. However, textbooks have a wider market than monographs, as they are bought both by end users and by institutions. As a result of content licensing, an additional market has been created: there is at least a potential market for end users to buy access to textbooks, a market that has been addressed by some of the aggregators, notably Questia (see section 7.5.8).

A slightly different area of academic publishing is the literature survey, or more inelegantly the 'crammer'. Tackling a subject in a couple of hundred pages or less, the crammer aims to provide an overview of the subject, a brief review of the literature and a bibliography, so that the student does not have to read any monograph at all. Such titles are produced by several publishers, including OUP, Routledge, Pearson and Continuum. Unlike monographs and textbooks, they are highly substitutable, given that for the purpose of most students one crammer is as good as another. Aggregating services often provide several collections of such titles. When providing digital versions of such content, quantity can be more important than quality: as more titles are added to the series, the series brand becomes as important as, or even more important than, the author name. This is the case with a series such as the Very Short Introductions from Oxford University Press.

Reference books are to a large extent substitutable. Basic definitions of terms, subject dictionaries, bilingual dictionaries and encyclopedias, typically have competing titles. Despite publishers' efforts to make their reference titles unique, only a handful of reference works reach iconic status, where libraries will accept that work and no other; the *New Grove Dictionary of Music* is an example. In most other areas, user choice comes down to issues such as convenience and speed of retrieval.

Aggregated collections of commercial content are probably more substitutable than their owners would like. This would seem to be indicated when aggregators keep adding more content to a service: if the existing content had no substitutes, there would be no need to add further content. For more about business and finance databases, see section 7.2.

One way in which content licensing can introduce competition is by providing access to the same content in a different channel. End users will be pleased with this, publishers and content owners less so. End users such as students need to access, say, 20 books or journal articles for a course module. For each item, they can choose to purchase the print book (new or second-hand); they can license the content, borrow it from a friend, access the print copy from the library, or access a digital version from the library. In other words, there is a proliferation of means of accessing the content, and the end user has some flexibility in deciding which method to use. In the academic textbook market, if an aggregator sets the price for licensing a particular book title unusually high, end users can substitute one form of accessing that title for another. To an extent, the end user will place a value on convenience of use, findability and so on, but this does not prevent the different methods of access being substitutable. In addition, some users will recognise a benefit in having the content available in multiple formats, such as both print (for ease of reading) and online (for ease of searching).

The situation in the trade fiction market is rather different. Some titles are of course non-substitutable, but this is only true of a small number of in-copyright authors. For much fiction, all titles are in competition with each other: a reader will enter a bookshop to buy one fiction title, but many will purchase a different title if the first one is unavailable: in other words, users will frequently treat fiction titles as substitutes. The arrival of a new format such as the e-book reader might exert a downward pressure on price, as the different formats in which a book is available are competing with each other, as described above; however, the added convenience of the e-book reader might well ensure that a premium price is payable for the title in a convenient format.

Journal publishing has a monopoly aspect to it; for most purposes, there is no alternative but to read one specific article, which is the copyright of one publisher and which may only be available from one digital collection at any library (although Google Scholar, described in section 8.2.2, may provide other possible locations). The extent to which journal publishing is a monopoly can be seen by the steady increase in inflation-adjusted journal prices over the last 20 years. One response within the higher-education community is the rise of the institutional repository and open-access journals (see 'Open-access content' in section 5.11).

Monopoly issues are more significant where the content is both unique and has no readily available substitute. Some publishers and/or aggregators have created a content monopoly in providing the most complete collection of texts on one subject, for example the Chadwyck-Healey literature collections (see section 2.5.3). It may be that as the pace of digitisation increases, a wider range of content from several aggregators or publishers could become available by providing a federated search of several independent collections.

Unique content available from only one source constitutes a monopoly. This happens particularly in commercial publishing, but there are also examples of this with agencies loosely linked to but not forming part of the government, such as (in the UK) organisations publishing official standards (the British Standards Institute, BSI), maps (Ordnance Survey) or legal information, such as health and safety standards (IOSH, the Institution of Occupational Safety and Health). Organisations such as the BSI and Ordnance Survey receive government funding to support the publication of information, yet operate as a monopoly supplier in their market.

The cost of accessing public standards may also be an issue. Ironically, when Adobe moved the PDF standard to an open standard, managed by the International Standards Organization (ISO), the cost of acquiring the standard went up from zero (when it was downloaded from the Adobe website) to hundreds of Swiss francs, acquiring it from ISO (the International Standards Organization), a not-for-profit body that has little opportunity for revenue except by charging for copies of the standard.

5.5.1 Case study: Online standards from the BSI

Government-controlled information bodies run the risk of approaching monopoly status. The BSI is the UK national standards body, charged with producing and disseminating standards on behalf of government and industry. Today, digitised versions of these standards are available from several content sites, but in 2002 another information provider, Barbour Index plc, alleged that BSI was abusing its monopoly position by not granting access to other companies to disseminate these standards in digital form.[11] At that time, the only digital versions of British Standards were provided by a company called British Standards Publishing Ltd, a joint venture company 50% owned by BSI. The situation was resolved after the UK Office of Fair Trading (OFT) opened a formal investigation, which was closed in 2003 when BSI agreed to allow other companies to provide this information online. Clearly, it is in the interest of the consumer for standards information to be available via more than one channel, a situation that can require careful regulation of the market through bodies such as the OFT.

5.5.2 Case study: The right to watch horse racing

A judgement in 2008 ended the 20-year monopoly of a single company providing live TV transmissions of horse races in UK betting shops. The horseracing industry is organised around gambling, and bookmakers want to show live transmissions of the races in local betting shops. Since 1988, these broadcasts had been provided by a single company backed by the two largest bookmakers in the UK, William Hill and Ladbrokes. Betting shops pay in the region of £10,000 per year for the right to carry these broadcasts. But the racecourses felt they deserved a greater share of the revenue from such broadcasts, and after failing to reach agreement on a new deal, they funded the development of a competing service. The legal ruling allowed the new service to continue, judging that it had not broken UK competition law. As a result, transmission rights are now shared between two companies. The court victory showed that it is possible for parties involved in a monopoly to change the terms under which content licensing takes place, if they act collectively.

5.6 Dictionaries and encyclopedias

Subject encyclopedias and dictionaries are highly suited to screen-based access, as reference works are typically organised in self-contained units or sub-units, whether alphabetically or thematically organised. By comparison with a chapter of a book, which could be several thousand words long, reference content is typically more concise and has clear subdivisions (see, for example, the index of sections to the longer articles in Wikipedia). Moreover, the clear organisation of reference works means they can be placed in a collection of licensed content as a kind of stepping stone to more advanced content.

The ease and speed of retrieval of content from digital collections has made possible collections of reference content, such as Credo (see section 7.6.1). Such collections provide more than one reference title for many subjects, and so provide the user with the opportunity to compare several reference sources – something that would have been considerably more difficult to achieve using print-based content. In this case, digital publishing has increased the opportunities for content to be licensed, as well as saving users considerable time.

Access to dictionary content is an instructive case. For most content, the time to retrieve the information is only a small proportion of the total time spent with the content. But for dictionaries, searching is a major component of the information-retrieval process; in other words, the time taken to retrieve the information may be as great as or greater than the time spent reading it. One consequence is that for many types of dictionary, the digital version is so convenient that there may be no need to have the printed copy any more. As a result, most dictionary publishers are unwilling to have their content indexed by Google and the other major search engines: many dictionary definitions could be accommodated within the average length of a Google citation. Certainly, dictionaries are among the most frequently accessed titles in aggregated collections of digital content. This is especially true of bilingual dictionaries, which are essentially lists of equivalent terms rather than sets of definitions, and so have particularly short entries. Has the market for print dictionaries therefore disappeared? Of course not – the market has simply changed. Print versions continue to be used more for handy reference, while the largest editions of dictionaries, such as the *Oxford English Dictionary*, have substantial advantages when retrieved in digital form over the print version. The reasons for providing digital versions of dictionary content include:

1. Larger dictionaries are typically a large volume of several hundred pages. In consequence, they make extensive use of abbreviations and jargon that is poorly understood by users. Digital access removes the need for such concision.

2. Print dictionaries are cumbersome to use – many users have difficulty understanding the complexities of alphabetical ordering (which comes first, 'think tank', 'think-tank' or 'thinktank'?). Retrieval with a screen-based dictionary is usually faster than using the equivalent resource in print.

3. Words and meanings in a language change frequently. Hence print dictionaries become progressively more out of date over time.

Some examples of reference collections are described in section 7.6.

5.7 Textbooks

Publishers initially baulked at the idea of licensing textbooks, fearing that, instead of a sale of one copy to each student taking a course, all the students would now access the digital version and would therefore no longer purchase a print copy. Certainly, today there are relatively few textbooks available in digital form. However, the situation is not quite as clearcut as that. First, a print textbook has several advantages that maintain its usefulness even when a digital version is available. It is easier to read, it can be annotated, and it gives the user a clear idea of how the part fits into the whole (the user can see at a glance how long a chapter is, and how it compares with the others in the book). While many digital books include annotation features, these features are not widely used. Of course, the digital version has specific advantages of its own: full-text searching, and the possibility of links to external content, either a publisher-created website with further resources relating to the book, or to other third-party content. These features make the digital version an ideal complement to a print version; a case can be made for having both.

Many publishers today provide electronic versions of popular textbooks, including Cengage (an initiative called iChapters, which enables students to access individual chapters from titles), OUP (e.g. the *New Oxford Textbook of Psychiatry*), Elsevier and Macmillan. Pearson have included some of their best-selling textbooks, such as marketing titles by Philip Kotler, on CourseSmart (originally launched as Safari Textbooks Online), using the same technology as Safari Books Online (see section 7.6.5). Like Safari, CourseSmart offers titles from a range of publishers. CourseSmart (Figure 5.2) offers a variety of subscriptions, usually 180 days or 360 days, available either in a downloadable version or in an online-only version; the latter is not downloadable and requires an Internet connection for access. However, difficulties with licensing mean that many of the titles listed in the CourseSmart index turn out not to be available in specific territories.

Figure 5.2 CourseSmart: textbooks online

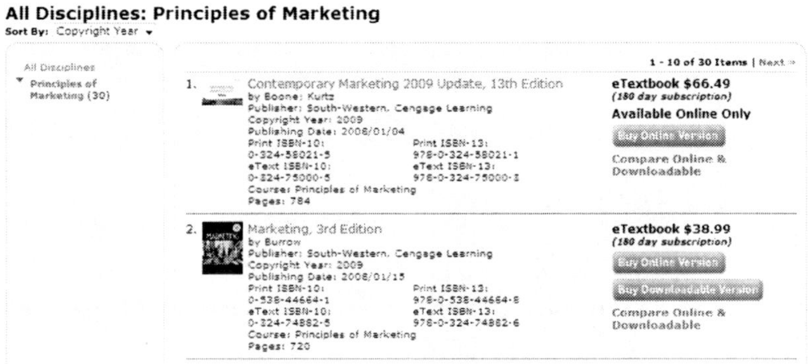

There is clear demand for textbooks in digital form: pirated versions of textbooks appeared as soon as the first e-book hardware was on sale. Several US universities have announced trials of electronic textbooks.[12] In the UK, JISC, the not-for-profit agency representing all of higher education, made 36 textbooks available free as part of a two-year experimental program, the National e-books Project.[13] The goal of this project was to establish how e-books are used. One remarkable fact revealed by this project is the low proportion of students who buy the

Figure 5.3 Customised textbook creation overview (McGraw-Hill)

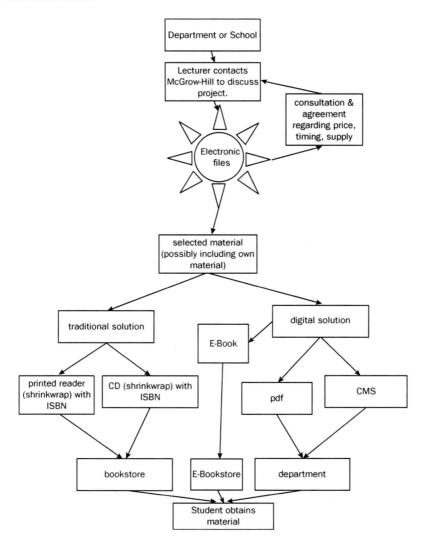

print edition of textbooks necessary for their course. Many of them rely on the library. The library, in turn, faces overwhelming demand for a single title with many students wanting to access it simultaneously. In a survey of some 20,000 students, the National e-books Project found that over 35% of students relied on library copies of textbooks, and 39% of them shared printed copies with others; less than 10% of students bought a print copy of a set textbook.[14] The idea of digital versions of textbooks cannibalising a substantial print sale therefore seems unlikely.

5.7.1 Customised textbooks

Some enterprising publishers are now offering customised textbooks – creating a new combination from existing textbook content. Some of these sites provide not only the licence to republish the content in this way, but also the means to create the new package. For example, McGraw-Hill Education textbooks can be manipulated to create a custom solution, which can be output as print as well as online (Figure 5.3).

The content is drawn from a database called Primis (Figure 5.4),[15] which also contains content from other publishers, such as Harvard

Figure 5.4 Primis Online: selecting content for custom publishing

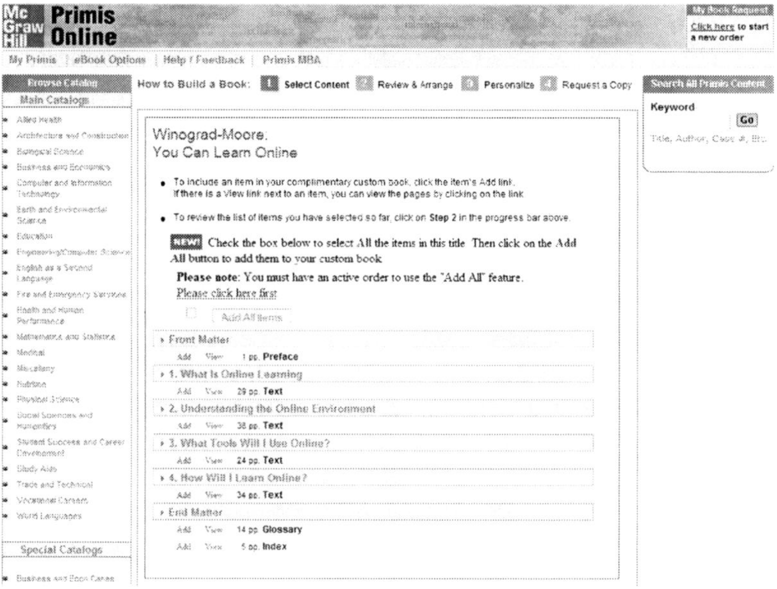

Business School Press. The process shows how different content from a single publisher could be mixed, including material created by the institution itself:

A pioneering project for customised textbooks was SCOPE (Scottish Collaborative On demand Publishing Enterprise), a project involving several Scottish universities, started as long ago as 1998.[16] This was followed by HERON (Higher Education Resources On-demand), aimed at setting up a collection of resources from which print and/or online textbooks could be created. Heron was taken over by Ingenta in 2002.

5.8 Free versus paid

This section looks at the business implications of free versus paid content. Should a publisher make all their content available free, as many newspapers have done? Or should they attempt to replicate their print model, by which content is only available to those who have paid?

One of the aspects of the Web that all content providers have to deal with is the often diametrically opposed goals of interested parties providing content. On the one hand, the idealistic creators of the Web believed in the free exchange of ideas and of content; the academic community is certainly responsive to this argument. On the other hand, commercial publishers and information providers have no interest in providing free communities of content without some means of monetising the relationship with the user, typically by charging for access to at least some if not all of the content. There are examples on the Web of both extremes, and many intermediate points between the two.

An example of the free versus paid approach can be seen from websites dealing with places. Traditionally, this information would have been served by print reference titles; a good example of the genre is published by Columbia University Press, perhaps the most comprehensive single-volume guide to places of the world, *The Columbia Gazetteer of the World*. The digital version of this title has the entire content restricted so that access is available only after payment. For non-subscribers, the entire experience of the Columbia Gazetteer is a search box (Figure 5.5).

Anything beyond that is restricted to subscribers. The site provides no information about what might be available to subscribers, and hence represents poor marketing. Would-be users are unlikely to be persuaded to buy on the basis of the log-in screen they are shown.

Figure 5.5 Columbia Gazetteer of the World: search screen

For printing and accessibility, please visit the Text-Only Version of this site.

CONTRIBUTORS	ABOUT THE GAZETTEER	CONTACT US	Choose one of the following:
ABOUT COLUMBIA UNIVERSITY PRESS	MEET THE EDITOR	HELP	⊙ TYPE OF PLACE SEARCH
			⊙ PLACE-NAME SEARCH
			⊙ WORD SEARCH A full text search

Enter all or the first part of a place-name _____ ● GO

Equally, the site misses the opportunity for users to get involved in updating and correcting what could be the most powerful location-based information site on the Web.

A very different approach can be seen at the freely available database GeoNames, launched in 2002 (Figure 5.6). GeoNames is an ontology (classification) of data about places, derived from Wikipedia and other sources, and comprises some 6.2 million place names. Of course not all of these have equal levels of information, but for many places, the quantity of information available is surprisingly rich: what is more, all the data are available in machine-readable form, which means it is available for integration with other information sites. GeoNames provides an interactive map that enables users to zoom to all of its individual place entries, including names of streams, hills and individual buildings, all geo-located. GeoNames is available on a Creative Commons attribution licence (see section 9.16).

Figure 5.6 GeoNames interactive world atlas

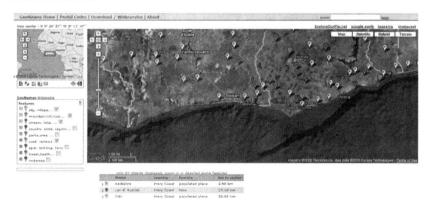

Clearly the free and the paid resources are in competition with each other, and it is by no means certain that the authoritative (paid) content can survive against the less reliable, but freely available content.

For content owners, the short-term strategy is to maximise usability and ease of access, and to make clear what content is available for users, should they choose to pay. In the longer term, paid content owners will need to think very carefully about what value they can add to their paid content, and how best they can manage its growth, if they wish to avoid their market being eroded by free sites.

Managing the transition from free to paid is difficult: it is well known that introducing payment for content on a website that was formerly freely accessible causes a dramatic drop in usage. One effective strategy for content owners is to provide a reasonable sample to any would-be user, to demonstrate the value of the content. Many newspapers provide free access to the current issue, and then charge for access to the archive. With a good understanding of the market, even more can be given away. Thus, for example, the *Financial Times* makes a distinction between 'core users', who use *FT* content on a regular basis in their organisations, and 'general users', who use the content on an occasional basis. For the latter, access to the *FT* became free in 2008.[17] Of course, occasional users are all prospective subscribers.

For a consideration of a related issue, whether or not to index subscriber-based content via the major search engines, see section 8.7.

5.9. Content in the public domain

Material that is out of copyright may be freely copied and republished. Most free collections of content on the Web comprise material that is out of copyright. One would expect, therefore, that there would be little or no competition for out-of-copyright content, in any format.

This, however, is clearly not the case with print titles. The market for classic fiction by out-of-copyright authors is a flourishing one, with three or four editions of most classic titles available, ranging from a cheap unannotated edition to editions with a recent critical introduction and bibliography. All the editions would appear to be profitable. How is this possible? Publishers differentiate their titles by adding value (an introduction, notes, bibliography, an attractive cover); in other words, differentiation by metadata. The same principle applies for licensed content in areas where there is competition.

Whatever the status of the original text, metadata acquire a new copyright on publication, so the notes and introductions create a new intellectual property. However, even the text of out-of-copyright authors can have issues with copyright. It is perfectly feasible for a publisher to argue that the existing public-domain text is incorrect, and then make substantial revisions to the text as part of a new edition, and thereby claim that the revised text now forms a new copyright, as was the case with the Cambridge Edition of the collected works of D. H. Lawrence, from Cambridge University Press. Although Lawrence's work came out of copyright at the end of 2000, this edition remains in copyright, not just for the critical apparatus, but for the text itself.

Of course, even if the work is out of copyright, it is not available in digital form until someone, somewhere, captures it. Even the longest texts are not immune to competition, if funding can be found for a rival to capture the content, whether for commercial ends or by a not-for-profit interested party. Thus, for example, the *Patrologia Latina*, a vast collection of Latin primary sources, originally published in 221 volumes between 1844 and 1865, was captured by Chadwyck Healey and sold for several thousand pounds per set to academic libraries. But the entire set has now been recaptured and made available free by a Catholic organisation called the Cooperatorum Veritas Societas.[18]

There are several freely available collections of digitised content. The longest-established is Project Gutenberg, *http://www.gutenberg.org*, dating back to 1971, with content captured by volunteers; this remarkably early date makes Gutenberg arguably the first e-book publisher. Today, with only 24,000 titles digitised, it may seem a minnow compared with some of the more recent digitisation programmes, but Gutenberg remains one of the most famous content initiatives on the Web. Gutenberg is perhaps the most disinterested digitisation project; subsequent initiatives from Microsoft and Google were undertaken for more commercial reasons. A similar initiative to Gutenberg, but concentrating on reference works, is Bartleby.com (*www.bartleby.com*), founded in 1993. Unfortunately, these sites frequently make use of inadequate texts, which are often unreliable for students. Because of the (unsurprising) difficulty in obtaining copyright clearance from publishers to post content to a free site, many recent editions of classic titles are not available in the public domain, as explained above. Hence Gutenberg is not likely to be a serious competitor to a recent scholarly edition of a work.[19]

There are similar problems with another public-domain archive, the Universal Library Project, also known as the Million Books Project (*http://www.archive.org/details/universallibrary*). The resource itself states that 'many of these books are not complete or in good shape'. A further useful site, which does not hold any books, but provides an index to books available online, is hosted at the University of Pennsylvania, *http://digital.library.upenn.edu/books/search.html*, which reveals the surprising number of freely available texts available on the Web.

For literary texts, it is beneficial to have both primary text and commentaries accessed from the same package. Some aggregators of paid content have in consequence also provided primary texts, and sometimes several editions of the same text, for comparison purposes (see section 7.6.3).

5.10 Copyright content freely available

Rather than charge for copyright content, why not give it away free? It might seem perverse to discuss free content in a book dedicated to licensing content, but there are some situations where it makes perfect sense to make access to copyright content free of charge. This might be for marketing purposes, discussed below, or it may be in the context of academic or educational use, such as content in an institutional repository. Cases where content is given away without any restriction are rare; typically, the use of the 'free' content will be controlled under some kind of licensing agreement. Some content licences have been developed with the specific purpose of protecting rights while giving away the content free in certain contexts. An example is the Creative Commons licence, discussed in section 9.16. The examples that follow describe some cases of free content, and how that content is paid for.

5.11 Open-access content

Open access, the practice of providing content free of charge at the point of use, is now well established as one method for providing scholarly journal articles, although there is a long-running and often heated debate between adherents of traditional paid journals and their open-access equivalents. Some 10% of all peer-reviewed journals are open-access; a list is available at the Directory of Open Access Journals (*www.doaj.org*). Within information science, such well-known journals as *Ariadne* and *D-Lib* magazine are both open access (both are subsidised). One of the best-known open-access portals is BioMed Central[20] with some 200 open-access journals available at a single site.

The key issue with open access is funding: who pays for the publication? Typically (but not always) authors pay to have their content published (a 'processing fee', or in the case of BioMed Central, an 'article-processing charge'). Some open-access sites operate on a different principle, being funded by an external agency, without charging contributors to publish articles; thus, *Ariadne* is funded by the Joint Information Systems Committee (JISC), the European Union and the Higher Education Funding Council (HEFC). *D-Lib* is funded by a several university libraries, plus CrossRef and some commercial organisations. Open-access publishing is encouraged, and subsidised, by several major research funding bodies, including in the UK the Wellcome Trust, and in the US the National Institutes of Health. In fact, the Wellcome Trust have made it (since 2006) a condition of funding that any papers from a Wellcome-funded research project are published via the open-access PubMed Central.[21]

5.12 Free content for marketing purposes

Serialisation, the practice of providing extracts from a work in a newspaper or magazine, is based on the principle that providing extracts from the work encourages sales as well as increasing the total revenue when the content is published in complete form. The heyday of the serial novel was the nineteenth century, with novelists such as Dickens and Hardy, although the first serial novel dates back to 1698.[22]

There is no guarantee that content will continue to have a market after it has been published in one market. It is sensible to think carefully before making content widely available.

One problem is where free access might replace the paid version altogether. The case of dictionaries is described above (see section 5.6). For most accessing of content from scientific journals, the abstract is all that ever gets read. US copyright legislation protects abstracts, while under UK copyright law, abstracts in scientific and technical areas can be copied without infringement of copyright.[23] In practice, abstracts are not republished in their entirety without permission.

In principle, the text of an article abstract could be restricted to subscribers, but the convention in academic publishing is that the content of abstracts is usually provided free of charge by publishers and aggregators, with any sale being made only when the full text is accessed. The availability of free abstracts is sustained by a smaller but revenue-generating market for the full text.

5.13 Content free at point of use: the cover mount

One specific case of providing content free is as a cover mount. The development of a mass market in publishing through newspapers and magazines was a tremendous boost to the content licensing market. Giving away licensed content with a newspaper is not new; it is another form of serialisation, as described above.

However well established serialisation may be, traditional newspaper staffers shake their heads at the process. Rebekah Wade, Editor of UK mass-market tabloid daily the *Sun*, remarked in 2005 that the newspaper's success depended more on the disks given away with it than on the quality of the journalism.[24]

How does it work? The newspaper gives away a free CD or DVD of a film, or a computer game. This might cost the paper £750,000 for the licence, plus the costs of manufacturing the disks. The cost is covered by the increase in circulation for that one issue, or in some cases, as with *Le Monde* in France, the cover mount is available at an additional price. Of course, from the newspaper's point of view, the exercise is only worthwhile if the occasional purchaser is then persuaded to continue buying the newspaper. Often, all that happens (particularly in the magazine market) is that the entire market switches to a situation where all the major players provide bundled content and none of them dares remove what seems now to be a necessary part of the purchase price. The home computer magazine market is an example of this phenomenon: most of the leading magazines provide a CD or DVD with bundled software with every issue. Initially only demonstrations of games were provided, but later full versions of games, and full versions of computer software – usually a release or two before the current version, with a discounted offer to purchase the current version; a notable example was a cover mount in December 2006 of QuarkXPress 5, at which time version 7 was the current available commercially. In other words, this software had a lower but nonetheless appreciable value in the market, which the vendor felt would be likely to generate additional sales of the latest version.

5.14 Providing free content to members

Licensed content can be given away as a membership benefit, either commissioned specifically for the new market, or repurposed for the new use. In 2004, the Building Research Establishment (BRE), the largest construction research laboratory in Europe, launched a monthly current-awareness bulletin called *Insight*. It provided technical updates about the built environment, provided by BRE's team of expert scientists. The Royal Institute of British Architects (RIBA), the professional association for architects in England and Wales, bought a licence from the content owner to provide this newsletter free of charge to their members at a password-protected area of the RIBA website. Membership benefits of this kind are a common win–win scenario for content licensing: the publisher reaches a market that would probably otherwise not be reachable, and the licence provides a benefit at an advantageous, or zero, price to the membership. Finally, a professional association is able to meet one of its stated goals in providing a benefit for all members, not only those who are within easy reach of the London-based central office or of local branches. In this case, the architects gained a valuable information resource that would not otherwise have been available. Many membership and professional associations now provide online licensed content of this kind. The British Computer Society, for example, provides collections of IT-related books and articles from aggregators for members (Figure 5.7).

Figure 5.7 Content as a member benefit: the members' library for British Computer Society members

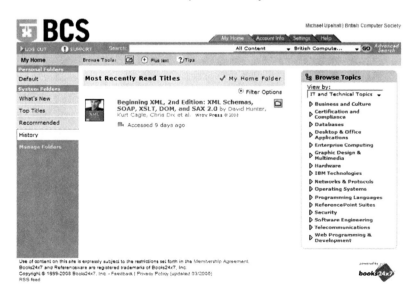

5.14.1 Case study: better rugby coaching

Providing targeted content ready for immediate use is a widely used strategy for publishing to teachers, but there are many situations where ready-to-use content can have a market. Amateur sports clubs across the country have regular training sessions for their teams, but their coaches may not necessarily have the time or resources to prepare detailed tactical and skills training for each session. A small UK-based newsletter publisher has published for several years print-based training plans, each of them one or two pages of A4, for use by rugby and soccer clubs (*www.newsletters.co.uk*). Each weekly issue contains enough content for one or two training sessions. With digital delivery, it became possible to deliver by email a couple of A4 pages of PDF that can be printed out via a local PC. But in addition to the cost savings provided by not having to pay for postage, the publisher was able to license to the Welsh Rugby Union (WRU) a selection of digital training plans, which were then provided free of charge to amateur clubs via a website. For the WRU, this initiative provided a clear benefit to all clubs and helped to meet the association's goal of developing the game. The content-licensing sale would not have existed had it not been for the prior digitisation of the resource. Of course, the publisher has to be satisfied that any 'leakage' of sales will be outweighed by the increased exposure to the product from a sale of this kind.

5.15 For and against licensing content

The decision to license content or not is affected by many factors, discussed at various places throughout this book. For convenience, I have summarised some of the most common arguments given by content owners about their attitudes to licensing. Arguments in favour of selling digital rights include:

- Digital sales will enhance the total sales revenue.

- New technology creates new markets, and licensing content enables the content owner to gain a share of this new market. The provision of information is moving inexorably to digital delivery. If publishers do not enter this new market now, they will miss a vital opportunity.

- If a content owner does not license their material, other competing content owners, whether offering free or paid, existing or new material, is likely to gain market share by licensing their content first, and/or by creating a portal. As described above, substitutability does play a part in at least some areas of the book market. Library budgets are not infinite, and the purchasing allocation for titles might well be exhausted before many publishers have got round to making their content available digitally.

Arguments against licensing digital content include:

- Sales of the licensed content may cannibalise print sales.

- Licensing to aggregators may harm the publisher's brand (this is often used as a justification for the publisher creating a portal of their own – see section 6.9).

- Licensing may alienate authors and creators (less likely today, although it was a significant problem in the early days of licensing – see section 9.1).

- Licensed content can easily be pirated (see section 10.25).

The possibility of cannibalising existing sales is the oldest argument, and for a print publisher who sees every hard-earned copy sold in print as a guarantee of survival for the coming financial year, it would seem an appealing one. However, there are plenty of examples in the print world that prove, if not the reverse, that at least the situation is not so simple. The Organisation for Economic Co-operation and Development (OECD), an international non-governmental organisation, published in 2007 a new edition of one of its best-selling titles, both free as an e-book on the Internet and in print form. The print sales were in the region of two-thirds the level of sales of the previous edition. In other words, a decline in print sales, but given that the content was available for free, it is fascinating that sales did not disappear completely.[25] A similar example is that of The Stationery Office (TSO), the privatised publishing company that sells print editions of UK Government legislation. Today, all UK legislation is made available for free by the Office of Public Sector Information on the Web within 24 hours of enactment by the UK Parliament,[26] but TSO continues to provide print editions of Acts of Parliament, and these continue to make money. The 2008 UK Budget was available in print for £45, and free on the Internet. These examples suggest that there can be a coexisting market for a print edition, for example for official and regulatory content.

Remarkably, there is even a precedent for creating a print product after a digital original has been published. Some blogs, which are typically created as ephemeral comments and responses to events as they happen, have been successfully republished in print; for example, Macmillan UK have republished selections from the blog of Richard Charkin, their former MD (*http://charkinblog.macmillan.com/*) in print form.[27]

Notes

1. See 'Bear Stearns updates News Corp. model to reflect Dow Jones acquisition', 2 January 2008, *http://www.tradingmarkets.com/.site/news/ Stock%20News/951164/*
2. *http://www.miptv.com/*
3. See *http://koreacontent.org/*
4. For more about the EU content programmes, see, for example, *http://cordis. europa.eu/econtent/mmrcs/mmrcs.htm*
5. *http://www.library.yale.edu/NERLpublic/index.html*
6. *http://supc.procureweb.ac.uk/*
7. *http://www.nesli2.ac.uk/*
8. *http://aljc.swets.com/*
9. *http://www.jisc-collections.ac.uk/media/documents/jisc_collections/business% 20models%20trials%20report%20public%20version%207%206%2007.pdf*
10. See *http://news.netcraft.com/archives/web_server_survey.html*
11. See Office of Fair Trading Press Release, 7 July 2003, 'British Standards Institution agrees to grant online licence', *http://www.oft.gov.uk/news/press/ 2003/pn_94-03*
12. For example, University of Texas, October 2008: 'Major US University Trials Electronic Textbooks', *http://www.sitepoint.com/blogs/2008/10/08/ major-us-university-trials-electronic-textbooks/*
13. *http://www.jiscebooksproject.org/*
14. *http://www.ucl.ac.uk/infostudies/research/ciber/observatory/ciberentrysurvey. pdf*, Table XXVII.
15. See *www.primisonline.com*
16. See, for example, Scottish Collaborative On-demand Publishing Enterprise (*http://www.socresonline.org.uk/3/1/scope.html*) 1998.
17. See Griffin, Daniel: 'Closer Encounters', *Information World Review*, October 2008.
18. See Documenta Catholica Omnia, *www.documentacatholicaomnia.eu*
19. See Paul Duguid, 'PG Tips', *Times Literary Supplement*, 11 June 2004.
20. *http://www.biomedcentral.com/*
21. 'Wellcome Trust announces Open Access plans', press release 2005, *http://www.wellcome.ac.uk/News/Media-office/Press-releases/2005/ WTX025191.htm*
22. Shawn Crawford. *No Time to Be Idle: The Serial Novel and Popular Imagination* (1991).
23. UK Copyright, Designs, and Patent Act 1988, Section 60. London: The Stationery Office.

24. Quoted in *Sunday Business Post*, 5 March 2006 (*http://archives.tcm.ie/businesspost/2006/03/05/story12333.asp*)
25. Toby Green, Head of OECD Publishing, posting on liblicense-l@lists.yale.edu at 12 January 2008.
26. See, for example, all 2008 Acts of Parliament at the Office of Public Sector Information site, *http://www.opsi.gov.uk/acts/acts2008a*
27. *Charkin Blog: The Archive*. London: Macmillan, 2008.

6

Converting, hosting and access management

The next three chapters look at some aspects of licensing in more detail. This chapter looks at the process of capturing or converting content, then how it is packaged and offered for purchase to the end user, either as a single title or as an aggregated collection of titles. Chapter 7 considers aggregators in more detail, while Chapter 8 looks in detail at content retrieval.

One of the most important decisions in the licensing process is how the content should be provided to the user: should it be delivered as a single item, or as part of a larger collection, as a library or bookshop does? Should the content owner host the content themselves, or should they use a specialist third party?

A collection of content can come from a single publisher or from several; the collection can have one theme or comprise many topics. It can be organised in many different ways, for example by age range of anticipated user, by educational sector (higher education, further education) or by location (North America, Europe). Although much emphasis is placed today on the optimum retrieval of content, via techniques such as search-engine optimisation (SEO), it is equally important to make the right decisions about an appropriate collection for the content.

6.1 Data capture and conversion

It is rare for content to exist in a format suitable for immediate digital exploitation. It may comprise printed text on paper, which means it needs to be captured, or it may exist in a format that does not lend itself to secure digital retrieval, as is the case with word-processing files. The first stage, then, in the content licensing process is to ensure the data are captured or converted to the required format. For many publishers, these decisions are taken on their behalf by an aggregator, but it important for the content owner to know what decisions are being taken and how the data are to be captured, as the flexibility of the content, and indeed subsequent licensing deals, may depend on decisions taken at this stage. For a full comparison of the major formats for holding data, see section 10.10.

Data capture or data conversion? There is less of a difference than might be expected; the same specialist companies do both operations, and the same questions usually have to be asked. The publisher might begin with a legacy collection of print-based content that has to be digitised completely, or might have content that exists in one of the common page-make-up formats such as Quark or InDesign. In both cases, a faithful replica on screen of the print original may or may not be appropriate for the task. The work of the data capture company is to ensure not only that content is captured or converted, but also that it is tagged with appropriate codes for it to be indexed and retrieved successfully in digital form. To that end, some kind of analysis is required of how that content is to be retrieved and delivered.

For example, the content will need to have metadata that identify the author, the publisher, the date of publication and so on. In many cases, there may already be a table of contents, but this, as well as lists of illustrations and figures, will benefit from being converted from a printed list of page numbers to machine-readable links that enable the user to jump to the relevant points in the text. In other words, the data capture should only begin after decisions have been taken about how that content is going to function.

Data capture is often carried out in countries with lower labour costs, such as India or the Philippines, but while the capture itself might be cheaper, there is the additional cost and difficulty of managing an operation some considerable distance away – it is unlikely that staff will be available on the phone during European or US working hours, unless dedicated staff working Western hours are employed. The price of conversion also varies with the speed of conversion required – rapid turnaround costs considerably more.

Conversion is charged by the number of keystrokes, in addition to the complexity of the operation. Most conversion companies quote a rate per thousand keystrokes, which is simple enough to convert to words. Roughly speaking, there are approximately five characters per word in English, and allowing for one keystroke per word for spaces and punctuation, a reasonable estimate for the number of keystrokes is approximately six times the number of words: divide the total keystrokes by six to get the approximate cost of capture per word. Tables, graphics and other non-text items will be excluded from this measure, so should be quoted separately. These also require consideration – what format are they to be captured in? Are they to be held together with the text or separately?

6.2 Data capture: scan or rekey?

Data capture of existing content can be achieved either by rekeying the text, or by scanning it and using optical character recognition (OCR) to convert the scan to a digital file. In some cases the capture is done twice and then software is used to identify any differences, to improve the accuracy of the process; this is called 'double capture' or 'double entry verification'. Scanning is cheaper than rekeying as long as the content can be scanned with few or no errors, which is not always the case when the original version is in poor condition, for example when the printed characters are faded or distorted, or the printed work uses unusual characters or typefaces, or the source has handwritten annotations. Both scanning and rekeying have their advantages:

- Scanning is more effective when the originals were printed on good-quality paper and using high-quality printers; this is not the case with old newspapers, for example.[1]

- The best combination of OCR software and scanners achieves an accuracy of over 97%, a figure that increases over time with improvements in scanning technology (an independent survey in 2001 measured the success rate for over 40,000 pages of nineteenth- and twentieth-century titles at 96.6%[2]).

- Images typically have to be captured in a separate process, even if the text is scanned. The settings for capturing images are typically different from those for capturing text.

It is best to obtain two or three quotes and recommendations from external capture agencies, but to leave the choice of capture method to them, as they will have current knowledge and experience of both methods. As with all other areas in technology, any recommendations will change over time, since technology improves the ability of scanners and software to interpret captured content.

Whichever capture method is used, appropriate metadata should be created along with the text, such as the date of the capture. This can be invaluable for tracking problems in the capture process, and can enhance the content by automatically adding metadata – for example, it is often possible to add codes automatically for headline, title, document author and so on.

6.3 How to choose a data capture or conversion company

There are many data capture companies, and it is a straightforward matter to get two or three quotes before selecting a supplier. Price, however, is only one criterion, and possibly not the most important one. Other factors to bear in mind for the comparison include:

1. The format for the capture should be clearly stated by the capture company, e.g. PDF or XML. If XML, the company should specify which DTD or schema is being used (see section 10.10).

2. If the data are captured in XML, then the data capture company should guarantee that the data have been parsed (check that the capture is valid XML) and validated (check that the XML conforms to a specified DTD). Some companies provide enhanced validation tools to ensure the smoothest possible transmission of data between the capture company and the publisher.[3]

3. The capture company should provide a sample of the capture that can be processed in advance, the same way as the bulk of the content will be, to ensure that the capture process fits the purpose. Parsing and validation are two useful tools that can be used to check the capture (see section 10.4).

4. Try to get recommendations from other people and companies with recent experience of data capture – it makes sense not to choose a company about which nothing is known. Mailing lists can be a good place to compare suppliers. It is not a good idea to try an unknown capture agency for a major conversion job.

5. Make sure the chosen data capture company gives a clear statement of proposed workflow and project management responsibilities, particularly who is to manage the project once it is underway. The person who sells the data capture contract may be based in the UK or

the US, but if the capture itself is done on the other side of the world, and there is a three-way loop for information to pass between the publisher, the local office and the offshore keyboarding company, that may be one stage too many as far as the publisher is concerned.

6. Clarify how illustrations will be captured. The data conversion company should provide examples of how text and other media are captured, and how the links between the two are managed. In addition, images should be checked for scanning quality. The supplier should understand how to deal with issues such as moiré effects (distortion that sometimes occurs when scanning images that that are themselves scans of an original). Scanning of images should be done to an appropriate resolution for the final use, such as web-based publishing.

7. Establish how illustrations will be linked to the text. Scanning to PDF maintains an image of the page, inclusive of any graphics, but more elaborate data conversion may involve capturing all illustrations separately so they can be made available for reuse. In this case, illustrations will need to have metadata that can be used to link them to relevant points in the text.

8. Check how print cross-references and links will be managed. The conversion may include such changes as creating hyperlinks from a table of contents, or creating hyperlinks from terms in an index.

9. If there are data protection issues, the capture company should provide a policy specifying how secure the operation is, for example where copies of the data will reside during the capture operation, and when and how these data will be destroyed at the end of the process.

Less important, perhaps, than the above, though still valuable, are criteria that are often prominently displayed in the agency quote, such as the quoted level of accuracy of the capture. Of course price and accuracy are important, but most capture agencies will quote similar figures for accuracy, and it is often the case that an agency can only charge significantly lower prices for capture if the capture process happens without variation from the original specification. Unfortunately, the biggest problems during the capture process often arise because of changes in the specification, for example the publisher only realising what they want to do with the data after the content has been captured, which means (potentially) an additional keyboarding or conversion stage. Such changes typically cost far more than any variation in the basic keyboarding charge between the cheapest and the most expensive supplier. The moral is to have a clearly agreed specification and an approved sample, rather than to choose suppliers based only on rate per keystroke without checking all the other criteria listed above.

In some cases, the aggregator may offer to manage the data capture or conversion on behalf of the publisher. Of course, because of economies of scale, the aggregator can negotiate cost-effective prices for capture, because aggregators can usually negotiate a low price for data capture. This does not mean, however, that the publisher will benefit from these prices, nor that the content delivered will meet the publisher's requirements, as the aggregator's capture requirements may well be different from those of the publisher. Roughly speaking, if a publisher requires more than 20–30 books to be captured, it is worth setting up a capture process and data management direct with a data capture agency rather than relying on an external aggregator to manage the task.

Ideally, the content owner should be considering further licensing opportunities, and capturing content in a format that facilitates these. If the content is unlikely to be subdivided into units other than a page, then PDF should be sufficient. More complex content that is delivered in different subsections, for example with or without graphics, may best be held in XML. Of course, the content owner is attempting to prepare their content for platforms and channels that may not yet exist, but one of the reasons why XML has become widely adopted is because it is a format designed specifically for content conversion to new formats in as flexible a way as possible (see section 10.3).

6.4 Chunking

One reason for thinking through how the content will appear is because of limitations on readability. Users do not want to scroll through huge amounts of text. Providing content in PDFs gets round this problem by simply adopting the pagination of the print version. This can, however, raise as many question as it solves – a page of print is not always very readable on screen; most PCs do not have a portrait-format screen, so it is necessary to scroll even to read one page.

Acts of Parliament are an example of the problems presented by screen display. UK legislation (and this will be similar in all legislations) comprises very lengthy documents, sometimes with several hundred pages of text. When such a long piece of text is delivered to the user in a browser, it takes an unacceptably long time to load, and a long time to scroll from one end to the other. If content is not to be served up as a set of PDFs replicating the pages of a printed book, then some other mechanism has to be used to slice the content into reasonably manageable units. The solution of slicing the content at appropriate intervals, which can then be linked forwards or backwards as appropriate, is known as 'chunking'. It is typically carried out when the document is captured or converted for online publication. When a full-text search retrieves a hit from the Act, only the relevant chunk is delivered to the screen, which means an acceptably fast loading time to the screen. Chunking may also be used for lengthy fiction and non-fiction that is not held as PDF pages.

6.5 Intermediaries

Few publishers have the in-house skills to produce websites, and few information professionals have the skills to create content delivery platforms. Libraries will have authentication systems, but these may be incompatible with the various content delivery systems they provide. It is common to pass all this work to intermediaries, companies specialising in hosting, delivering information and authenticating access. These companies either provide single-product or single-publisher sites, or they aggregate content from several sources into one big package. Aggregators are compared in detail in Chapter 7; the remainder of this chapter considers general principles of hosting and aggregation.

6.6 Aggregators vs. single suppliers of content

One of the fundamental questions when licensing content is whether to license the content to an aggregator or to host it directly. On this point the content licensing industry seems to be moving in two different directions at the same time. In audio, video and software utility licensing, there is a trend towards major licensing sites pulling together ever-increasing quantities of content; for example, following the success of iTunes, Apple has now launched the iPhone App Store, selling a wide range of software utilities for the iPhone.[4] It is via the App Store that utilities such as Stanza (see section 4.9) have been widely disseminated.

On the other hand, in the book-licensing market, in addition to collections by aggregators, there are an increasing number of sites created and managed by publishers to host their own content. Formerly, only the largest content owners could fund the considerable investment required to create and manage a hosting service, as well as managing the sales process. Today, the increasing revenue from digital sales and the falling cost of setting up a hosting service have made it feasible even for small publishers to provide their own content delivery service. Of course, a proliferation of sites is a problem for the end user, who would prefer a single point of access for many different sites.

6.7 Selling content directly

Strictly speaking, selling content directly to the end user is not content licensing, but in the context of this book, it makes sense to consider it as one of the various ways in which content can be delivered to users. Many of the issues that have to be addressed when licensing content are the same for hosted content, and as we shall see later in this chapter, the distinction between licensing via a partner and selling direct to end users is often small. There are even examples of content owners becoming licensors as soon as they have built their delivery platform (see the case study on GMB Publishing below).

The greatest control over electronic sales is achieved when the publisher has a dedicated online bookstore that can provide content as complete books but also as smaller units, as well as providing time-based access to content. The Taylor & Francis online bookstore is an example (see *http://www.ebookstore.tandf.co.uk/*), providing content in a variety of formats, and also offering subscription packages, as well as providing page and chapter micro-purchase. This bookstore was created by Digital Publishing Solutions (since 2006 part of Value Chain International, VCI), who provided an innovative online bookstore capability for several publishers; others include Bloomsbury, Cambridge University Press and McGraw-Hill. This service was initially provided by rental: publishers pay a monthly fee, and a commission on sales, combined with a contract to capture the publisher's content. This service was one of the first to provide a full range of content delivery options, for example purchase by chapter, or by period of time (for 24 hours, or for a month).

Many publishers provide a single-publisher online store in this way. The drawback of such a solution is that there are thousands of publishers, so potentially thousands of publisher online bookstores, and it becomes difficult for publishers, however clever their website design skills, to ensure that their site is findable. For most publishers, a neutral site providing the full range of delivery options would be preferable; as far as the end user is concerned, a licensed-based site that holds many publishers' content in one place is far more convenient.

6.7.1 Case study: GMB Publishing

Global Market Briefings (GMB) (*http://www.globalmarketbriefings.com/*) is a company that has been transformed through content licensing. Founded in 2004 as a management buy-out from general business publisher Kogan Page, GMB at launch comprised almost nothing but a series of books entitled 'Doing Business With', with each volume covering one country. It soon became apparent there was considerable demand for the content in these books, beyond the original market, if they could be delivered in digital form. This demand included sales of individual chapters, as well as entire books. Despite having only two full-time staff, the company created an online bookstore for selling its content, and then in 2008 launched a subscription-based site providing research reports, as well as enabling related content licensed from third parties to be included. Hence within four years, the company had moved from digitising its content, to selling it to others, to acting as an aggregator. GMB's experience with content licensing also showed how the price of content can vary dramatically depending on the market it was selling into. In the book market, a single chapter will sell for a only small proportion of the entire work, yet in a different market sector, such as a market-research website, a chapter on, say, the oil industry in Uzbekistan could sell for several times its original price in book form. This demonstrates the fundamental principle that content can have widely differing values in different markets, and how even the smallest publishers can benefit from digital delivery.

6.8 Single-publisher content sites

A content site can be built around a single product, such as the *Dictionary of National Biography*, or by combining several titles from the same publisher, for example Elsevier (Science Direct), Oxford University Press (online collections such as Oxford Reference Online, and Oxford Scholarship Online), Macmillan (*Nature Encyclopedia of Life Sciences*), Informa (*Routledge Encyclopedia of Philosophy*, *International Who's Who*) and Cambridge University Press (Cambridge Histories Online). The distinction between single-title sites and aggregated collections is not watertight; for example, Oxford Music Online includes *The New Grove Dictionary of Music*, *The Oxford Companion to Music* and *The Oxford Dictionary of Music*, although to many users it is best known as 'Grove' and treated as if it contained only that title.

All of the publishers mentioned above developed their own platform. Among other things, to have a complete portal involves licensing (or building) a hosting operation for the content, and an authentication mechanism, plus having a dedicated sales and marketing team. However, the benefits of a dedicated portal are substantial:

- All revenue comes direct to the publisher.

- The publisher has complete control of branding.

- Additional metadata and navigation tools can be built exclusively for the site – the publisher is not dependent on third-party coding, and in fact it is in the publisher's interest to differentiate the portal from other aggregated sites.

The drawbacks, however, include:

- The site owner must be responsible for sales and marketing of the service, as well as running an access-management system for the content.

- Such a solution only works if the content is compelling enough to draw users to the site. Content that is valuable but not unique may sell via an aggregator, but will not attract users to a dedicated site.

6.8.1 Case study: Oxford Reference Online and Oxford Scholarship Online

Both of these sites are managed by Oxford University Press (OUP). Oxford Reference Online (ORO) was launched in 2002, the same year that OUP dramatically withdrew most of its reference titles from aggregated sites such as Xrefer (today called Credo Reference). Instead, it created its own collection of reference works, *www.oxfordreference.com*, initially with some 100 volumes, all of them digital versions of titles that had originally been published in print, covering humanities, social sciences and some science. Subsequently, the service was split into a premium general collection and specific subject subgroups (such as literature and Western civilisation). ORO has been successful in the market, despite its initially patchy coverage, having few visual resources, and suffering from inconsistent cross-referencing (since none of the initial volumes was conceived to appear in a single collection) and an apparent lack of any editorial input to the print volumes when they were transferred to the digital platform. Overall, ORO has been an excellent example of brand development through digital publishing. The service has been supplemented by the Oxford Digital Reference Shelf,[5] which provides perpetual access to individual reference titles, sold on a title-by-title basis for a single payment per title.

Oxford Scholarship Online (OSO) was launched in 2003. It provides electronic access to already published academic monographs from OUP in a number of subject areas, initially philosophy, religion, economics and politics, with other subject areas added subsequently. In 2008 it comprised the fully searchable text of some 2,000 OUP titles. It is sold to institutions as a subscription licence, in the same way that aggregators license content from several publishers. One innovation of OSO has been adding Digital Object Identifiers (see section 10.24) at chapter level, which makes linking to individual chapters possible for use in reading lists. OSO raises the following issue: is it possible for one publisher, even the world's largest academic publisher, to provide a collection restricted only to its own titles? This may be possible for a collection of introductory reference titles, but is unlikely for a collection of monographs. It would not be surprising if OSO begins to host other publishers' content, and to act as an aggregator.

6.8.2 Case study: Cambridge Companions Online

This is a paid subscription service comprising some 280 book titles, all from Cambridge University Press. Each title comprises several essays by prominent scholars in an academic field, for example *The Cambridge Companion to Zola* or *The Cambridge Companion to Feminist Theology*. All are available at a dedicated subscription-based website,[6] including full-text searching. The series can be bought as a complete collection, or as a smaller subset concentrating on literary or philosophical titles. The content is provided as PDFs of the pages.

Cambridge Companions are not unique, nor particularly innovative for their technology. However, it is interesting as a successful example of an academic publisher taking a well-known print genre, the collection of academic essays, and adapting it to digital publication. Cambridge Companions aim to make key essays available in convenient form for students, and because each article was commissioned for the series, and never repurposed, it was possible to set up the entire series with rights cleared for digital dissemination. Moreover, the publisher realised that to publish one or two or even 20 collections of essays is not a saleable package; but with over 200 titles in the series, the collection can be sold in its own right to academic libraries. The series creates a new electronic market that differs from subject-based dictionaries or encyclopedias. Cambridge Companions do not claim to be complete (their list of authors is selective, and it is not difficult to spot gaps in the coverage of individual volumes), but the series as a whole can be sold as a coherent package, and has been very successful. This is quite an achievement: in a single package, libraries gain a wide-ranging collection of humanities content for undergraduates.

6.9 Subject-based portals

Portals are collections of content on a single or small number of themes. Portals can be created by individual publishers, libraries or academic departments. They may (but need not) include full-text content. An excellent example of the value of portals as subject 'gateways' is the series of JISC-sponsored subject-based portals that link to a wide range of freely available resources in that subject. Intute (Figure 6.1) is organised in four main groups, of which, for example, the Intute[7] Arts and Humanities hub (formerly the wonderfully named Humbul Humanities Hub) lists over 21,000 related websites, including worksheets and exercises. Other Intute portals cover science and technology, social sciences, and health and life science. Unfortunately, Intute only links to free sites; there is a great need for such neutral, annotated guides to paid content resources as well.

The origins of Intute lie in the JISC-funded Electronic Libraries Programme (eLib), which developed a series of subject-based portals, such as SOSIG (the Social Science Information Gateway) and EEVL (Edinburgh Engineering Virtual Library).

Figure 6.1 Intute: arts and humanities

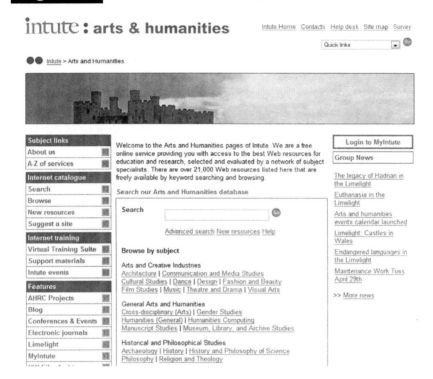

6.10 Aggregators

The principle of aggregation is simple. Content is easier to find when contained in a large collection, and the bigger the collection, the more users an aggregator is likely to attract. It is easier for libraries to do a deal with one aggregator that can provide 5,000 titles, than with ten aggregators that provide only 500 titles each. Hence the biggest collections tend to be the most successful. Aggregators exist in most content-licensing markets; a detailed look at individual aggregators can be found in Chapter 7.

In principle, the biggest aggregator should gain all the traffic, and put its smaller rivals out of business, but in practice there is space in the market for differences in emphasis. In addition, not all content owners license their content to all aggregators: each has different terms and conditions.

Because aggregators license, rather than buy, the content they provide, they have the same problems as any distributor: they are dependent on, but have little influence over, the content they provide. Any brand enhancement of individual titles will be to the benefit of the publisher rather than to the aggregator, so there is more incentive for the aggregator to promote the aggregated service than the individual titles within it.

A further drawback for the aggregator is the continuing risk that the publisher will change its strategy and withdraw its titles from the aggregated collection; this happened in 2002, when Cambridge Scientific Abstracts withdrew its databases from Dialog and from EBSCO Host. Similarly, the London *Financial Times* removed its content from some of the largest commercial aggregators in 2008. The *Financial Times* explained that it preferred to form commercial agreements direct with its major end users, such as law firms, rather than via aggregators.[8] This is a justifiable strategy for content owners, but a major headache for the aggregator.

6.11 Hosting and dissemination platforms

Several companies specialise in the hosting and dissemination of content. For example, the heavy-duty requirements of streaming audio and video delivery mean that publishers or hosts often outsource this aspect of content delivery. Another reason for outsourcing hosting is simply because the task of running a content website and ensuring it remains available at all times is one best managed by dedicated online companies, which have delivery skills, rather than publishing skills.

Companies providing solutions in this area include Ingenta, Semantico (SIPP) and Atypon (Atypon Link, Atypon Premium).

6.11.1 HighWire

HighWire Press (Figure 6.2; *http://highwire.stanford.edu/*), a division of Stanford University Libraries, is one of the largest journal hosting companies. Founded in 1995, it initially provided online journal subscriptions 'unbundled', that is, available separately from the print edition of the journal. It subsequently pioneered link-resolving technology, and several other features regarded as standard for journal publication, such as provision of usage statistics (see section 10.26). It is today one of the largest dissemination platforms, including some 140

Figure 6.2 HighWire Press: journals available free

publishers and over 1,200 journals. Although it is a commercial organisation, HighWire includes over 1.8 million freely available full-text articles, typically science articles that are over 12 months old.

6.11.2 Ingenta

Ingenta is an online content dissemination and hosting company. Its IngentaConnect Web platform (Figure 6.3)[9] provides a repository from which some 250 publishers deliver their content, and with some 25 million articles available. Ingenta has its origins in providing a commercial version of a bibliographic service, BIDS (Bath Information & Data Services), which it acquired shortly after launching in 1998.

Figure 6.3 IngentaConnect

Ingenta's strategy was to provide a neutral platform for content dissemination between publishers and libraries, not favouring any one publisher unduly. It also provides website development and management for publishers, enabling them to create own-brand sites including authentication and e-commerce. Ingenta has had a varied corporate and financial history, gaining and then losing some major hosting accounts,[10] but its merger in 2007 with Vista International looks likely to ensure Ingenta's longer-term financial stability.

6.11.3 Atypon Systems

Atypon Systems (*www.atypon.com*), founded in 1966, is a privately owned US-based company that provides hosting and delivery systems for publishers. Its content hosting service, Atypon Link, provides smaller publishers with a platform to deliver their content online. Atypon Premium is an administration tool that manages, for example, CrossRef, a site maintained by publishers to create and manage links between scholarly content. Atypon Premium is also used by Blackwell/Wiley Synergy, and (since 2007) provides the platform hosting JSTOR (see section 7.4.4).

Atypon acquired Extenza e-Publishing Services in 2005. Extenza, launched in 2003, was an attempt by Swets, a library supplier, to provide an independent outsourced hosting service for smaller journal and book publishers that lacked the resources to host their own content.

6.12 Access management

If content is to be licensed, there needs to be some way of controlling access to it. Restricting access to specified users is a process called authentication. Methods of authentication include:

1. *Passwords.* These require regular management, and are a security risk if the same password is used for all users accessing the content from a single organisation – there is a high risk that users will share their passwords with others. On the other hand, passwords enable log-in from any PC, so they are convenient for remote users – as long as they can remember their password.

2. *IP authentication.* Access is restricted to users logging in from computers that have an IP address within a certain range, for example, all users from a given university domain, such as 'lon.ac.uk'. This is widely used, although little more secure than passwords. IP authentication is simple to implement, but is easy to circumvent, for example, using proxies. It is also a rather blunt tool, as it is difficult to restrict access to a subgroup within the larger group.

3. *Federated access management.* Access is via use of a single authentication to provide access to several resources. The best-known example of this is Shibboleth. Although initially complicated to set up, Shibboleth is more secure than either of the above. In addition, federations are easy for users and can enable a single campus log-in that provides access to many services.

Other widely used tools for authentication of content sites include Athens, Kerberos and EZproxy. For very high-value content, more sophisticated methods of authentication include systems increasingly used in online banking, whereby to access the content, in this case details of a bank account, the user needs to provide a password, a PIN number and in addition a security token generated by a hand-held device; discussion of these is beyond the scope of this volume.

6.12.1 Athens

Athens is a UK-based authentication system, in use for several years by the majority of higher-education institutions in the UK. Athens is managed by Eduserv, a not-for-profit company. Created in 1996, Athens is a directory of usernames, independent of IP addresses, which means a single Athens user can log in from any PC. When the user logs in, their ID is checked either by Athens central administration or by a local organisation such as a university. Users have a limited lifespan, typically 18 months (although this can be renewed), and are allocated access to resources by being a member of one or more groups.

Originally, Athens had limited capability for single sign-on, that is, the ability for a user to log in only once in order to gain access to several different services, rather than have to provide a separate username and password for each service from an institution. This problem can be solved by linking a group of content services in a federation, so that any successful access to any member of the federation provides access to other parts of that federation. Once logged in, users no longer have to answer the question 'who are you?' to gain access to services, because the system knows where the user has logged in from and what permissions they have.

JISC ceased its support for Athens in July 2008, believing that institutions are better served by using Shibboleth (see below). Interestingly, Eduserv's response was to launch OpenAthens, a federated version of the Athens system. Eduserv continues to offer OpenAthens, currently at a price below that of Shibboleth,[11] and to work with Shibboleth. Both OpenAthens and Shibboleth make use of SAML (Security Assertion Markup Language), an XML-based standard for exchanging authentication information. Both of them use the UK Access Management Federation, which is supported by JISC for higher and further education.

6.12.2 Shibboleth

Shibboleth is an international open-source project to create an architecture for federated authentication of users. Shibboleth is 'attribute-based', which means it can check a user's level of authorisation, so that, for example, a lecturer can view content not accessible to a student from the same institution. Shibboleth is in a process of slow development; the project was begun in 2000, and the service launched in 2003, but is only today becoming more widely adopted, with version 2 launched in March 2008.[12] The difference between Athens and Shibboleth is that the former is a proprietary system, and the latter an open-source one, to achieve the same goal. Long-term, Shibboleth is the way forward. It is open-standards based, it is truly international in scope, and it is more secure than Athens or a simple password-based system. Plus, it will have continuing technical development. However, although OpenAthens is proprietary, it is easier and cheaper for many institutions using Athens to stick with their existing supplier for the present.

6.12.3 Other access-management systems

Kerberos dates from the 1980s, so is a pioneer of authentication. It is used both in free and in commercial software. It is widely used for authenticating access to software programs; for example, it was used as the authentication system for the Windows 2000 operating system.[13]

EZproxy[14] is a proxy server and authentication system owned by the Online Computer Library Center (OCLC; since 2008). It can be integrated

Figure 6.4   The Captcha system

Comments (0)

There are no comments on this article

Back to top

Add a comment

Your name

Your comment

n o *r c k e d*

Please enter the characters you see in the image:

Submit

with larger-scale packages such as Athens and Shibboleth, but it can also work in smaller library environments where no other authentication system is running, simply checking the library's database of registered users. It is mainly used in the US.

6.12.4 Captcha

The Captcha system (Figure 6.4),[15] developed at Carnegie Mellon University in 2000, is a further kind of access control, checking that the user is a human and not an automatic device that gains access to a protected site for nefarious purposes; frequently, seemingly unimportant but unprotected sites find their comments section filled with junk. Captcha avoids this problem by requiring users to key in some letters or numbers that are displayed in a form that a machine cannot interpret.

Notes

1. See Michael Lesk, 'Document Conversion' in *Understanding Digital Libraries*. London: Elsevier, 2004.
2. 'Measuring Search Retrieval Accuracy of Uncorrected OCR', Harvard University Library, 2001, *http://preserve.harvard.edu/resources/ocr_report.pdf*
3. For example, XML Probe from Griffin Brown (*http://www.xmlprobe.com/*).
4. *http://www.apple.com/iphone/appstore/*
5. *http://www.oup.com/online/digitalreference/*
6. *http://cco.cambridge.org/public_home*
7. *www.intute.ac.uk*
8. *Financial Times* press release 6 May 2008, see *http://www.ftadmin.co.uk/version1/FinancialTimesAnnounces6.html*
9. *http://www.ingentaconnect.com/*
10. See, for example, 'Rowse steps down as Ingenta CEO', *Information World Review*, 22 October 2004.
11. See Tim Buckley Owen, 'Athens still in ID fight', *Information World Review*, September 2008.
12. See the Shibboleth site at *http://shibboleth.internet2.edu/*, including a video demonstration.
13. *http://technet.microsoft.com/en-us/library/bb742431.aspx*
14. For more about EZproxy, see ALA TechSource Newsletter March 2008 (*https://publications.techsource.ala.org/products/archive.pl?article=2616*).
15. See Luis von Ahn, Manuel Blum and John Langford. 'Telling Humans and Computers Apart Automatically', *Communications of the ACM*, 47:2, February 2004.

7

Aggregators in detail

Aggregators range from some of the world's largest information companies (LexisNexis, Dow Jones Factiva) to small websites holding one or two resources provided by a third party. Both are taking advantage of the principle that a bigger collection of content is usually more attractive to end users than a small collection. Aggregators may choose to collect a wide range of content, or to specialise in a small subject area in depth.

The aggregation principle is used by thousands of websites that act as a portal, that is, they point to and/or pull together content from a variety of sources (as, for example, with Intute, discussed in section 6.9), although licensing rarely plays a part in the aggregation of content on these sites.

Not only are the collections of the major aggregators big; they are getting bigger still. A recent survey of aggregated databases found that since 2001, the number of titles in Gale's largest interdisciplinary database had doubled, and the number of titles in EBSCO's Academic Search Complete had increased from 3,390 titles to 9,524.[1]

It may be questioned, given the huge size of these resources already, whether the increase in quantity improves the overall quality to a similar degree.

7.1 Types of aggregator

Aggregators come in several flavours. In addition to the citation database aggregators who provide collections of information about works, today often combined with full-text content, there are data aggregators, companies collecting and disseminating information about individuals, plus corporate aggregators, who provide information on companies. Examples of corporate aggregators are Dow Jones Factiva and Bloomberg.

A more recent kind of aggregator is a feed aggregator, which merges news headlines from websites, blogs, articles, etc., in a variety of sectors to produce a new product. This, of course, is only following on the Web the pattern that was established by print-based news agencies many years ago. In online form, aggregated news headlines are controversial, because they may be syndicated (paid for) or simply copied without payment. There are thousands of feed aggregators, based on a wide range of technology; Google Reader is one of the better known. The buying and selling of content for reuse by feed aggregation software is called Web syndication, a name that acknowledges the role of syndication in print journalism (see section 2.1). For more about attempts to regulate feed aggregators see section 10.22, on the ACAP initiative.

This chapter considers aggregators in three main groups: commercial (which comprises business and finance, legal, and news), education and e-book aggregators. As some companies provide aggregated services in more than one of these groups, there will be some overlap. Nonetheless, each of the three groups has distinctive characteristics.

7.2 Business and finance, legal, and news aggregators

These are the heavyweights of the aggregation world, with vast, high-priced collections, and with blue-chip corporate clients. Many of the major aggregators have a different emphasis, for example, Bloomberg on financial data, LexisNexis and ThomsonReuters on legal information, Dow Jones and Bloomberg on business information, and Dialog, Dow Jones Factiva and LexisNexis on news, but they all overlap to some extent. All provide content for access not by unskilled users but by trained information researchers, using highly sophisticated search engines. The large aggregators typically load and manage their own content databases.

Although the aggregators are separate, they often make deals to share each other's content in areas where there is a clear gap. For example, in 2005 LexisNexis signed a deal whereby it provided Factiva content to its legal market customers.

7.2.1 LexisNexis

LexisNexis, part of Reed Elsevier and founded in 1970, is one of the largest collections of aggregated content. It is divided into legal content (the 'Lexis') and more general news and business content (the 'Nexis'). It delivered its first online content in 1973, and became best-known for its collections of complete US and UK statute law, together with updates from case law and (in the UK) statutory instruments, as well as statutes for several other countries. LexisNexis also offers a wide range of databases for academic (LexisNexis Academic) and public libraries, and a corresponding database for school students, LexisNexis Scholastic.

7.2.2 Dow Jones Factiva

Dow Jones Factiva provides mostly newspaper and business information, with a full-text search engine interface. Dow Jones & Company originated as a news agency in 1882, and was privately owned until its purchase by News Corporation. Apart from the Dow Jones Indexes, which dates back to 1894, its greatest asset is the *Wall Street Journal*, available exclusively on the Dow Jones online service. Factiva was founded in 1999 as a joint venture between Reuters and Dow Jones, and was merged into Dow Jones in 2006. Dow Jones Factiva was acquired by News Corporation in 2007.

7.2.3 Dialog

Dialog, one of the pioneers of online business information (see section 2.4.1), specialises in news, business, and patents and trademarks information. Following its takeover by Thomson in 2000, Dialog lost market share for some years, partly as a result of lack of investment, even though it contained at one point more news sources than any other aggregator. Its takeover by ProQuest in 2008 (see section 7.4.2) may revitalise it.

7.2.4 Bloomberg

Bloomberg was a new entry to the financial information market that rapidly gained market share from more established companies such as Dow Jones and Reuters. It was created in 1982 (under the name Innovative Market Systems) by Michael Bloomberg, delivering real-time share data from a proprietary terminal, the 'Bloomberg', leased to the client. This terminal displays information from many sources on a single screen, enabling financial analysts to make rapid informed decisions.

Bloomberg began delivering business news from 1990, and today, with some 10,000 staff, it also publishes magazines, and has a radio and TV station. Bloomberg largely provides its own data, but also licenses some content from other sources, for example Platts Global Alert. Bloomberg's success has been through continuing innovation to meet changing customer needs, although the proprietary platform delivery has remained a constant; it was only in 2006 that Bloomberg started to provide content on Web-based platforms, instead of exclusively via its proprietary interface.

Traditionally, there is an argument that the content provided by services with a proprietary interface are more reliable. However, running a private-interface subscription-only service does not make Bloomberg immune to what happens on the Web; it interacts with free services such as Google, whether intentionally or not. For example, there was an incident in September 2008 when Google displayed an article relating to the bankruptcy of United Airlines in 2002, without a date stating that the story was six years old. This story was posted to Bloomberg Professional, and United Airlines shares fell dramatically within a few minutes, since readers assumed the events described referred to the immediate present rather than six years earlier, before trading was halted and the error revealed.[2] In other words, it cannot be assumed that content is inherently more trustworthy if it comes via a subscription site rather than via the Web.

7.2.5 Thomson Reuters

Thomson Reuters, the result of a merger between Thomson Corporation and Reuters in 2008, is a major provider of electronic information through its Westlaw (and, in the UK, Sweet and Maxwell) legal databases, and tax and accounting information, as well as financial data (Thomson ONE). Thomson Reuters and Bloomberg each have about a one-third share of the financial information market.[3] The company has focused for several years on electronic delivery. Its major products include Web of Science, ISI Web of Knowledge and several medical/healthcare databases.

Thomson formerly owned Dialog (sold to ProQuest in 2008) and its Thomson Learning sector was sold in 2007 (see section 7.4.3). One area where Thomson is increasing its coverage is in late-breaking financial news. It purchased a European financial news agency, AFX, in 2007, and has launched a service providing news stories via a private subscription service aimed at professionals.

7.3 Comparing the business and finance aggregators

Comparing the big aggregators is difficult, partly because typical users are highly skilled professional searchers who have learned to make best use of the complex indexing services provided. As with the Web, the information may be there, but the user has to be skilled enough to find it. As also with the Web, it is a challenge for any search engine to be sufficiently powerful to disambiguate unstructured information that has little useful metadata. A recent report by Megan Roberts in *VIP* Magazine[4] (December 2006) compared Factiva, Thomson Business Intelligence and LexisNexis, and revealed how difficult it is to run an effective comparison between them. There are several reasons for this situation:

- The markets for such services are far from being examples of perfect competition. There are only a handful of providers with sufficient content to provide the resources required by the major clients.

- The information users are typically very large organisations. The cost and effort of switching vendor is considerable when, as here, the organisation is running hundreds or thousands of saved searches each day, each of which would need to be rewritten if the user tried to run them on a different aggregator's service. It is difficult to compare aggregators when there is a substantial cost to change supplier.

- As would be expected in a market with only a handful of suppliers, there is a tendency for vendors to compete not on price but on services, rather like the situation with airlines before the rise of the budget carriers.

- A further important factor that limits competitiveness is a lack of clear information about pricing and range of content in the market, which would enable users to evaluate rival sources. It is rare for any user to take the time to carry out a comparative assessment by running the same search on three different platforms.

- The databases themselves have powerful but highly sophisticated search engines, and the complexity of using these products should not be under-estimated. The vendors themselves employ specialist search advisors whose job it is to demonstrate the most effective use of the search tools.

Megan Roberts suggested five criteria for differentiating between vendors:

- customer service, including support and training
- retrieval rate
- unique articles in the results

- ease of setting up alerts

- how hits are displayed – keywords in context (KWIC), or the first few lines of the article containing the hit.

The number of unique articles in the results may be a questionable measure of value: a database that reports 20 not-very-relevant hits is not necessarily better than a database that reports one good match. Other factors to bear in mind when comparing these aggregators include:

- *Shared feedback from other users.* As with any sophisticated software, the users themselves will collectively have far more knowledge of the product than the vendor, if only they can share it. The difficulty is to locate public sites where such knowledge is made available.

- *Skill at creating alerts.* Again, this is knowledge that can be shared. Openly available databases such as MEDLINE have freely available alerting services, such as PubCrawler,[5] which has the wonderful tagline 'it goes to the library – you go to the pub'.

Many law firms subscribe to two or more services. For example, a comparison between LexisNexis and Westlaw was carried out by a US survey of over 700 law libraries early in 2008[6] and found that the majority of law firms and law schools subscribed to both. The survey revealed considerable overlap between the two services, and questioned whether libraries needed two similar information tools. This suggests a market that is not very price sensitive.

7.4 Academic content collections

This group of aggregators contains collections of academic and educational content. Also included here are two government-funded organisations involved in the acquisition and delivery of content to the education community, JSTOR and JISC Collections. Aggregators typically manage acquisition of academic content using an advisory board of librarians, department heads and consortia staff; for example, the LexisNexis Academic Advisory Committee comprises 13 external members,[7] mainly reference librarians from academic collections.

7.4.1 EBSCO

EBSCO Publishing, founded in 1986, is one of the largest aggregators, with some 15 separate subject-based collections. Its private ownership has insulated it to some extent from the roller-coaster changes in structure and ownership that have taken place in the commercial database arena, and with some of its major competitors in academic database provision. EBSCO provides content for academic, commercial, public and government sectors. EBSCO is also heavily involved in other parts of the information distribution business: it is the world's largest subscription agent, managing journal subscriptions for publishers, in print and in electronic form, as well as providing subscription access for libraries.

Like all the major aggregators, EBSCO is continually enlarging its content by acquisition of whole lists as well as licensing individual titles; for example, in 2006 EBSCO reached agreement with ABC-Clio to manage online publication of ten of ABC-Clio's history databases.

EBSCO's largest database is Academic Search Premier,[8] comprising over 13,000 journals either in full-text or indexed and abstracted. It is the most widely used database by US college students. EBSCOhost is the EBSCO journals platform.

7.4.2 ProQuest

ProQuest is one of the largest aggregators in the market. Since 2006 part of the Cambridge Information Group, it has its origins in microfilms for academic and public libraries, capturing newspapers and academic dissertations – it was founded as long ago as 1938, as University Microfilms (subsequently UMI). After a spell under control by Xerox, the company was sold to Bell and Howell, and started digitising the full text of newspapers in 1996. In 1999 the company acquired Chadwyck-Healey (see section 2.5.3). From 2000 the company pursued an aggressive acquisitions policy, taking over several other collections and aggregators, but a major financial problem was announced in 2006 when under Sarbanes-Oxley requirements the company revealed accounting irregularities between 2001 and 2005. Subsequently, in 2008, a former ProQuest executive was charged by the US Securities and Exchange Commission with accounting fraud that lost the company more than $437 million in market capitalisation.[9]

Under new ownership, ProQuest has continued its expansion policy in the areas of news and business with the acquisition of Dialog (see above) in 2008. A particular strength of ProQuest is its collection of dissertations and theses, as well as specialist collections of literature, drama and theology. Other collections include ABI-Inform (business content) and ProQuest Newspapers. ProQuest also publishes some reference collections such as KnowUK and KnowEurope, which originated with Chadwyck-Healey.

7.4.3 Cengage Learning

Cengage Learning was formerly the Thomson Learning division of Thomson Corporation, sold in July 2007 to venture capital investors to finance Thomson's merger with Reuters (see section 7.2.5). It includes well-known publishers such as Gale and Nelson; the Gale name is used for several products. Cengage combines publishing in its own right and database collections of third-party content, so many of its collections include home-grown content as well as licensed material. Among the Cengage range of over 100 databases is the well-known 'InfoTrac College Edition', a database of articles made available to students as part of the purchase price of a printed college textbook. Their major databases for the academic market are Gale's Expanded Academic ASAP and Academic OneFile.

7.4.4 JSTOR

JSTOR is unlike other aggregators in that it is a not-for-profit organisation. Funded partly by the Mellon Foundation, and today self-funding, it provides an online archive for academic purposes to thousands of journals and other digital content. It was founded in 1995, and is managed by a board of trustees from higher-education institutions. By acting as a purchasing consortium on behalf of higher-education institutions, JSTOR can license content for lower prices than the institutions could acting separately. In this respect JSTOR is the US equivalent of JISC. In addition, JSTOR provides a model of scholarly information provision that other aggregators can emulate. Typically, JSTOR hosts scans of the original journal article, typically up to a few years before the current issue (what it terms the 'moving wall', as the date is constantly changing, and can be set by individual publishers to suit their preference), and was a pioneer in digitising journal archives back to their first issue. JSTOR provides a royalty-free non-exclusive perpetual licence to publishers' content. Libraries are charged for access; publishers receive income from the journal use, but also benefit from not having to pay for the digitisation of the content.[10]

7.4.5 JISC and JISC Collections

JISC, the UK-based organisation providing technology for higher and further education, is not primarily an aggregator, but among its many other roles, it facilitates the delivery of content to its core UK market.

JISC hosts some content for publishers, through a series of data centres, but for the most part it negotiates education-wide licences, through a separate (but wholly owned) company called JISC Collections. JISC Collections now licenses content for UK schools in addition to further- and higher-education institutions. Any institution that wishes to can subscribe to a JISC-adopted title at a standard price negotiated by JISC, based on the number of full-time students.

Content licensed via JISC Collections is beneficial for all parties: for libraries, because it ensures a competitive consortium price for access to content; for publishers, because once content is accepted by JISC, the publisher no longer needs to market their content to individual institutions, and because total sales are almost certainly higher than could be achieved by selling directly; and for users, because the adoption of common standards for delivery and authentication reduces the cost of implementation and makes information retrieval simpler and more powerful.

JISC and JISC Collections run many research projects, which provide invaluable information on how electronic resources are used, for example the national e-books observatory project described in section 5.7. It also funds the provision of some information delivered free to the education community; for example, it provides 21 titles from the Gale Virtual Reference Library to every further education institution in the UK.[11] Another JISC project aims to create a single UK institutional repository search.[12]

7.5 The e-book aggregators

Several new aggregators have been created since the late 1990s. Many were founded on the enticing premise of creating new business models via a Web-based service, and some were genuinely innovative. Perhaps confusingly, they have been branded 'e-book' companies, as all the aggregators provide digital versions of books. Most provide content to institutions, but a few are pitched mainly or entirely at end users. If any one aggregator has a feature that distinguishes it from the others, then within a few months a similar feature will typically be offered by rivals. Thus, for example, most of the aggregators now offer a private hosting platform by which publishers can create an 'own-label' portal for their content without aggregating it.

To find out more about specific e-book platforms, JISC provides an Academic Database Assessment Tool at *http://www.jisc-adat.com/adat/home.pl*. This site compares information about five e-book aggregators: E-book Library, MyiLibrary, NetLibrary, Dawsonera and ebrary. Although useful, the comparison reveals that the rival systems have more similarities than differences. All provide MARC (machine-readable cataloguing) metadata, all have restrictions on printing, copying and pasting, and all provide Athens authentication – there is not much to choose between them, except that they all have slightly different collections of content, and some differences in the market at which they are aimed.[13]

How widely used are e-books? Obviously there are wide differences depending on the type of book resource, but a 2007 survey by the Publishers Communication Group of a wide range of academic, government and corporate libraries revealed that they would double their spending on e-books in 2008 compared with the previous year.[14] Clearly, institutions are making increasing use of e-books.

7.5.1 ebrary

ebrary was founded in 1999 by Random House, Pearson and McGraw-Hill. Based in Palo Alto, California, their major sales are to libraries. For libraries, they offer a range of subscription packages. A notable deal from ebrary was an agreement with the UK Southern Universities Purchasing Scheme in 2006, which provides some 30,000 titles in a single package for participating higher-education institutions.

Ebrary works by users preloading a reader. This cross-platform plug-in program, ebrary claims, prevents any download of content to the user's PC. The reader has personalisation features, enabling users to save bookmarks and notes. A Java-based application within the reader enables the user to search in the ebrary database indexes, enabling portions of text and/or images to be copied, and a personal 'bookshelf' to be created where the user can see titles of interest.

Ebrary provides general academic and public library collections, plus subject-based groups such as business, careers and Datamonitor industry reports. It provides integrated searching with library collections. Separate engineering and business libraries, selling via company-wide licences, were launched in 2008.

Initially, under the ebrary model, the library did not own the titles, but paid for each access, but a perpetual access model is now offered as well.

7.5.2 E-books.com/E-book Library

This Australian-based service, founded in 1997, comprises two separate services: *www.e-books.com* (launched in 2000), a collection of some

100,000 e-books selling direct to end users as individual copies, and Ebook Library (EBL; *www.eblib.com*), an aggregated collection for academic libraries. Some 60% of e-books.com sales are in the US, and perhaps surprisingly, fiction is the best-selling subject area for e-books .com. They also provide bookstore capabilities for publishers, for example an online bookstore for Cambridge University Press.

EBL, launched in 2004, sells to academic libraries and has more or less equal sales across three major areas – Australia and New Zealand, North America, and Europe – so unsurprisingly there is an Australian/NZ emphasis in the content. This service features:

- multiple concurrent access (several people can access the same book at the same time)
- chapters for short-term lending.

A basic premise of the EBL scheme is that the content and the e-book lending platform are purchased separately. Libraries own the e-books they purchase just as they own whatever else they acquire for their collections. The price of the e-book is set by the publisher. Libraries buy the EBL platform separately, for a one-time fee, and pay an annual hosting fee. For all books, there are restrictions on printing and downloading, and a range of licensing models.

In 2007 E-books launched 'eb20 Technical Services', which provides technology for publishers to deliver electronic titles direct to their customers.

7.5.3 MyiLibrary

MyiLibrary is a UK-based library aggregation service owned by US-based Ingram Digital Group. They have a collection of around 100,000 titles, and claim to be adding a further 1,000 per week. The service was launched by Coutts Information Services in 2004, and was already growing rapidly when Ingram acquired both Coutts and MyiLibrary in 2006. Quite separately, Ingram Digital also provides an e-book platform for publishers to host and distribute their own content.

7.5.4 Dawsonera

Dawson Books is a long-established UK-based supplier of print volumes to libraries. This service from Dawson Books provides some 40,000 e-book titles, all available on a perpetual model, with no annual subscription payable. Although the service has mainly been marketed to Dawson customers, it is not necessary to have a Dawson print account to use Dawsonera. As with the other e-book services, Dawsonera provides PDF downloads, while the complete title is held on the Dawson site. It is even possible to download entire titles so that they can be read offline; the Dawson site says that 'Of course, after download, the student can't keep the e-book forever. Access will be denied after a few days.' A type of inter-library loan operates for readers to 'borrow' titles that the subscribing library has not purchased but which are held in the Dawson catalogue.

7.5.5 NetLibrary

Based in Boulder, Colorado, NetLibrary (*www.netlibrary.org*) is today a division of OCLC (Online Computer Library Center), publisher of WorldCat and Dewey Decimal Classification. NetLibrary provides content delivery to institutional libraries, corporations and government agencies. It has some 100,000 titles in digital form, mainly academic, from over 400 publishers, licensed to around 14,000 libraries. Like several other companies in content licensing, NetLibrary has had a chequered history. In 2001, when the company was only three years old, but already had 40,000 titles licensed, and 125 staff, it filed for chapter 11 administration, having failed to attract further venture capital funding from its initial investors. It was subsequently bought out of bankruptcy by OCLC, who made substantial revisions to the NetLibrary licensing agreement.

7.5.6 Books 24/7

Books 24/7 is part of e-learning company SkillSoft. It is one of the smaller general aggregators, with some 21,000 titles available, many of them grouped in professional areas such as business, engineering, IT and finance. Its Referenceware service is a subscription-based system aimed at end users, providing full content plus summaries of business books, as well as videos, tutorials and other learning material.

7.5.7 Questia Media

Houston-based Questia Media is an innovative online aggregation service that is aimed at end users. Claiming to be 'the world's largest online library of books', it caused quite a stir when it was launched because of the ambitious stated growth plans – at a time when many aggregators looked to license tens of titles, Questia wanted to capture publishers' entire lists. Founded in 1998, Questia survived a shaky start after exhausting all its venture capital funding only nine months after launching the site. Despite that inauspicious beginning, however, Questia survived and now claims to have 67,000 digitised titles available, plus journal and newspaper articles. Questia sells directly to anyone, although in practice it concentrates on humanities books for students (85% of its total user base). Its sales pitch is simple: for a monthly fee, users can access course content, even if all the print titles are out on loan at the college library. The target age range is higher secondary school (UK)/first two years of college education (US). Questia seems now to have reached a critical mass and to be more stable.

7.5.8 Case study: Questia's business model

Questia, the Houston-based aggregator, is an interesting example of market extension in content licensing. Market extension is the capability, in this case by an aggregator, to create new markets where none existed before. In principle, the end-user market aimed at by Questia – the student who needs to revise and is happy to pay for instant access to titles – is not one that takes away sales from publishers (who will probably not have sold a copy of the textbook to this student anyway) or from libraries (who probably already have copies of the books the student needs, both in print form and possibly also in online form from one of the other aggregators). If that is the case, then every Questia sale is additional to all the other channels by which content is provided to students. There is some evidence that these sales are complementary rather than substitutes for textbook purchase. Given the evidence of the JISC National e-books Observatory Evaluation in 2008 (see section 7.4.5), Questia is targeting the majority of students who did not buy course titles in print.

Having helped to create a student retail licensing market, Questia now needs to look for additional revenue. One possible strategy may be to keep the student as a subscriber after he or she leaves college.

7.6 Specialist and subject-based aggregators

Subject-based collections of content have always existed, for example MEDLINE,[15] a collection of healthcare-related scholarly journal articles (which in fact includes a number of newspaper and magazine articles). Some aggregators have chosen to launch single-subject collections that are sold independently. Instead of aiming for a general collection, where success tends to be measured in tens of thousands of titles, these aggregators have chosen to create a collection in a single subject, or covering only a specific type of work. Some of these services are examined below; inevitably, single-subject aggregators will typically have a much more coherent collection in their given subject areas, and can reasonably claim to have more precise knowledge of how and where their content is used in that area.

7.6.1 Credo Reference

Credo Reference is an independent aggregator, founded in the UK, but now running jointly in the UK and the US. Credo is unique because it focuses entirely on reference works; it has a small but focused collection of resources, which are typically used more frequently than other types of content, so while its collection is measured in hundreds of titles, rather than the tens of thousands of the general aggregators, it can claim nonetheless to have a very high usage rate compared with other aggregated services. Subject matter includes monolingual and bilingual dictionaries, arts, social sciences, and science; users include public libraries and academic libraries. Because of its niche focus, Credo has the advantage of creating a targeted interface for accessing and cross-referencing reference-type content, including a timeline and 'Concept Map'.

Credo was founded in 1999 as Xrefer. It is another content-licensing company that has changed its fundamental strategy yet survived. When launched, it comprised both a free and a paid service, although the free service was the part that was talked about in the press, as in 1999 there was widespread uncertainly about pricing models on the Web, and many argued that only initiatives that were free at the point of use could survive. When it was clear that the free model was not working, Credo switched to a subscription-only service, and established a more solid revenue model.

It initially hosted many titles from Oxford University Press, but OUP withdrew these in 2002 to create its own reference service, Oxford Reference Online (see section 6.8.1). Despite losing almost half its collection, Xrefer survived, and in recent years as Credo it has grown its content coverage substantially.

7.6.2 Alexander Street Press

Alexander Street Press, based in Virginia, US, was founded in 2000 by Stephen Rhind-Tutt, formerly with SilverPlatter, and then head of Chadwyck-Healey Inc. It specialises in authoritative and comprehensive collections of primary resources in areas where there is little or no direct competition, including Black American history, theology (*The Digital Library of Classical Protestant Texts*), women's history and drama. With the acquisition of a streaming audio company, Classical International Ltd, in 2004, it began licensing music tracks.

7.6.3 Logos

Logos (*www.logos.com*) is one of the success stories of the licensing world. Founded in 1991 by two employees of Microsoft, it originally distributed content on CD-ROM. Logos has always specialised in theology. It has often been praised for its ambitious and imaginative use of technology, creating its own software and interfaces for downloading and reading e-books as long ago as 1995, as well as creating a remarkable interface that shows several different texts of the Bible and related commentaries on the same screen (Figure 7.1). One consequence of studying the Bible is that the search software has to retrieve and

Figure 7.1 Logos Bible comparison: five versions compared

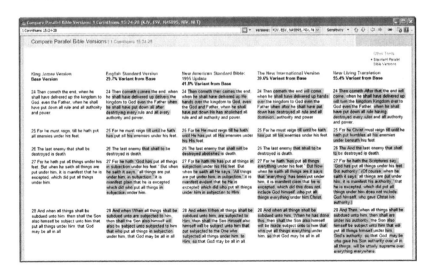

display scripts such as ancient Greek and Hebrew. Nor did Logos have any problems with large-scale collections, for example, the 9,000 pages of Karl Barth's *Church Dogmatics*, or McArthur's New Testament Commentaries, digitised from 26 volumes of print.

The Logos site demonstrates how, by combining several copyright and public-domain texts in a comparative edition, a unique value-added service is thereby created that is considerably more powerful than the individual resources in print form.

7.6.4 Case study: licensing the eighteenth-century way with Logos

One of the most remarkable publishing techniques used by Logos is a reintroduction of a very old way of selling books – sale by subscription, which Logos calls the 'prepublication alert' or 'prepub' (Figure 7.2). Under this system, Logos proposes a new licensed title to its existing customers. If the customer signs up in advance of publication, they benefit from a substantial discount on the published price. Only if enough customers are interested is the title actually put through the conversion process and published. The process is similar to the eighteenth-century practice by which a book would be announced, but not commissioned until there were sufficient subscribers. In the case of Logos, if there are insufficient orders, the pre-pub is cancelled and customers have paid nothing. Logos claims it has hardly ever needed to cancel a title put forward for publication in this way, which is a credit to its publishing team. For the customer there is no risk – money is only deducted from their credit card when the product ships. For the publisher, there is no risk of hundreds of printed copies lying idle in a

Figure 7.2   Logos 'Pre-pub' alert

Tony Evans Collection (16 Vols.)

The church is bombarded with messages from the broader culture about how to achieve happiness, success, and satisfaction. And none of these messages takes into account the transforming power of a saving faith in Jesus Christ. Internationally recognized speaker, pastor, and author Tony Evans has set out to change that. The books in the 16-volume Tony Evans Collection address a range of practical issues that Christians face—relationship conflict, divorce and remarriage, sexual purity, single parenting, gambling—as well as important theological topics, such as grace and the kingdom of God. This collection includes the entire 11-volume Tony Evans Speaks Out series, along with four books on relevant theological themes—all written from a sound biblical perspective and from the heart of a pastor. [More Info]

Status: Gathering Interest ▩▭▭▭▭   (Production can proceed at 100%)

warehouse, and the system has the advantage that it keeps the aggregator in close contact with customer requirements. It is an excellent example of innovation that demonstrates that content licensing is not just about signing licensing agreements.

7.6.5 Safari Books Online

Safari Books Online (*http://safari.oreilly.com/*) is a collection of computing titles and articles. The initiative was set up by publishers O'Reilly and Pearson in 2001. It carries books by each of these publishers, as well as titles from several other publishers. Thus, Safari is both a portal and an aggregator.

Safari is an excellent example of adding value to the content-licensing process to differentiate its titles from more general aggregation platforms. There are several ways in which users can vary their access. Books can either be read on screen, or chapters can be downloaded in PDF form. Titles are 'borrowed', rather than purchased, which means they are downloaded to the user's 'bookshelf'. Once borrowed, a title must remain on the user's bookshelf for 30 days. Users can choose either of two models: the 'Library' model, with unlimited access to all titles, or for a lower price, the 'Professional Bookshelf' model, enabling the subscriber to 'borrow' ten books in any month. In 2008, Safari added the ability to download PDF chapters to the iPhone and iPod.

7.6.6 Case study: Safari – a new way of using content

Safari represents a genuine attempt to respond to the needs of readers in the digital age. Computing titles are rarely read all the way through; instead, chapters or sections are read, often from several titles. Hence, Safari provides powerful search and preview capabilities (Figure 7.3): hits are shown in context, but for each title, a table of contents is provided, and the first paragraph of each section within a chapter is displayed before the user selects that content. Safari offers a genuine advantage over bookshops (and other aggregators) because it enables users to preview individual chapters before committing to read the full text.

The portal provides content ranked at several levels of difficulty, including introductory guides, authoritative texts and 'how-to' manuals. These introductory guides will have three or four competitors from rival publishers, for example a guide to the latest version of Windows, or a

Figure 7.3   **Example of Safari search results**

title on an aspect of computing. They may or may not be the best introductory guide, but this matters little for a purchaser looking to acquire a rapid overview of the subject.

Safari is an excellent example of a neutral site aggregating content from several publishers, but providing a more compelling offering than any single publisher could offer, even O'Reilly, which has one of the most impressive English-language computing lists.

One implication of the Safari model is the need for publishers to provide extensive metadata for content from within the book to be retrieved and displayed separately. By using these rich metadata, Safari can provide several methods for finding content, including an impressive hierarchical index, which organises book sections into subject categories, for example, chapters on 'Web development', 'business' and 'programming'.

Safari has already begun extending this model to include additional content that does not fit within the book model, for example, Roughcuts, which cover a topic such as 'analytics' in fewer than a hundred pages; in addition, there are 'Short Cuts', for content that is very topical, for example 'Web 2.0 Mashups and Niche Aggregators'. There are also videos, 'how-to' guides and market-research reports.

Notes

1.   Aggregated Interdisciplinary Databases and the Needs of Undergraduate Researchers (Barbara Fister, Julie Gilbert, Amy Fry, *portal:* Libraries and the Academy *(July 2008), http://homepages.gac.edu/~fister/aggregateddatabases.pdf*

2. See '2002's News, Yesterday's Sell-Off' *Washington Post*, 9 September 2008 *(http://www.washingtonpost.com/wp-dyn/content/article/2008/09/08/AR2008090803063.html)*.

3. 'Thomson Reuters braces for showdown with Bloomberg', *International Herald Tribune*, 23 June 2008, *http://www.iht.com/articles/2008/06/23/business/23thomson.php*

4. Megan Roberts, In-depth product review in *VIP* Magazine, Issue 37, December 2006, see *http://web.vivavip.com/go/vip/37*

5. See *http://pubcrawler.gen.tcd.ie/*

6. 'Law Librarians and LexisNexis vs Westlaw: survey results' Stanford Law School Legal Research Paper no 23, July 2008. *http://www.law.stanford.edu/publications/projects/lrps/pdf/lomiowayne-rp23.pdf*

7. See *http://academic.lexisnexis.com/online-services/academic-product-management.aspx*

8. *http://www.ebscohost.com/thisTopic.php?marketID=1&topicID=1*

9. See *http://www.sec.gov/news/press/2008/2008-147.htm*: 'SEC Charges Ann Arbor-Based Company and Former Executive in Accounting Fraud Scheme'.

10. See Sarah E. Sully, 'JSTOR: An IP Practitioner's Perspective', *D-Lib Magazine*, January 1997, *http://www.dlib.org/dlib/january97/01sully.html*

11. See *http://www.jisc-collections.ac.uk/gvrl*

12. See *http://www.mimas.ac.uk/focus/08jun/newsletter-p2/#intute-repository*

13. See also Armstrong and Lonsdale, 'Aggre-culture: what do e-book aggregators offer?' *Update, April 2008. (http://www.cilip.org.uk/publications/updatemagazine/archive/archive2008/april/ebooks.htm)*

14. Publishers Communication Group, Library Budget Predictions 2008 (November 2007), p. 20 *(http://www.pcgplus.com/Resources/Library BudgetSurvey2008.pdf)*

15. See MEDLINE Factsheet, *http://www.nlm.nih.gov/pubs/factsheets/medline.html*

8

How content is searched for and (hopefully) retrieved

This chapter is about content access and retrieval. A consequence of the proliferation of content that has been unleashed to the world is that search and retrieval become all-important. In the days when a TV set could receive only a handful of channels, finding the right channel was not so important. Today, when a cable- or satellite-linked TV has several hundred TV channels, but only ten numbered buttons on the zapper, the method by which the user accesses, say, channel 825 becomes more important. A separate problem is to know what is being broadcast on that channel: TV guides have become exercises in information retrieval, with over 50 channels listed for each day.

If TV channels represent a problem, the Web has the same problem many times over. It is often said jokingly that the answer to any question can be found on the Web, as long as the user knows where to look. The rate of growth of websites is slowing, but the total number is still increasing, with an estimated 70 million active websites worldwide in February 2009,[1] compared with 7 million in 2000.[2]

The implication for content owners and distributors is clear: content licensing can only be a success if the content can be found. Content owners, publishers, information service providers and aggregators all have an interest in providing effective search tools. And, for better or worse, any discussion of searching today has to begin with Google.

8.1 The role of Google

Google has changed the world in more ways than one. Quite apart from introducing a new word to the English language, as in 'I'll Google it', it has changed forever the way we think about retrieving content. The art and science of searching have moved from a small community of skilled professionals, who knew how to construct elaborate search strings using a precise set of terms qualified by Boolean operators, to a world in which anyone keys in a single term, and expects an immediate (and successful) result. It is no accident that the 'I'm Feeling Lucky' box has remained a feature of Google for several years, as this represents the dream of the average user. Moreover, when the user does not get the required result, their next strategy is typically to start again with a new search. Traditional searchers would be horrified at such a technique, and would start to ask whether Google has had a deleterious effect on information-retrieval skills. It is not the way one would search for titles via an online public-access catalogue (OPAC). Nonetheless, whatever the correct method of searching may be, Google is always there, and everyone is familiar with it: so familiar that many search engines seem frightened to diverge from the Google model, and to provide any other kind of search tool.

It is fascinating to see research on students' and academics' use of search tools to retrieve academic content, and to discover that the majority of academics start just where the undergraduates start, that is, with Google, rather than dedicated subject-based search tools. It is worth remembering how many information professionals turned up their noses at using Web-based search engines in the early days of the Internet; for example, one typical study reported gravely: 'Some researchers question whether the Web really is a unique searching environment worthy of separate study.'[3] Google has not got substantially better, but it indexes more pages, and everyone uses it.

The ubiquity of Google has had several effects on users' perception of searching:

1. All searchers now have expectations about the nature of searching, based on their experience with Google. Any deviation from the Google methodology therefore has to be justified and explained.

2. Searchers expect to get results, not 'no hits'. For Google, and for e-commerce sites such as Amazon, a zero response usually represents failure (although for a skilled searcher, 'no hits' may be a perfectly satisfactory conclusion to a literature search).

3. Searchers expect a rapid, if not immediate, result. Google users expect to find their result in two passes only: first, the word search, and then, if necessary, a quick trawl of the top ten or so hits displayed in context.

4. Google does have an advanced search screen, but it is hardly ever used, except by information professionals. Therefore, most search

tools on content sites try to provide a simple search tool that provides immediate results.

5. Google indexes only a part of the total content available online. It excludes content at private sites, hidden behind security walls, but can also exclude whole sections of publicly available websites. It is sometimes stated that the major search engines only index the first 100 KB of any site. This figure is incorrect, but it does seem to be the case that search engines use some kind of truncation when they index very large websites – and so fail to reveal what might be vital content for users.[4] For more about what Google indexes, see section 8.7.

Of course, Google is not the only search engine, but the points above apply equally to the next two most widely used search engines, Yahoo and Microsoft Search.[5]

8.2 Getting round the limitations of search engines

Despite Google's dominant market share, some less widely used search engines provide different and in some cases better results than Google. Northern Light Search (*www.nlsearch.com*), for example, is aimed at providing only business search information, and often provides better results in this area. Meta-search engines, such as Dogpile (*www.dogpile. com*), aim to search across several search engines and then collate the results, but the resulting display is sometimes not entirely clear.

Providing more metadata in websites might appear to be a way of improving retrieval, yet, paradoxically, Google chooses largely to ignore the fields available in HTML for describing content, such as the "meta" tag, because it has little confidence in most web-creators' ability to tag their content accurately and honestly (see also section 10.28).

Improving the quality of metadata on websites is of course not within Google's control. Nonetheless, some of the most interesting attempts to overcome search-engine limitations are coming from Google itself. Google now has several initiatives that aim to make more of the world's content available for searching, notably Google Book Search and Google Scholar. Google's initiatives have affected both the technology and the business of content delivery, and have impacted powerfully on content licensing.

8.2.1 Google Book Search

Google Book Search (Figure 8.1; *http://books.google.com/*) is a collection of information about books, using metadata from the books and sometimes content from within the books. It is closely linked to the Google Books Partner programme, by which publishers are encouraged to put details of, and content from, their titles into Google. Google Book Search, launched as Google Print, contains the searchable text of several hundred thousand titles. These titles have been provided by publishers, or scanned from the collection of several major academic libraries in the US and Europe. This project began in 2004, following deals with various university libraries, including Stanford, Harvard and Oxford (The Bodleian Library). The project is controversial because it originally included titles in copyright, as well as out-of-copyright content (see below). Google provides publishers with the option to decide how much of their content should be searchable, although they request that the entire content should be captured. The business model is two-fold: first, publishers share in contextual advertising on the pages where the content appears, and secondly, publishers benefit by promoting sales of the print copies from links to bookstores. Google Book Search has links whereby a book can be tracked to the nearest available copy, using OCLC's WorldCat.

Figure 8.1 Google Book Search

Currently, Google offers publishers, in return for allowing them to index the full text, a link to an e-bookstore where that book can be purchased, and four possible levels of textual detail from the book to be displayed:

1. Full view – the entire content of the book is available and can be downloaded. This applies mainly to out-of-copyright titles.

2. Sample pages view – a small selection of pages is available for view, because the publisher has given permission, if the book is in copyright.

3. Snippet view – this typically displays the keywords in context (KWIC) when the user searches within the content. This establishes whether the requested term is contained in the book or not.

4. No preview – the term is searched for within the title, but the key word in context is not displayed. Even such a limited result can be useful, because it is often highly valuable to know if a term appears somewhere in a book (especially if the book does not contain an index). It is worth pointing out that many paid content delivery services do not show the key word in context.

Google Book Search caused considerable controversy among publishers and libraries. Should third parties such as Google be allowed to capture large quantities of copyright content? Following a highly publicised class action lawsuit in 2005 by the US Authors Guild (followed by a separate suit from five major publishers), Google restricted its capture programme (used both in Google Book Search and in Google Scholar) to out-of-copyright titles. The suit was resolved in October 2008 by a settlement between the parties, rather than a full legal judgement in court. Google agreed to set up a 'Books Rights Registry', a scheme by which authors of in-copyright works receive a share in the revenue from the hosting and delivery of pages from their books; libraries and colleges that display in-copyright content from Google are expected to pay a fee (although public libraries will be granted free access). This is a similar system to that in use by The American Society of Composers, Authors and Publishers and Broadcast Music Inc. for music performance (see section 4.7); these organisations manage a 'pot' of income that is then redistributed to participating members who own the content. In addition, Google will pay a proportion of any revenue (63%) from book sales at these sites to participating publishers. The settlement only applies to the USA, but it is reasonable to think that a similar agreement can be reached in other countries. At a stroke, a new book-licensing market was created.

This settlement represents a major development in Google's activities, as henceforth it will participate in a paid process in this area, in effect becoming a content licensee, promoting and selling book content to a paid market (including many libraries) in return for paying fees to publishers – that is, a new content-licensing market. By reaching an out-of-court settlement, no legal precedent was established that might alter the validity of Google's activities; but clearly, both sides in the dispute, authors and publishers, as well as Google, are happy to create this new paid market for their content.[6] One outcome of the decision was a clarification of what constitutes fair use in terms of display of in-copyright book content. Under the terms of the settlement, up to 20% of a copyright title can be displayed by Google without payment.[7] Some publishers and libraries expressed concern that Google should have access to such a large body of in-copyright content, but there is no reason why other search engines should not offer publishers an identical service. Publishers may earn some revenue from titles that are out of print but still in copyright if they are included under the scheme, and can of course opt not to include their books in the Google Partner programme. There is no doubt that the Google Book Search settlement has created a potential revenue stream where none existed before.

The controversy over indexing works in copyright goes to the heart of the clash between the Web, with its ethos of providing everything for free, and the traditional world of paid content, where copyright works are protected and copying is controlled. The Web was developed by academics who believed in the free exchange of information, and although it is today enormously commercialised, the culture of free content on the Web has persisted, and there are still demands to make information more freely available. Others point out that commercial organisations such as Google or Amazon are making considerable sums of money out of this provision of 'free' information. And, of course, as economists say, there is no such thing as a free lunch: free content is being paid for by somebody, somewhere.

There is a powerful lobby in favour of indexing in-copyright books in their entirety for searching purposes. From an academic point of view, the more resources on a subject are available to students, the better. For an academic library, it would be considered ideal for the student to have access to every word that has ever been written about *Hamlet*. As far as Google is concerned, the more content it can include, the better, and nobody at Google would complain if all the text written by and about Shakespeare were freely available (on Google, of course) for students to access. This is the view of Lawrence Lessig, a respected commentator and advocate of full access, commenting in 2005:[8]

> Google Print[9] could be the most important contribution to the spread of knowledge since Jefferson dreamed of national libraries. It is an astonishing opportunity to revive our cultural past, and make it accessible. Sure, Google will profit from it. Good for them. But if the law requires Google (or anyone else) to ask permission before they make knowledge available like this, then Google Print can't exist. Given the total mess of copyright records, there is absolutely no way to enable this sort of access to our past while asking permission of authors up front. [...] Google's use is fair use.

Lessig's comment pre-dates the resolution of the Book Search dispute, but it now appears likely that most copyright books will be indexed in full, but with all parties, including the publishers, benefitting financially from the arrangement. If the settlement is generally agreed, then all publishers would sign up to the system by default, which is far more practical than having to seek permission to index every new book.

Other related content-acquisition initiatives, although with a lower public profile, include the Open Content Alliance,[10] a not-for-profit group set up in 2005 to create a collection of digitised public-domain works, set up in response to Google Book Search, and Microsoft Live Search Books and Academic, two programmes that ran between 2006 and 2008, under which Microsoft scanned some 750,000 volumes in partnership with major academic libraries.

For more about copyright and how it affects licensing, see Chapter 9.

8.2.2 Google Scholar

Google Scholar, launched in 2004, is aimed at academic markets. It includes scholarly content such as journal articles and abstracts, but not (it claims) textbooks or monographs.[11] It provides not only bibliographical details, but usually a full contents list, some text from the book, selected frequently appearing quotations (called 'popular passages') and references from scholarly literature. In the case of open-access journals, the full text is provided; for paid journals, Google offers (with the publisher's agreement) to provide paid access and to pass payment to the publisher. Unlike Google Book Search, Google currently receives no payment for passing orders for books or articles to the publisher.

Google Scholar has several rough edges, as might be expected from a service labelled 'beta' (see section 11.10). Despite these imperfections, Google Scholar is an interesting service that may provide an important opportunity for content owners to display their intellectual property, especially since the resolution of the Google Book Search dispute (see section 8.2.1).

8.3 Amazon Look Inside

Amazon's goal in adding enhancements to an e-commerce catalogue is to add value and to make its role in the content acquisition process a key one. Its initiatives, notably Look Inside (Figure 8.2), provide genuine enhancements to the search process. It is feasible to envisage the Amazon search interface being the ideal starting point for selecting and licensing any kind of digital content. It is well known, for example, that Amazon has become the de facto source of ISBN information, as the official national ISBN agencies charge for access to this information.

Most people will be familiar with Amazon's Look Inside (launched in 2003 as SearchInside), which has a similar functionality to Google Book Search, except that it takes place inside a book-buying portal. In the case

Figure 8.2   Amazon Look Inside

of Amazon, every title that has searchable text is captured with the approval of the publisher, who controls the quantity of text visible. Of course, Amazon has a clear business model that (at least for the present) fits with that of publishers: the service was set up to encourage book purchase. Look Inside demonstrates that being able to identify what is inside a book can be a powerful incentive to buy either the print copy or an online version, whether purchased or licensed.

Amazon provides an increasing number of other enhancements to the search process, some automatic and some customer-generated. For example, many books have reader reviews. Automatic enhancements include (currently only available on the Amazon US site) a list of people, places or events mentioned frequently in the book (for example, *Gibbon's Decline and Fall of the Roman Empire* includes Marcus Aurelius, Asia Minor and the Red Sea). 'Statistically improbable phrases', phrases that would be unlikely to appear in other books, are shown; thus, *The Hound of the Baskervilles* includes the term 'yew alley'. Finally, there are lists of tags associated with the book, other books cited by this book and so on. All of these features are most likely created without any manual intervention, but are valuable tools for identifying content with inadequate manually-created metadata.

Amazon has created some 15 or 20 enhancements in all, some of which may be useful, some not; it would appear that consumers can now demonstrate which, if any, of these features provides a genuine enhancement to the search process.

Figure 8.3 HarperCollins 'Browse Inside'

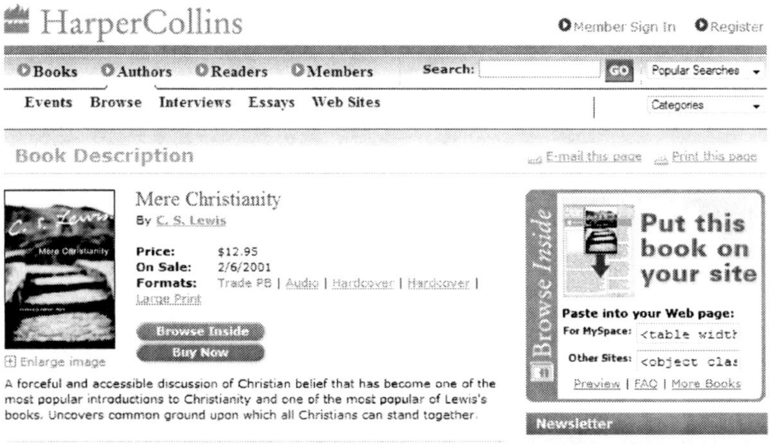

With Amazon's entry to the e-book reader market (see section 4.13), it is clear that Amazon intends to play an increasingly important role in content delivery, both via the reader and from its website.

The initiatives of Google and Amazon towards providing content show the interaction of technology on the content-licensing market: both companies make use of the activity of searching to influence content delivery – in other words, where users search, there can we provide.

Some major publishers have responded to the Google and Amazon initiatives by launching a similar service for their own titles: Random House has launched 'Insight',[12] while HarperCollins has launched 'Browse Inside' (Figure 8.3), including the capability to place a book search tool onto a third-party website. However, publisher-specific tools of this kind have only limited value.

8.4 Paradigms for digital content retrieval

Today we take for granted that the contents page of a book can be found at the front, while the index is at the back. But there is no inherent reason for this ordering; books in French typically have the contents page at the back. Again, books in French more often show the book title on the spine of the book running from bottom to top, while English book spines typically run from top to bottom. Despite these minor variations, users are familiar with a 'book' paradigm that enables them to navigate the contents rapidly. This is why browsing a book is convenient and quick.

Unfortunately, the paradigm of how content is retrieved has not yet been fully established for digital content. There may be a contents list, but there is typically no index, apart from a full-text search capability, which any indexer will point out is not as useful as a good human-created index. Even the way in which full-text searching is implemented varies widely between apparently similar services, which causes confusion, especially when the user is not told how the search is implemented. For example, Witte and Cargill,[13] in a comparative review of searching in five aggregated content collections, state:

> All five resources begin with a single box simply labelled 'search' … none but Gale give any notion of what is going on, even though what is going on is not the same in every case … the syntax behind the simple box is at least slightly different in every instance, and it is sometimes radically different.

In other words, competing services have substantial differences between them, so much so that it can disorientate the user. The following sections look at some of the main configurable capabilities of search engines and how they may differ.

8.5 Common retrieval techniques

Many users assume that the way Google does things is somehow the 'correct' way; yet the simple search box used in Google and followed by many aggregated services is not as simple as it looks. As licensed content will typically be provided with a search interface similar to the one shown in Figure 8.4, it is worth understanding a little more about how the effect of simplicity is achieved, and what searching is actually taking place.

Typically, a search engine has the following characteristics, all of which are explained in more detail below:

- A search box accepts one or several terms, without restriction
- Natural-language searching
- Common words are eliminated when searching
- Stemming
- Hits displayed in context
- Ideally, a maximum of two clicks to reach the content.

All of Google's considerable experience of searching and retrieval comes into play when a term is searched. Below are listed some of the main

Figure 8.4   The 'simple' search interface

features that Google and the other major search engines typically provide. The features described below are for indexing a single collection of texts; there is no consideration here of the tools that Google uses to rank hits based on its estimation of the relative importance of the sites; in other words, these comments apply equally to a collection of websites, and to a collection of content items such as an aggregated book collection. Many books have been devoted to this topic, and the related issue of how to get a site appearing higher in search engine rankings; neither is considered here. The search engines used in aggregated content collections may differ from Google, but it is necessary for everyone to understand the Google model to be able to understand how, and why, a different search engine works.

8.5.1 Number of hits

Google, like most of the major search engines, displays the number of documents it searches, and how many hits were found, with the implication that the more documents are searched, the better the search engine. But is this an indication of the quality of the results? When a new search engine, Cuil,[14] was released in 2008, its selling point was that 'Cuil searches more pages on the Web than any other search engine – three times as many as Google and ten times as many as Microsoft.'[15] Reviewers were not convinced that simply searching more pages produced better results. It is not as if Google is parsimonious in the number of pages it indexes: a recent search on Google for 'Microsoft' produced no fewer than 701 million hits.[16] Of course, all but one of those hits are irrelevant as long as the one most users want, Microsoft Corporation, appears at the top of the results. In other words, methods for sorting described here are typically seen as more important than the total number of pages searched.

8.5.2 Multiple-word searching

If the user keys several words in the search box, all are searched for. Most search engines will process the words both as a string (a series of words in a specified order) and as a collection of words in any order. The former is much more specific than the latter; if multiple words are searched in Google, the engine retrieves hits for the string before hits for the words in a different order. Hence a search for 'man bites dog' should retrieve the phrase 'man bites dog' before the phrase 'dog bites man' (which has a rather different meaning).

Another important operation carried out by Google is to search for multiple words using implied AND before implied OR. Google searches for multiple words assuming they are linked by a Boolean AND before searching for the words assuming they are linked by OR. For example, a search for 'apples oranges pears' retrieves documents that contain all three words in preference to documents that contain only two of the terms, and finally documents that contain only one of these terms.

8.5.3 Natural language searching

Key in a full sentence such as 'What is the capital of Denmark?' When searching its index for terms, the search engine ignores stop words (words such as 'is' or 'the', which are not indexed because they are too frequently used in English to be able to differentiate searches). This leaves 'capital' and 'Denmark'. This can be seen by searching first for 'what is the capital of Denmark?' and then 'what capital Denmark' – the results are usually very similar. Google does not reveal its stop words, but a good approximation is shown at *http://www.ranks.nl/resources/stopwords.html*. Most search engines have a configurable stop word list.

8.5.4 Hits displayed in context

Google displays the hit 'in context', typically displaying a few words before and after the hit itself. This enables users to spot such difficulties as homonyms, where one word has multiple meanings, as in 'bridge' (the card game) or 'bridge' (the structure). The search engine itself cannot distinguish such differences; all it can do is display the context so users can judge for themselves.

8.5.5 Relevance ranking

A search for the single word 'Hamlet' will usually display a hit in the title before a hit in the text. Thus, a search for the word 'Hamlet' usually displays websites that have 'Hamlet' as their title before mentions of Hamlet in full text. Search engines typically have a complex scoring system that ranks hits according to their presumed relative importance, including book titles, chapter titles and so on. Multiple relevance ranking, particularly for a multiple-word search, can be configured, but it can be very complicated to adjust.

8.5.6 Proximity searching

A user who searches for 'capital Denmark' is likely to be interested in hits where those two words appear next to each other. So the engine ranks more highly hits where the terms are next to each other, and will typically display hits by proximity level – the closer the terms, the higher the hit is ranked. Some engines can have the proximity level defined, e.g. within five words.

8.5.7 Stemming

A search engine using stemming automatically expands a search to include inflected and related forms of a word. Thus, a search for 'look' will automatically retrieve 'looked' and 'looking'; irregular forms are also taken into account, so a search for 'mouse' will retrieve 'mice'. Stemming may be an advantage or a hindrance, depending on how it is implemented; 'industrious' and 'industrial' are very different terms, and it might be unhelpful in some contexts to search for both when one is keyed. Hence some control over stemming is important when setting up a search engine for a content collection.

8.5.8 Searching against a preloaded index

Amazon and Google both use this technique (Figure 8.5), which surprises users when the system appears to be intelligent: the user keys in

Figure 8.5   'Did you mean' dropdown

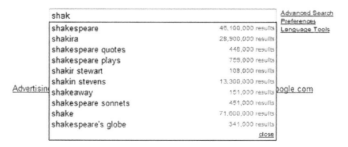

'Browne', and the engine responds 'Did you mean "Brown"?' This is achieved by the engine having a preloaded A–Z index of terms, which is updated regularly. If a search is similar but not identical to a term in the index, the result is to suggest that term to the user. This can be weighted to show only more popular terms.

One benefit of a preloaded index is that it can help users who have difficulty with spelling, and can make searching for foreign words easier.

8.6 Limitations of the Google model

One might think that applying all the above procedures in the right order would produce the perfect indexed resource, but that is not necessarily true. Much depends on the collection being searched. Google is designed for searching the largest possible collection, and aims to provide a hit or hits whenever possible; it is rare that Google finds nothing, unless the user makes the search over-specific. But in many circumstances, too many hits represent a poor result. For most content collections, a specific search with a limited number of hits is preferable to a broader, less accurate search. Here are some additional search features either not handled by Google, or that could be handled differently for a 'walled-garden' repository of content:

- *Stemming*: inappropriate use of stemming can produce too many irrelevant hits. Searching the Cambridge Companions for 'Orientalism' retrieved many hits for 'orient', which is not closely related.[17] In this case, removing some of the stemming would improve the search.

- *Saved searches*: most of the major commercial databases provide the ability to save a complex search and subsequently rerun it. This is beneficial when a very precise search is carried out on a collection of content that is regularly updated.

- *Search within results*: neither Google nor Amazon provide the opportunity to search within results, which can sometimes be a powerful way of locating the required result. Again, this feature is widely implemented in major commercial databases.

- *Sorting results by criteria other than relevance*: for archives of newspaper articles, for example, it is often helpful to index stories by date of publication rather than by relevance of hit.

- *Federated searching*: the ability to search across multiple databases with a single search. Unfortunately, different proprietary databases use very different search strategies, and considerable behind-the-scenes work is required to federate them. Ideally, a collection should have a single interface to a wide range of different proprietary databases. Just as federated access (see section 6.12) is increasingly used in the academic world, so federated searching is seen as increasingly a requirement. In the business and commercial world, this is done by search engines such as Vivisimo (*http://vivisimo.com/*) and Copernic (*http://www.copernic.com/*), often combining searching of Web-based resources with local files on the desktop. Indeed, Google itself offers the same functionality with Google Desktop Search, which can search across files on the user's PC, either separately or combined with searching the same time on the Web.

- *Adding semantic features*: the ability to disambiguate terms would be a major enhancement for a search engine – for example, the ability to distinguish hits for 'Java' (the computer language) from 'Java' (the region). For a fixed repository of content it is sometimes possible to use metadata to make the search more specific. For more about semantic links, see section 11.10.

- *Adding a web index*: indexing the full text is not the same thing as providing a proper index; there is a school of thought that a Web-based index would be a useful complementary navigation tool.[18] Usually the book index is abandoned because, the argument goes, it has been superseded by the full-text indexing from a search engine. As we have seen, this can produce rather variable results, while a human-generated index is the work of a skilled practitioner who makes an effort to identify and to resolve problems in retrieval – by disambiguating homonyms, for example.

8.7 Controlling Google searches

Google does not index hidden pages: most walled-garden sites, in which the content is only accessible to those who have paid to come in, are not indexed. However, users have some control over what Google and other search engines may or may not index.

It is possible to have subscriber-only or paid content indexed by Google, via its 'first click free' system. Under this system, Google can, at the owner's request, index subscription-based content as long as the first hit can be displayed free. Any subsequent hits are not displayed; instead, the log-in form to the subscription area is shown.[19] Yahoo has a similar service. In fact, for some customers, the major search engines have at times allowed what is called 'cloaking': allowing search engines to trawl subscriber-based content, and then displaying a different result depending on the status of the user – subscribers are shown the content, while non-subscribers see a log-in page. Cloaking was used, for example, to index subscriber-only pages on the *New York Times*[20] until 2007, when the newspaper switched to free access.[21] In principle, cloaking is not allowed by search engines, but clearly a process analogous to cloaking is used for non-subscribers seeing hits but not content with some collections, such as JSTOR, a subscription-based archive (Figure 8.6). Searching in Google for a full-text reference to a JSTOR article without a subscription displays only the first page of the article containing the hit – but not necessarily the hit itself. For subscribers, this is an undoubted benefit, as they have a federated search to their subscribed resource every time they search with Google. This happens because Google signed an agreement in 2006 with JSTOR to index its content.[22] For non-subscribers, it is probably an annoyance.

In the case of HighBeam Research (Figure 8.7) and EBSCO Host, both of them subscription-based aggregated collections, article titles are indexed in Google but not the content. Again, the first few lines of the article are shown; the effect is very similar to cloaking, although in this case the full text is not searchable (see Figure 8.6).

There are cases where Google does not appear to have fully indexed some complex sites that owners have requested to be retrieved.[23]

Figure 8.6 **Search Engine indexing of subscriber content**

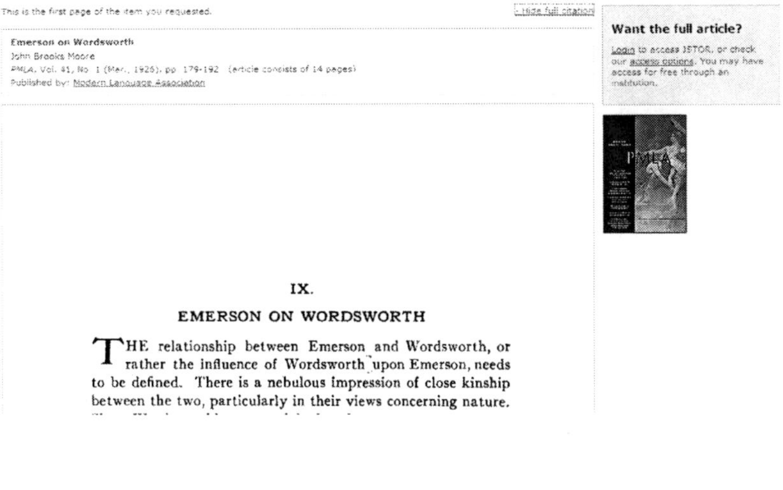

This is the first page of the item you requested.   Hide full citation

Emerson on Wordsworth
John Brooks Moore
PMLA, Vol. 41, No. 1 (Mar., 1926), pp. 179-192 (article consists of 14 pages)
Published by: Modern Language Association

Want the full article?
Login to access JSTOR, or check our access options. You may have access for free through an institution.

IX.

EMERSON ON WORDSWORTH

THE relationship between Emerson and Wordsworth, or rather the influence of Wordsworth upon Emerson, needs to be defined. There is a nebulous impression of close kinship between the two, particularly in their views concerning nature.

Figure 8.7 Searching a subscription-based resource by indexed title: HighBeam

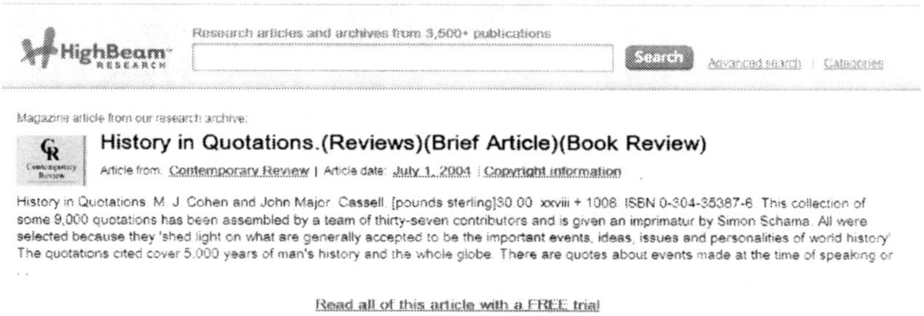

Conversely, content owners might sometimes want to ensure that their hidden content is never indexed or visible. Any content provider should check carefully how much of their paid content is discoverable by the major search engines, without prior permission having been given.[24] Sometimes this happens when a web page is deleted, but because content is cached by Google, the page remains searchable even after the original page is removed. Some ideas for removing content from indexing can be found in the article 'Removing your materials from Google'.[25]

Notes

1. Netcraft Web Server Survey 2009, *http://news.netcraft.com/archives/web_server_survey.html*
2. 'Trends in the Evolution of the Public Web' *D-Lib Magazine* April 2003 (*http://www.dlib.org/dlib/april03/lavoie/04lavoie.html*), based on OCLC figures from the Web Characterization Project.
3. Jansen, B.J. and Pooch, U. (2000) 'Web user studies: A review and framework for future work.' *Journal of the American Society of Information Science and Technology* 52:3, 235–246.
4. See Serge Bondar, 'Search Engine Indexing Limits: where do the bots stop?' (April 2006), *http://www.sitepoint.com/article/indexing-limits-where-bots-stop/*
5. See 'U.S. Core Search Rankings, February 2008', Search Engine Watch, *http://searchenginewatch.com/3628837*
6. 'Breakthrough in Google Book Search Case', *Managing Intellectual Property*, 31 October 2008, *http://www.managingip.com/Article/2039039/Breakthrough-in-Google-Book-Search-case.html*
7. 'Markets Declare Truce in Copyright Wars', *Wall Street Journal* 17 November 2008.
8. *http://lessig.org/blog/2005/09/google_sued.html*
9. Now renamed Google Book Search.

10. *http://www.opencontentalliance.org/*
11. See publishers' help pages at *http://scholar.google.co.uk/intl/en/scholar/ publishers.html* (accessed 11 November 2008).
12. *http://www.randomhouse.biz/webservices/insight/*
13. Witte, Sarah and Cargill, Mary (2008) 'Selected Reference Works, 2007–08', *College & Research Libraries*, 69:5.
14. *www.cuil.com*
15. *http://www.cuil.com/info/*
16. On 12 November 2008.
17. See review of Cambridge Companions Online in *The Charleston Advisor* 9:1, July 2007.
18. See Browne, Glenda and Jermey, Jonathan (2004) *Website Indexing*. Adelaide: Auslib Press.
19. See *http://www.google.com/support/news_pub/bin/answer.py?answer= 40543&topic=8871*
20. See 'Getting the New York Times more search engine friendly', Search Engine Watch, 15 June 2006, *http://searchenginewatch.com/3613561*
21. 'Times to Stop Charging for Parts of its Web Site', *New York Times*, 18 September 2007.
22. See 'JSTOR's Google Effect', JSTOR News, March 2007 *http://fsearch-sandbox.jstor.org/news/2007.11/google.html*
23. See Hagedorn, Kat and Samelli, Joshua (2008) 'Google still not indexing hidden Web URLs', *D-Lib Magazine* July/August, *http://www.dlib.org/ dlib/july08/hagedorn/07hagedorn.html*
24. See 'Hackers turn to Google to find weakest links', *New Scientist* 1 August 2003, *http://www.newscientist.com/article/dn4002*
25. Google Hacks #100 (13 March 2003) *http://oreilly.com/pub/h/220*

9

Copyright, royalties and contracts

Any licensing deal, whether between content owners and publishers, between publishers and aggregators, or between libraries and aggregators, is created via a contract (an agreement between two parties) that then grants a licence (a unilateral permission by one party only that grants rights to other parties). This chapter aims to explain what a typical licensing agreement covers, and provides some examples of what rights owners like to offer, and what rights libraries and users like to require. It does not attempt to provide model contracts; some examples of these are referred to in this chapter, or listed in the Further Reading section at the end of the book.

Any kind of content licensing contract will typically cover such areas as:

- Term of licence
- Extent of licence
- Sublicensing
- Updates to the content
- Technical support (if relevant)
- Warranties and indemnities.

Copyright legislation changes frequently, and this chapter does not set out to provide precise advice for any territory or legislation; for example, a recent major review in the UK was the Gowers Report on Intellectual Property,[1] published in 2006, which recommended some changes in UK copyright legislation. Rather, the intention is to give some general principles that should be considered when creating or negotiating any licence. Although this chapter discusses contracts and makes recommendations, it is sensible first to examine any precedents that relate to the specific type of contract being discussed, and to obtain specific legal advice if the situation is exceptional, and/or if any major variation to these standard agreements is contemplated.

9.1 Agents

Often, specialist agents are involved in contract negotiation. In general, agents act as intermediaries between the various links of the licensing chain. Two examples are:

- Subscription agents, who typically negotiate subscriptions to journals on behalf of publishers. They typically have a substantial expertise in contracts. The largest subscription agents are of course aggregators.

- Content licensing agents, who manage the relationship between aggregators and publishers, finding content licensing deals for publishers, recruiting publishers to license their titles for aggregators and often negotiating contract agreements.

The benefits of using agents is that they have current expertise in a specific market, most importantly a good working knowledge of licensing agreements and typically best practice. Hence, they can save time for both libraries and publishers. The Association of Subscription Agents and Intermediaries (ASA) (*www.subscription-agents.org*) maintains a list of subscription agents. Among its initiatives, the ASA has supported the introduction of electronic data interchange (EDI) for journals.[2]

9.2 Author contracts

Authors and content creators, whether the work comprises text, artwork, music or video, use publishers or aggregators to ensure the widest possible sale of their intellectual property. Any sale of the content is a benefit to the author, so it follows therefore that most authors are happy to see their work licensed for digital sale. In this chapter, the term 'author' should be interpreted broadly to mean the content creator.

9.3 The legacy problem

When new content is created, any contract with the author should of course state the rights and royalties for digital licences of the content. As with any contractual negotiation, it is easier to agree licensing clauses in advance of the anticipated use.

Things are more complicated when dealing with content previously published in print for which no digital rights were ever established: the legacy contracts. A typical publisher will have a collection of new and old agreements, signed over a period of many years, which means that there may exist hundreds of different versions of the author contract, each based on the legal view at the time the contract was signed, and often without any awareness of digital publishing and content licensing.

In this case, before any licensing can take place, the agreement of the author to digital distribution must be obtained. It is time-consuming for publishers to discuss the position with each author individually, and in practice, many publishers opt for what is called a 'passive' or 'tacit' agreement. The publisher writes to the author explaining what is proposed, with a request that the author contacts the publisher in case of disagreement. If the publisher hears nothing, they assume that the author accepts. In the meantime the content is licensed (usually as part of a deal involving many titles). If the author subsequently objects to the licence, for example over the royalty rate offered, or with any other part of the proposed agreement, their content is removed from any content licensing deal until the difficulty is resolved. With few exceptions, this procedure has worked well in practice, even though organisations representing authors have raised concerns about publishers taking unilateral decisions on behalf of their authors.

Orphan works, content for which the copyright position is uncertain because the author is unknown or cannot be contacted, are discussed in section 3.5.

9.4 Primary and subsidiary rights

Publishers distinguish between primary rights and subsidiary, or secondary, rights, which are any rights beyond the initial form of dissemination agreed. So, for example, a book contract treats publication of the book as a primary right, but the rights to make a film out of the book as a subsidiary right. Subsidiary rights include translations, performance rights, photocopying, serialisation (selling the rights to reproduce the content in sections in a periodical publication), recording rights, and film and radio adaptation rights. The revenue from rights is, in the case of books, typically passed by the publisher to the author, after deductions to the collecting society that has collected the money. Hence, in the UK, the Copyright Licensing Authority collects money from users of photocopying machines and passes it to publishers, who in turn pass it to authors.

Are the digital rights for intellectual property a subsidiary right? Contracts vary on this point. Some publishers view licensing verbatim texts via an aggregator as part of the normal sales of the title, earning the same royalty for the author as on sales of the print version. But this view varies from that of the Random House vs. Rosetta Books judgement of 2001.[3] Rosetta Books, a small start-up company, published e-book editions of some well-known Random House authors, including William Styron and Kurt Vonnegut. Random House, as the publisher of these authors in print form, sued for copyright infringement, but Judge Stein denied Random House's case, arguing that online sale was an entirely new right, different in kind to a subsidiary right. The consensus position today seems to be that electronic rights are considered separately from other primary or subsidiary rights.

9.5 Electronic rights

Electronic rights are the rights to the content when published in digital form, which is usually online but which can include other formats such as CD-ROM and DVD-ROM. These can be distinguished between verbatim rights, where the work is reproduced in its original form (with or without pictures and graphics), and multimedia rights, in which the content is used as part of a new compilation. Multimedia rights are sold less frequently than verbatim rights, and it is difficult to generalise about them as the nature of a multimedia compilation can take many different forms; the proportion of the value of a multimedia title that can be ascribed to the text, or the illustrations, will vary between individual titles.

Typically, therefore, content licensing means the licensing of verbatim electronic rights. A typical contract for such rights is considered below.

9.6 What to look for in a contract

First, consider who drew up the contract. The party that draws up the contract is likely to pay most attention to safeguarding their own position. Therefore, for organisations looking to use a model contract, it is a good idea to start with a model contract that has originated from an organisation in a similar situation: for publishers, another publisher; or for a library, another library. For example, some consortia have drawn up model licences for licensing content from aggregators to provide within the institution;[4] authors' societies have drawn up model contracts for authors to license their work.[5] The freely available contracts at Licensing Models[6] were sponsored by subscription agents EBSCO, Otto Harrassowitz and Swets, and were intended to be neutral, that is for use by both libraries and publishers, without being favourable to either party. This agreement was in turn partly derived from another freely available neutral contract template, the JISC Model Licence between UK education institutions and publishers,[7] which derives from a framework agreed between publishers and libraries.

The following sections cover clauses that are typically included in any content-licensing contract; these are sometimes known as 'boilerplate' clauses.

9.6.1 Exclusivity

Authors often sign exclusive deals with publishers. Exclusivity for audio recording contracts may mean that recordings can only appear on one label, or that music compositions can only appear from one music publisher. Like other rights, exclusivity can be reserved for one format only (such as print) or for one channel only (such as e-book).

Similarly, an author or creator can license their content exclusively, for example to a single aggregator. However, there is less justification for exclusivity when signing licensing deals. Publishers will justify exclusivity because they then have the greatest interest in promoting that author or artist. In contrast, it is not in aggregators' interests to promote one author, or one publisher, over another. Exclusive rights tend to be applicable when, for example, a new platform or format is being launched, and the licensee wishes to populate that platform with content. Unless the circumstances are exceptional, there is little reason for the content owner to agree exclusivity when licensing. Often, a request for exclusivity is in reality an attempt by an aggregator to prevent content being licensed to a rival aggregator (some aggregator contracts state explicitly that content must not be licensed to other named aggregators); this is a questionable strategy and certainly not in the interests of the market, the publisher or the end user. If a publisher feels exclusivity is important, then probably the content should not be licensed at all but delivered from a publisher's own site, because only in this way can the content branding be fully under the control of the publisher.

9.6.2 Term

The term is the period during which the licence agreement lasts. Music-recording contracts may last for a number of years (typically seven years), or for a number of albums. Book-publishing contracts are typically for a title or number of titles, without time restriction. Aggregated content deals are usually for a number of years; note that the actual term may be longer than the agreed term, because if a publisher licenses content for three years to an aggregator, and at the end of the third year the aggregator licenses the content to a library for one year, then a further year will elapse before this latter deal comes to an end.

It is difficult to generalise about an appropriate term: aggregators typically want a long-term licence, while content owners prefer a shorter term. Certainly, licensing content for less than two years makes it difficult for an aggregator to sell the content effectively; aggregators need time to inform users that new content is available, and it can be several months for this information to reach the libraries, let alone the end users. However, a long licence term may be equally restrictive: the publisher should be regularly reviewing the best strategy for licensing their content. A typical agreement is between three and five years, with optional renewal by mutual consent.

9.6.3 Perpetual access

Many licensing deals to institutions offer more than one kind of deal. Perpetual access is where the content is offered to the institution for a one-time fee, with the content then available to the institution without termination. Subscription access, by contrast, provides access only for an agreed time. Perpetual access does not mean that the aggregator or licensee has the right to continue selling new licences in perpetuity, of course.

9.6.4 Cost of hosting

Some aggregators charge institutions an 'annual maintenance fee' (or similar wording) in return for hosting the licensed content so it is available for perpetual access. It is worth checking by how much this annual fee can change – often such a fee is limited to the rate of inflation.

9.6.5 After termination

Check on the position after termination of the agreement: what rights does the licensee have over the content from this point? This is typically covered by a perpetual access clause (above).

Note that even when a print edition is purchased, the rights of use may be constrained. For example, when an individual buys a print copy of a title, they may not buy the right to do what they want with it. A single-user subscription to a print journal (which usually costs considerably less than an institutional subscription) cannot legally be donated to the local library for public access there, because the appropriate rights were not bought initially: a single-user licence cannot be converted into an institutional licence simply because a few years have elapsed.

9.6.6 Applicable law

Many content-licensing agreements straddle national borders. A French publishing company, for example, may sign an agreement with a US-based aggregator to provide content worldwide. Which legislation is therefore appropriate for the agreement? The parties have a legal right to choose a jurisdiction, at least in Europe under the Rome Convention of 1980.[8] The simplest option, therefore, is to choose one or other of the jurisdictions between the two parties. This avoids the problem of attempting to interpret a contract with different assumptions, based on the relevant legislature. Usually, the jurisdiction chosen is that of the party that draws up the contract. At times a neutral jurisdiction is chosen, one that is not where either party is based. This may be because the local jurisdiction may refuse to handle any cases below a certain aggregate value of transaction.

9.6.7 Future technology

This is the clause in a rights contract that attempts to encompass all possible forms of reproduction. It is common for copyright agreements today to include the phrases 'electronic, or mechanical' to describe copying, but in an effort to include possible technologies that have not yet been introduced, contracts for new content will include such statements as the following (from a typical music-licensing agreement for soundtrack music):

> to exhibit, record, reproduce, broadcast, televise, transmit, publish, copy, print, reprint, vend, sell, distribute, perform and use for any purpose, in connection with the motion picture as defined herein, whether or not now known, invented, used or contemplated.[9]

In practice, most content-licensing deals have wording that relates to rights in a limited number of specified rights, such as a retail e-book edition, or CD audio rights or library aggregation rights.

9.6.8 Most favoured customer

Some contracts between aggregators and publishers specify that the price agreed with the publisher must be as low as the best price offered to any other aggregator. However, such a clause can raise several difficulties. First, a 'most favoured' clause often clashes with a 'non-disclosure' clause (see below); the publisher must reveal the price agreed (if any) with other aggregators, and there may be clauses in the other contract stating that the price is not to be revealed to any third party. Secondly, it is often difficult to compare the prices for licensing content between two different agreements because of the differences in the way each deal is structured.

'Most favoured' clauses are also used to attempt to ensure parity across different formats: the aggregator requires the publisher to provide content on as good terms as any offered for the content to be sold via any digital medium. In this way, one format, such as an e-book, will not be superseded by another format simply on the grounds of price. Some aggregators state that such a clause should operate retroactively: if the publisher signs a subsequent deal for the content in any digital medium on better terms, they must amend the terms with the first aggregator. Such a clause would be very complicated to administer and impractical for any publisher making sales to several aggregators.

More importantly, such a clause could be interpreted as anti-competitive by authorities, on the interpretation that such a clause could prevent a content owner favouring one licensing platform over another. Hence such clauses are best avoided by the publisher.

9.6.9 Non-disclosure of price and best terms

Some licensing contracts state that the licensee is not allowed to disclose the price paid for the licence. Quite apart from potentially conflicting with any most-favoured customer clause, described above, many libraries and institutions will have difficulty with such a clause, since as a public body they are required under Freedom of Information Acts to reveal such information on request.

9.6.10 Advance payment

Some aggregators offer an advance, or guaranteed minimum revenue in the first year of licensing. Such offers provide an independent estimate of the value of the content. Advances and guarantees tend only to be offered when the content has an established brand name, based on a strong sale in other media.

9.6.11 Who pays for capture

When an aggregator licenses content, that content may need to be captured or converted. The cost of this capture may be provided as part of the contract by the aggregator, or chargeable. Even if the content already exists in digital form, some conversion may well be required, as it is unlikely that the content can be repurposed without amendment. The contract should state clearly which party is responsible for capture and/or conversion. Separately, it should be established in what format the content will be captured (see section 10.10).

9.6.12 Reporting requirements

Aggregators should be asked to provide regular reports of usage and statistics on who is using the content. Aggregators are usually reluctant to reveal details of title usage by institution, but there is no reason why publishers should not be given usage details for title usage overall. Equally, institutions ought to be able to see which titles are the most frequently consulted. For more about tracking usage, see section 10.26.

9.6.13 No subcontracting

The aggregator may request rights to sublicense content to a third party, for example another aggregator. Maximising sales is of course in the publisher's interest, but some sublicensing deals might result in the content being sold in markets that the publisher may be reaching in other ways, and with a different financial model. It is advisable for publishers to have control over specific segmented markets; hence the publisher should state that no subcontracting should take place without the publisher's prior permission.

9.6.14 Interlibrary loans

Some institutions request permission to fulfil interlibrary loans using digital content. This could be a problem if the library has a large number of interlibrary loans, or is providing such a service to some users on a commercial basis. One solution, similar to that used with photocopying arrangements for interlibrary loans, is to place an upper limit on the number of such loans that can be made without any financial recompense, such as five per year for any journal.[10] Publishers and aggregators vary on this point regarding digital licensing; the position should be stated in the contract.

9.6.15 Reciprocal clauses

Reciprocal clauses are of the type 'if A, then B', followed by the reciprocal clause 'if B, then A'. They follow the general rule in a contract that it is reasonable for both parties to have similar rights: for example, if A must give three months' notice of termination to B, then in a similar way B should give three months' notice of termination to A.

It is worth checking any contract to see if there is a missing example of reciprocity, particularly if the contract was created by the other party: look to see that for any protection afforded to one party, a similar protection is afforded to the other.

A similar concept to reciprocity is used in many open-source software contracts – that for any condition accepted by the user of such software, the same condition is applied to the user's clients.

9.6.16 Indemnification

Indemnification clauses absolve one party of financial loss as a result of the other party's action or error. Thus, for example, licensing contracts between aggregators and institutions include a clause to indemnify the licensor (the aggregator) from any errors made by the licensee (the library). A typical clause is:

> The licensee indemnifies the licensor against and costs arising from claims relating to misuse of the licence.

This could happen if, for example, a library allows content to be accessed by thousands of users outside the institution because it had failed to set up its authentication system properly. But there should at the same time be a reciprocal clause indemnifying the library from errors by the publisher or aggregator:

> The licensor indemnifies the licensee against and costs arising from claims that the work has infringed the copyright of a third party.

It is possible, for example, that the library could have an action brought against it for infringing copyright, when in fact it was the publisher (or aggregator) who had not cleared all the appropriate permissions.

A further question to ask with indemnification clauses is: who pays the costs? In both the examples above, the indemnifier bears all the costs of a claim, even if the claim turns out to be spurious. It would be better to reword indemnification clauses to make clear any costs are borne by the party that caused the infringement, and for good measure, to restate the clause so that it is valid for both parties:

> Each party is responsible for its own negligence and indemnifies the other against costs arising from claims caused by wilful misuse or breach of the licence, to the extent that the party is responsible for the misuse.

A further pragmatic addition here would be to add a clause that enables either party to put right a breach within a reasonable time, so that (for example) the publisher is given five days to remove the offending content, or for the library to fix the access problem.

9.6.17 Guarantee of availability

Aggregators providing content to institutions should state what the availability of the service is (which may be unhelpfully described in percentage terms, or more usefully as the maximum number of days in any year when the service is not available) and what, if any, compensation will be offered if this availability target is not met. High percentages sound impressive, but may not in fact be as challenging for providers as they seem. For example, a 99% availability percentage means that the service is allowed to be unavailable for 3.65 (1% × 365) days per year.

9.6.18 No republication

Publishers are reasonably concerned that the licensing of their content does not create a new work, for example by republishing sections of a textbook in a new compilation. This can be avoided by a clause that states the aggregator is not entitled to republish the work in any form other than verbatim, and in its entirety. If the content is to be used in compilations, this should be specifically stated. Republication of short extracts is covered by fair use, below. Such a clause prevents, for example, images from a copyright work being extracted and reused in a new work.

9.6.19 Rights to search

Aggregators typically want their content to be searchable by search engines. However, publishers may have concern about how much of the content should be displayed as a result of this search: what is displayed in a hit can vary (see section 8.7). This clause should specify how much of the content can be displayed, for example the sentence in which the hit is found, or five words either side of the retrieved word.

9.7 An alternative to contracts?

An interesting recent development in contracts between libraries and publishers is the SERU Initiative.[11] SERU stands for 'Shared E-Resource Understanding', which indicates the intention behind this approach, which is an attempt to do away with contracts for specific deals but to work within a shared framework. The SERU initiative is managed by NISO, the US National Information Standards Organization.

Given the increasing quantity of content being licensed, but at the same time the increasing complexity of contracts, and the need for a separate contract for each licensing deal, it is sensible to consider an alternative way of agreeing a licence. The SERU Agreement[12] was published in February 2008, the result of a collaboration between publishers, aggregators and industry associations, including the Association of Research Libraries (ARL) and ALPSP, the Association of Learned and Professional Society Publishers.

SERU attempts to replace contracts for smaller deals, simply by agreeing a framework for licensing to take place. Most importantly, because SERU is not in itself a licence, but an 'understanding', it is not signed, and does not use legal language. Nor does it include such details as price, and start and end dates, which are covered by a separate letter between the parties, which states 'this agreement follows the SERU guidelines'. It is not intended that SERU is modified in the course of any licensing agreement. The SERU Agreement is refreshingly easy to read after the complexities of most contracts for licensing.

9.8 Fair use

Contracts often refer to the principle of 'fair use', or 'fair dealing', the reproduction of small portions of the work for a different purpose to that originally intended by the work. For example, a work of criticism will quote from the source it is commenting on. In an academic library context, fair use could be argued as using small portions of the content in lecture or course notes. Fair use can also mean (in US copyright law) parody or artistic expression.

The problem is, what constitutes a 'small portion' of a work? Quoting five lines from the latest James Bond film is unlikely to distort the market for the publishers of the screenplay. But if the entire script is reproduced, the publisher will claim that their market has been taken away. Fair use, in other words, implies that there is no harmful impact on the normal commercial exploitation of the content.

In practice, each area of intellectual property tends to have a rule of thumb, which, even if it has not been tested in courts, forms the basis for working practice. For example, dictionary compilers often follow the rule that fair use comprises no more than five definitions taken from any other dictionary. In the case of audio copying, fair use may comprise as little as three notes lasting two seconds.[13] There is typically no fair use at all for reproduction of video extracts of major sporting events; for example, the English Football Premier League sued YouTube for allowing video clips of goals (lasting only a few seconds) to be shown.[14] Since fair use is a generally accepted concept, there is no need to make separate reference to it in contract agreements, as they tend to state the obvious; for example:

> Licensee is entitled to make copies of the work under the Fair Use terms of national copyright legislation.

9.9 Copyright term

Copyright is designated by a © sign for books, and by a → sign for recordings.

Broadly speaking, any work (written or composed) is the copyright of the person who created it. Copyright in the UK and in the US lasts for 70 years after the death of the person who created the work. If the work involves a recording, then there is a separate copyright for the recording itself. Thus, for example, for a recording of a work by Debussy, no permissions are payable to the composer, who died more than 70 years ago, or to his estate, but payment must be made to the performers for their recording (also known as 'mechanical rights'), a right that currently last 50 years. This also applies to recordings of live events, authorised or otherwise.

Similarly, for works of art, there are separate permissions for the work itself, and for the photographic reproduction of the work. To reproduce a painting by Titian involves no payment to the sixteenth-century artist, of course, but picture agencies and galleries will charge for providing a photograph of the painting, and for the right to reproduce that photograph.

The above is a very brief summary. Cornell University has a useful website outlining the situation with copyright term and the public domain in the United States at *http://www.copyright.cornell.edu/public_domain/*; a similar site for music is *www.pdinfo.com*, the Public Domain Information Project.

9.10 Licensing payments

For subscription licence deals, aggregators typically pay royalties in the following way. The aggregator licenses a collection of content from many publishers. Libraries that subscribe to this content pay the aggregator a price typically based on the number of people in the institution who will access the content (see below for how user numbers are calculated).

The aggregator then takes a proportion of this revenue, typically 50%, for their administration costs. It then divides the rest of this revenue 'pot' between the participating publishers. It may be divided equally by the number of titles or by the values of those titles, or more equitably it may divided according to actual usage of the titles, as some titles will inevitably have higher usage than others. Publishers should check which of these methods is used.

In the case of e-books sold to libraries, access for more than one user at a time is typically sold by multiples, just as a library might buy two or three print copies of a popular book. This principle applies both for subscription sales and for perpetual licences: multiple perpetual licences can be bought that enable more than one user to access the content at the same time.

9.11 What is a user?

What constitutes a user should be stated clearly in any agreement. Thus, for a higher-education institution, the contract should specify the situation with:

- Part-time students
- Full- and part-time academic staff
- External access via a single password
- Students outside the country where the licensing is taking place
- Students taking short-term vocational courses
- Public access via a terminal in the library
- Distance-learning students with remote access to content
- Walk-in users to the institution library
- Visiting/associate academic staff.

Some of these will coincide with the institution policy for other access, but some will not. Agreements tend to be based on a calculated 'full-time equivalent' (FTE) number of students.

For a business, there are similar cases to be clarified:

- Part-time workers accessing the content remotely
- Foreign branches of the company
- Associated companies
- Customers of the company.

9.12 Collecting societies

Collecting societies are organisations that collect rights and copyright fees from content users. They include copyright clearance agencies and rights organisations.

Copyright clearance agencies, also known as reproduction rights organisations (RROs), collect fees for reproduction from photocopying and scanning within institutions, typically businesses, schools and universities, and libraries. These agencies are a form of content licensing for content owners, and are a valuable source of revenue, as they enable publishers to collect payment for a use of content that would otherwise be difficult to trace. An example is a textbook publisher receiving revenue from academic institutions photocopying extracts for class distribution. The publisher registers their content with the agency, and the agency distributes revenue, typically by requesting that the institution that carries out the copying keeps a log of which titles are copied. These agencies also attempt to control the extent of photocopying and reproduction, as can be seen for the detailed instructions provided at their websites (see below).

Collecting societies may have the exclusive right to collect royalties in a territory (the usual European model), or they may have a non-exclusive right, the typical US model. The relevant organisations are, in the US, the Copyright Clearance Center (CCC; *www.copyright.com*), and in the UK, the Copyright Licensing Agency (CLA; *http://www.cla.co.uk/*). These agencies collect payments on behalf of authors (in the UK, the Authors' Licensing and Collecting Society, ALCS) and publishers (in the UK, the Publishers Licensing Society, PLS). The CCC and CLA also manage rights for copying of digital content in some of their markets. The CCC, for example, publishes useful guidelines for copying of periodicals in US libraries (known as the CONTU Guidelines).[15]

For music, performing rights organisations collect revenue on behalf of performers. The three major performing rights societies in the US are ASCAP (American Society of Composers, Authors, and Publishers),[16] BMI (Broadcast Music Incorporated)[17] formed to compete with ASCAP, and SESAC.[18] Similarly, there is more than one collecting society in the USA for mechanical rights. The largest is the Harry Fox Agency,[19] but there is also AMRA (the American Mechanical Rights Agency).[20]

In the UK, the mechanical and performance collecting societies are, respectively, the Mechanical Copyright Protection Society (MCPS) and the Performing Rights Society (PRS); these work together as an operational alliance.

Synchronisation rights tend to be negotiated individually rather than via the collecting societies described above.

9.13 Perpetual access

What happens when an institutional licence comes to an end? Can an institution and a publisher or aggregator guarantee the continued access to content if the publisher takes the digital content out of print, as it were? As explained earlier, CD-ROMs and printed books have one feature in common: on completion of the agreement, the library owns a physical copy of the published work.

For many institutions moving to online journal acquisition, if the subscription is terminated, the institution faces the unpleasant situation of no digital access even to back issues, which print versions would provide. Many libraries have argued that they should be able to purchase content with the exact equivalent of print: the right to access it in perpetuity. A perpetual-licence clause in a contract provides that the aggregator or publisher, in return for a small continuing fee, agrees to keep the title available.

What then if the publisher or aggregator ceases to maintain the perpetual access site? For example, aggregators may cease trading. To overcome this issue, many libraries have sponsored initiatives to ensure continued supply of archive copies of journals, including CLOCKSS and Portico.

9.14 Perpetual-access initiatives

CLOCKSS, an initiative launched in 2006, combines libraries (including Stanford University and New York Public Library) and publishers (Elsevier, OUP, Taylor and Francis).[21] CLOCKSS, derived from an earlier project, LOCKSS (Lots of Copies Keep Stuff Safe), provides an archive of content no longer available from the publisher. It is designed to jump into action whenever there is what is termed a 'trigger event', for example a publisher discontinuing online access to a journal. At this point, a digital copy of the journal, held by several library servers distributed around the world, is made available to the participating institutions. The situation is similar to escrow copies of the source code of software, which are held at a neutral location and only made available to purchasers in the event of the software vendor ceasing trading.

The long-term funding of such an initiative has yet to be determined, but it seems clear that the purchasing institution will be funding the continuing publishing activity. There is talk of CLOCKSS being funded by a levy from publishers, but that has not yet been agreed. Until then, the initiative remains funded by grants, both public and private, but without any long-term guarantee.

Portico[22] is a similar not-for-profit collaboration, launched in 2005 by the Mellon Foundation, Ithaka, Library of Congress and JSTOR, which aims to keep back issues of journals available even if the publisher no longer provides them. Again, the long-term funding model is not yet clear. The two initiatives differ in that Portico holds content in a standard form, while CLOCKSS stores the content in the publisher's original form.

9.15 Licensing free content

As discussed above, there are several situations in which content may be made available free of charge (see section 5.8). Some contracts have been designed specifically for situations where the content is provided free, notably the Creative Commons set of licences (see below).

The practice of giving away software is long established. The best-known equivalent to open-source software for content licensing, the Creative Commons licence, was created along the lines of the standard for open-source software, the Free Software Foundation's GNU General Public License (GNU GPL). Software is provided without payment, but under certain conditions for the licensee. Many software developers use this method because, for example, they see a better route to gaining a reputation and success by giving away their software, without having to budget for sales or marketing. Word of mouth, or reputation-based, sharing sites are a powerful way of disseminating software for a single developer or for a small team. For the intellectual property owner, the advantages are obvious: the user base can grow very quickly, more quickly than by using conventional marketing (unless a very large budget is involved).

Moreover, open-source software has an additional advantage. A better program is a benefit to all; so feedback from one user can help make the product (the software program) into something better for all other users. In fact, the more people use a software program, the more robust it is likely to become. An example of a commercial organisation giving away software is MySQL.[23] This, the most widely used open-source database, is available for free download. The business model of the company that provides it and that owns the copyright, MySQL AB (now part of Sun Microsystems), is that the code is given away free, but the company charges commercial rates for training, consulting, technical support and creating additional features outside the product roadmap. Those activities fund the 100 or so engineers who work on updating, mainstream product development and so on. There is no reason why a similar model should not exist for licensed content.

9.16 The Creative Commons licence

Creative Commons (a not-for-profit organisation, *www.creativecommons. org*)[24] aims to overcome some of the limitations of current copyright legislation, and to provide machine-readable means for the retrieval of relevant content under the licence. Creative Commons was founded by a group including Lawrence Lessig, who released at least three of his books under a Creative Commons licence (*The Future of Ideas*, 2001; *Free Culture*, 2004; and *Code: Version 2.0*, 2006); similarly, Eric Raymond's *The Cathedral and the Bazaar* (2001 – appropriately enough, a book about the rise of open-source programming) was also published using this licence.

Creative Commons allows the free reproduction of intellectual property in a non-commercial context, but reserves the right to commercial exploitation. It aims to provide a middle-point between full copyright and public domain. It comprises a range of licences, and even has a remarkable 'build your own licence' tool, so its users can create an appropriate licence for their specific content. The fundamental difference between Creative Commons and putting content in the public domain is that the copyright owner retains the copyright of the work.

The conditions under which Creative Commons agreements grant licences typically include (note that these may not apply to every one of the Creative Commons agreements):

- Rather than being sold outright, content is provided under a perpetual non-exclusive licence. The licensee can redistribute the content as long as the same terms apply to further licensees.

- Credit for the work is required: the author is happy to give away the content as long as users are aware of the identity of the creator. This system is used by several trade and professional associations, who want to share their content, but want members to be aware of its origins.

- The content can be used for non-commercial purposes only, with commercial rights reserved.

It is not necessary for all open-source agreements to include all the above conditions; thus, the software program MySQL is distributed freely for commercial use.

9.16.1 Case Study: MIT OpenCourseWare

The Massachusetts Institute of Technology (MIT) is one of the most prestigious higher-education institutions in the US. MIT released a handful of its courses on the Web free of charge in 2002, and by 2007 almost its entire curriculum material had been published. MIT uses the Creative Commons licence to release the material for non-commercial use. The initiative is funded by several foundations.

Today, MIT produces material not only for higher education but also for US high schools, and includes versions in several languages, including Chinese, Spanish and Portuguese. The content comprises lecture notes and details of student assignments. As each course costs in the region of $10,000–$15,000 to produce, what is the benefit for the provider, a privately endowed institution? Perhaps MIT would argue that this initiative increases the reach of the institution, and thereby conforms to the institution's educational mission. The majority of users of MIT OpenCourseWare are those who are not able to attend the institution in person; MIT estimates that 60% of the users of OpenCourseWare are based outside the US, mainly in India and China. If any OpenCourseWare student were offered a full-time place at MIT with sufficient funding, they would jump at the chance. This initiative, then, does not reduce the desirability of attending MIT; if anything, it enhances it.

For MIT, the key part of the Creative Commons licence was that the MIT name appears in any use of the content.

Notes

1. See *http://www.hm-treasury.gov.uk/independent_reviews/gowers_review_ intellectual_property/gowersreview_index.cfm*
2. See *www.icedis.org*
3. The judgement is available on the Rosetta Books website at *http://www. rosettabooks.com/casedocs/Decision.pdf*
4. See, for example, NERL Generic License at *http://www.library.yale.edu/ NERLpublic/licensingprinciples.html*
5. See, for example, The EPIC model authors' contract at *http://www.epicauthors. com/contract.html*
6. *http://www.licensingmodels.com/*
7. *http://www.jisc-collections.ac.uk/model_licence.aspx*
8. Rome Convention 1980, 4.1 (see *http://www.rome-convention.org/instruments/ i_conv_cons_en.htm*).
9. See *http://www.djmixsource.com/film-synchronization-contract*
10. See CONTU (National Commission on New Technological Uses of Copyright Works) Guidelines on Photocopying under Interlibrary Loan Arrangements, *http://www.cni.org/docs/infopols/CONTU.html*
11. *http://www.niso.org/workrooms/seru*

12. Available at *http://www.niso.org/publications/rp/RP-7-2008.pdf*
13. Bridgeport Music, Inc. vs. Dimension Films, United States Courts of Appeals, June 2005.
14. 'YouTube facing football lawsuit', BBC News, 4 May 2007, *http://news.bbc.co.uk/1/hi/business/6627135.stm*
15. See *http://www.copyright.com/Services/copyrightoncampus/content/ill_contu.html*
16. *www.ascap.com*
17. *www.bmi.com*
18. *www.sesac.com*
19. *www.harryfox.com*
20. *http://www.amermechrights.com/*
21. See *http://www.clockss.org/*
22. *http://www.portico.org/*
23. See Arnö, Kaj (2005) 'MySQL's Quid pro Quo', *http://blogs.mysql.com/kaj/2005/09/27/mysqls-quid-pro-quo/*
24. There is also a UK site at *http://creativecommons.org/international/uk/*

10

Under the hood: the technology of licensing

To license content would not appear to be a technical problem, so why should a book on content licensing need to include anything on technology? Simply because the business and technology of licensing are intimately related. A publisher could license content to an aggregator and leave all the technical details to the aggregator, but this could hardly be considered effective long-term management of their intellectual property, because the way the content is captured and disseminated has a strategic implication on the business. It is not surprising that there is a strong correlation between the most successful licensors of content and their willingness to understand and to take advantage of the technical challenges involved. As we have seen earlier, any historical assessment of publishing will show how content and technology have frequently interacted in the most unexpected ways, for example when a technical innovation has provided market opportunities. The invention of printing is the obvious example, but the nineteenth-century serial novel (see section 5.12) provides another one: to maximise sales, many novels of the period published in this format have moments of suspense at the end of each weekly or monthly instalment, so the reader is motivated to buy the next issue of the magazine.

Another example of the content being influenced by the format can be seen in the development of recorded music during the twentieth century. When the long-playing disc was invented in the 1930s, to replace the earlier 78-rpm shellac discs, there were two competing formats: the long-player, running at 33 1/3 rpm, and the smaller 45-rpm format: the 12" long-player was launched in 1948 by Columbia Records, and the 45-rpm single by RCA Victor in 1949. Neither of these formats ever disappeared – they are both still with us today, and the two formats, that of the three-minute per side single and the 20-minute per side long player, created a framework for popular music that was the model for the next 30 years. In other words, each change in technology favours certain kinds of content.

Some understanding of technical change, and of how a text or audio track is captured, retrieved and then delivered to the end user, is valuable for anyone involved in the licensing process. Some content is more suitable for one format, for a single rather than an LP; other content can be adapted to suit several different formats.

There are two additional business benefits from knowing something about the technology used for content storage and delivery. First, marketing opportunities come about through technical change. It is commonplace in marketing and business textbooks that technology-led marketing, creating a product simply because the technology exists to make it happen, is poor business; but in the case of licensing content, taking advantage of a change in formats or platforms to obtain a new or better market share can in some circumstances be a perfectly legitimate strategy, especially for a new entrant to an established market. By keeping up with technical developments, each participant in the licensing process can identify business opportunities: can the content reach the user more easily using this or that format? Is it possible to simplify the requirements for rights clearance using a simple, effective technical solution? There is no need to be a technical expert to identify the impact a new technology is having on a market; ironically, the business impact is often unanticipated by the product developers and hardware manufacturers. Text messaging from mobile phones is an example, an innovation that was never taken seriously by the phone companies until they found users busy texting all their friends. Hence it is not surprising that many business commentators look for commercial opportunities out of recent web-based success stories such as Facebook.

There is no need to have a PhD in informatics to license content successfully; the aim of this chapter is to provide the reader with sufficient knowledge to understand the essentials of content-licensing technology.

10.1 Standards

What is the benefit of a standard? Cars have to drive on one side of a road or the other, and it does not matter much which side they drive on. However, if the world is divided into nations where cars drive on the left, and nations where cars drive on the right, the result is confusion and expense for drivers, manufacturers and authorities. A single agreed standard would make things much easier, but it is of course difficult to create a single standard once all the nations' road systems have been built.

There are few markets or industries where a single standard is universally adopted. As licensing content deals with delivering content to multiple platforms, it could hardly be expected that content owners would simply need to output to one platform. There are nonetheless approaches that content owners can adopt that minimise the difficulty of outputting for several different platforms and formats, and these are explained below.

It would be an oversimplification simply to list five or six major existing standards and leave it at that, with a recommendation to follow those standards. Unfortunately, the world of technology is not quite so simple. For some areas, no standard exists. More often, there are two or three different standards coexisting in the same sector, as happens with RSS feeds (see section 10.15); users can choose one or the other, or are forced to try to work with them all. It can be challenging to identify which standard to follow.

The relationship between standards and industry has always been fraught, and the status of standards in the computing industry is a rather intricate one. Information Technology is a domain where there are several international standards bodies, such as W3C, IEEE, OASIS and ISO, which, even if not in open competition with each other, do not always work in complete harmony. Given the risks and opportunities for manufacturers in supporting one or other standard, it is not surprising that major companies such as Microsoft, Intel and Apple attempt to create some standards, declare support for other standards and switch from one standard to another, sometimes with bewildering speed. Many pages have been filled by analysts trying to determine whether Microsoft is truly committed to XML in its Office software suite, or whether placing this or that standard in the public domain represents a step forward or not. Although standards are typically created by committee, these committees are formed of representatives from each of the major interested parties, and each committee member may have an agenda not shared by the others.

It is also worth remembering that standards only become standards when two things happen: a body creates a set of rules that defines the standard, and the standard becomes widely used. If a standard is not used, then it is not a standard in the everyday sense of the term. Many standards have been created for sound technical reasons, such as Brunel's broad railway gauge of 7 ft ¼ in, but were never generally accepted.

Nonetheless, many standards do become widely adopted, and as long as they are followed intelligently, they are the best path for everyone in the licensing process to adhere to. The next few sections describe the major standards in use in content licensing.

10.2 XML

XML, short for eXtensible Markup Language, is the best-known standard for the exchange of information. It originated in the 1960s from a vendor, IBM, as the Generalized Markup Language (GML), which subsequently became the vendor-independent SGML (Standard Generalized Markup Language), an ISO standard (that is, created and managed by the International Standards Organization), before being reconceived in the form of XML, a W3C standard.

XML is platform-neutral – it does not require a Mac or a PC to work; it is vendor-independent, and it is convertible, in that the individual characters can readily be converted to other codes for storage or for delivery. In addition, it has the advantage of being relatively readable, as text content within XML files can be read when source files are opened, as is the case with HTML (described below).

XML is based on some simple but clever principles. Both XML and recent versions of HTML follow a system of matching start and end tags to indicate different sections or different functions, such as <h1> around a title, as in <h1>Book Title</h1>. But while HTML has a small number of allowed codes, XML allows content owners to have any number of codes – there is no limit in XML. A content owner could, for example, want to identify all great soccer players in their content, by adding a new tag <great soccer player>: an example would be <great soccer player>David Beckham</great soccer player>. When the content is published, a search for great soccer players can then retrieve David Beckham with a single click of the mouse.

In this sense XML is a remarkably relaxed standard. Every user of XML is at liberty to create their own tags (technically known as entity labels). But this leads to a problem: XML is the preferred format for data exchange and interoperability, but if every content provider creates their own tags, then considerable conversion might be required to process some XML-coded content. What if another content owner decides to create a tag called <great football player>, using the term 'football' instead of 'soccer'? If every content owner insists on a unique set of tags then it will be difficult for content to be exchanged. Problems of this kind can be avoided or greatly reduced by agreeing not just to use XML but a particular 'flavour' of XML – a DTD or a schema (see below).

It is perfectly possible to convert between different flavours of XML, or to convert an XML file to HTML, so that it can be displayed on a website, using an XML-related language called XSLT (or XSL Transformations). Other parts of the XML 'family' include XPath and XQuery, tools for locating content in documents. The need for interoperability means that most industries tend to adopt a common specific set of tags within that industry, based around a single DTD (document-type definition) or schema; for more about these, see below. For example, in the newspaper industry, many newspapers use XML as a means of retrieving content efficiently from their archive. This is now endorsed by the increasing adoption of the News Industry Text Format (NITF) standard, which has been an XML standard since 1999.[1]

10.3 But why is XML so important?

Of course, there is more to XML than simply being able to code every instance of David Beckham's name in a document in an agreed way so that it can be retrieved later.

Most importantly, XML (like its predecessor SGML) separates function from appearance: it uses codes such as 'title' rather than 'italic'. So important is this emphasis of separating what the content does from how it appears, that XML documents can never be styled at all: an XML document always has angle-brackets throughout, and will only start to look styled when it is converted to something else. Although that insistence may make XML seem cumbersome, the reason for XML's success today is because the separation of style from content makes it so much easier to transform documents. This is why so many initiatives in content delivery, such as RSS (see section 10.15), make use of it. It is not essential, but it is much simpler, to do everything in XML.

Furthermore, XML can be used to ensure that some tags are mandatory, and that tags must follow the same order, for example that every chapter must have a title, and must include one or more paragraphs.

However, all is not entirely in agreement in the XML world. First, the take-up of XML in different areas has by no means been at an equal speed. Although, as mentioned above, the newspaper industry is using XML, there is an XML standard for transmission of stories, called NewsML, which has not been widely adopted. The use of NewsML would enable a whole news story, together with accompanying headline, pictures and links, to be rebuilt on a webpage, but in practice news stories tend not to be created in this way on websites. Another area of disagreement is over whether to use DTDs or schemas to describe documents.

10.4 DTDs and schemas

DTDs and schemas are two widely used ways of describing an XML document; they are not interoperable. Both enable a set of tags to be agreed by users within a specific domain. When an XML document is exchanged, for example when a publisher transfers content from an archive to a website, the tags all need to be intelligible to both parties. Typically, an XML document has all its codes 'explained' by some other document,[2] which is either a DTD (document-type definition) or a schema. For much content licensing, there is not much difference between the two:[3] they both provide a description of the codes used in the XML file, and most importantly, they both enable the document to be 'parsed' (that is, checked by machine to make sure that all the codes are accurate, for example that each opening code has a following and matching end code). Parsing can be used, for example, to ensure that data capture or conversion has been correctly carried out. A data capture company will capture content in XML, and then parse the data against the relevant DTD or schema to show that there are no errors in the coding. Both DTDs and schemas also enable documents to be 'validated', that is, checked that specific tags used in the DTD or schema are used correctly.

Both DTDs and schemas are widely used, although for some purposes there is a trend towards schemas. Schemas, for example, can make use of namespaces, which DTDs cannot do. Namespaces enable elements and attributes to be used across multiple contexts. Tags such as 'title' may be used for content in a newspaper and in a magazine, but with a different classification used for each. If content such as a news story is reused from one to the other, then some means of identifying the origins of the two fields is required. Namespaces enable this interoperability of content, without the need to rewrite XML each time content is shared.

As XML schemas develop, they provide more and better parsing tools, which help the content-creation process, and ultimately the content-licensing process, to take place more smoothly. Nonetheless, even the latest schemas do not include many simple checks on content, for example that a date field must be in the future, or past. For that reason, there are several commercial packages available, such as Schematron,[4] which provide enhanced parsing and checking tools for XML content.

In the longer term, XML will enable content licensing to provide much more sophisticated machine-based functionality. This does not quite mean that robots will deliver articles to the end user on a silver tray, but it is certainly the case that using XML enables content to be loaded to a repository and then retrieved in a very effective way. It is already the case that XML-based languages dominate the exchange of content in such diverse areas as medicine, meteorology and defence; if the Semantic Web, which is about understanding user needs and delivering personalised content, is to become a reality, then it is most likely to happen using XML.

10.5 Unicode

As with many innovations in computing, a simple assumption early in the history of technology led to considerable headaches later on. In this case, the problem is one of languages and characters: when computers were first developed, they used several different systems for coding numbers and letters, the best-known of which is ASCII (American Standard Code for Information Interchange). ASCII has 128 (2^7) characters, which is enough for most words in English. So, for example, when a user keys the lowercase letter 'e', the computer understands it as ASCII value 101. As computing became more international, accented characters and characters from non-European languages needed to be stored but had no universally agreed equivalent, as those characters were beyond the first 128 ASCII codes. For content in other languages than English, there was no guarantee that the coding convention used in one device, such as a CD-ROM, would follow the same system used in another, such as a computer screen.

The answer was to come up with a more comprehensive standard, which is Unicode, created by the Unicode consortium,[5] an association of the major computer companies. Even though Unicode does not cover all the written characters of all the world's languages, it has over a million characters encoded (2^{16}), which covers most purposes. Although Unicode is a single standard, not all applications need to use all characters, so most applications tend to use a subset of the entire set. The most common ones are UTF-8, the simplest, which has, helpfully, the same coding as ASCII for the first 128 characters; this means that ASCII and Unicode are interchangeable for those characters. The largest set is UTF-32, which covers most of the world's existing languages. The system has been so successful that even extinct languages such as Egyptian hieroglyphics are being encoded. Most current operating systems, such as Windows XP and Vista, use Unicode for character encoding.

10.6 Classifying content: taxonomies, thesauri, ontologies

Content is described using metadata, which are data describing data. So, for example, for a music track, the name of the performer, the date of the recording, the track title and the album title are all examples of metadata. Metadata enable the content to be classified and retrieved more easily. Note that the metadata are often held separately from the content itself: hence if an audio CD is copied, the track details that appear on the printed sleeve notes are not transferred to the copy.

Many widely used standards make extensive use of metadata, although users are not always aware of how to retrieve this information. For example, most digital cameras store a large quantity of metadata with every image taken (Figure 10.1), in a format called EXIF (exchangeable

Figure 10.1 Example of EXIF data for a digital photo

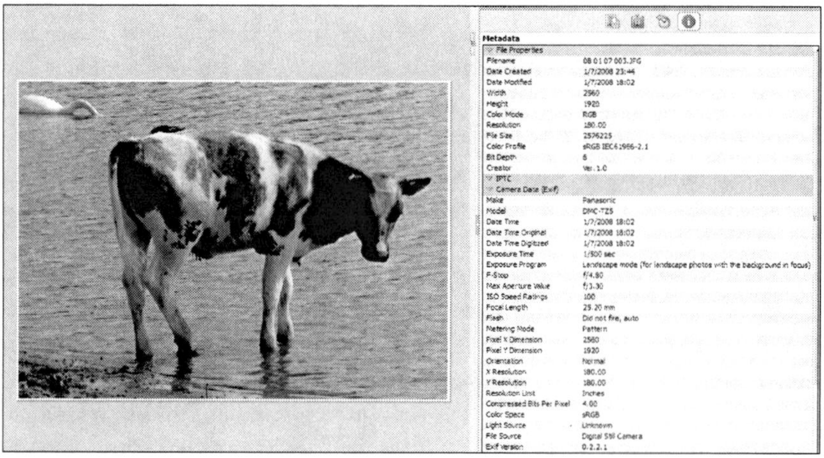

image file format), containing the name of the camera, the date and time when the photo was taken, and the exposure, as well as much other information.

Metadata are most useful when they are structured in some way. Three fundamental ways of organising metadata are taxonomies, thesauri and ontologies. A taxonomy is a grouping of things hierarchically in a tree structure; for example, apples and pears are both kinds of fruit. The justification for placing an object in one taxonomic class rather than another may be complex, but its position in the hierarchy is clearly identifiable in a diagram (Figure 10.2).

A thesaurus is a set of related terms, which may be divided into broader, narrower and equivalent terms. For example, a geology thesaurus (see Figure 10.3) may divide the term 'geologic history' into

Figure 10.2　A taxonomy

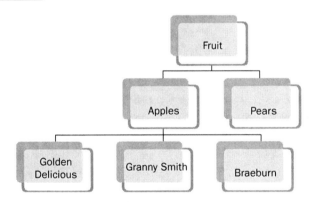

Figure 10.3　A sample thesaurus: geological terms

```
geologic history
    SN:    Record (and inferred reconstruction) of the origin
           and development of the Earth since its formation.
    BT:    Earth characteristics
    NT:    biostratigraphy
           Earth history
           lithostratigraphy
    RT:    geologic time scales
           geology
           paleontology
           paleoseismology
           stratigraphy
    UF:    chronostratigraphy
           geohistory
```

broader terms ('BT', for example, Earth characteristics), scope note ('SN', here 'record') and narrower terms (biostratigraphy):

Finally, an ontology is a set of agreed concepts within a domain, a superset of both taxonomies and thesauri, which has formal rules about the relationships of those concepts. Ontologies can potentially provide the most precise classification of content, and so can be used to manipulate content in powerful ways. Ontologies are of interest in computing because, unlike taxonomies and thesauri, they can be expressed in machine-readable form (see section 11.10).

Folksonomies are a very informal classification. Folksonomies originated with social bookmarking sites such as del.ic.ious,[6] which enables users to add a tag to describe any web page they have visited. The resulting collection of tags is not formal, and may have overlaps, as different terms may be used to mean the same thing, but they are easy to use, and, when represented in a 'tag cloud', they look impressive.

When preparing content for digital licensing, how detailed should classification be? A common error by content owners when starting a new project is to create an unnecessarily complex set of criteria for classifying content. As a result, when content creators (the authors) start to add more content, they find themselves spending too much time adding tags that are more detailed than the criteria that will be used for content retrieval. It is usually better to begin by relatively simple content tagging, as the needs of users tend only to become clearer over time, when they are more familiar with the content. When the metadata coding system is first set up, it is sensible to think about the possible tags that might be added later, but that does not mean that every conceivable tag needs to be added immediately.

Information architecture is the technique of designing and managing classification to facilitate access, and one of the tasks of the information architect is to determine the appropriate level of tagging to match user requirements, and hence to enable the search strategies that will be used to retrieve the information.

10.7 Content metadata: Dublin Core

There have been attempts to standardise content metadata, notably the Dublin Core, an agreed set of metadata for many types of content.[7] Dublin Core is an ISO standard, and comprises a set of core qualifiers, described in three groups: content (such as title, description and source); intellectual property (contributor, creator, publisher, rights); and 'instantiation' (date, format, identifier, language). Dublin Core is very widely used and so has achieved 'standard' status in the everyday sense; however, in practice, the standard is not very standard. Some of the fields are used in incompatible ways (for example, date fields are often not interoperable) while others, such as 'description', have not been widely used by search engines because self-declared descriptions are often misused by content owners to ensure they gain higher rankings from search engines. If content is tagged to Dublin Core specification alone, then that metadata is unlikely to be sufficiently unambiguous for automatic exchange with other content. Dublin Core needs to be supplemented by more rigorous and thorough metadata classification.

10.8 HTML

HTML must be the most familiar of all the standards discussed here – it is the language of all web pages. It is very easy to view, as the underlying HTML for any page can be viewed by clicking on 'view source' in any browser. At the same time as being easy to view, HTML is very easy to copy. Whole pages, or items from pages, such as images, can be copied and pasted into other applications. Hence, for commercial content-licensing purposes, HTML is not ideal.

HTML was created in 1989 with the development of the Web itself. One of its major innovations was the ability to jump from one place to another, within a document or to another document, the concept of 'hypertext', a trick on which the entire Internet has been based. Hypertext itself owed much to an earlier innovation called HyperCard, developed by Bill Atkinson for the Apple Macintosh in 1987. Interestingly, the originator of the term 'hypertext', Ted Nelson, explained that he created it to identify the source of a quoted document for rights-management purposes, to provide the owner with clear identification of the reuse – in other words, hypertext was initially developed as a way of identifying licensed content.

HTML was based on SGML (see section 10.2), but unlike SGML, gave the user some control over the format of the document.

HTML had the advantage of being simple to create, but it had the disadvantage that its use was dominated for several years by Microsoft and Netscape, creators of the two most widely used browsers, who added extensions to HTML with little regard for each other or for the development of a genuine universal standard. To be fair, Microsoft and Netscape were only two of the organisations attempting to develop HTML as a language – as one critic pointed out, 'imagine one hundred people trying to design a house'.[8] As a result HTML became (and remains) browser-dependent, which means that a web page may well look different when viewed through different browsers. The difference between browsers is less today than five years ago, but variations still remain. The W3C attempted to create a unified standard, and achieved a consensus on moving HTML, then at version 4.0, towards XML, by creating the new standard called XHTML. The XHTML 1.0 standard was published by W3C in 2000.[9] XHTML is something of a hybrid, not entirely new, but different enough from HTML to cause some headaches. It was designed to be a grown-up version of HTML that is more rigorous in its coding. Thus, for example, upper-case tags are no longer acceptable, as they were in HTML, and now it is not possible to omit end tags and assume they will be understood.

Why was this necessary? Because HTML's limitation is its very simplicity. It is just not comprehensive enough to describe the complexity of content that appears on most websites. Any site comprising more than a few pages requires a lot more than HTML to manage and to update. XML, being self-describing, can manage far more complex documents, even though XML by itself is insufficient for all the many tricks used today for publishing complex web pages: a website of any size will typically use additional tools such as JavaScript and Flash.

Another reason for creating XHTML was to make a start on resolving HTML's messy mixture of structural coding (describing what the content is doing) and presentational coding (e.g. "this <h1> heading should appear 3mm above the first line of text"). A good example is the use of italics. Early versions of HTML displayed italics using an <i> tag, like <i>this</i>. It was simple to do, but unfortunately the use of <i> is ambiguous. Are the italics being used to describe the title of a book, as in *Oliver Twist*? Do they show emphasis, as in 'I *told* you so!'. It is not difficult to find documents with several different meanings for the italic font that cannot be disambiguated using HTML alone. This means, for example, that it is impossible to create an index of book titles from a document that uses the <i> tag in multiple ways.

So it is clear that the simplistic tagging for appearance of HTML was never going to be sufficient for digital publishing. This is particularly important in the world of content licensing, which typically brings together content from many sources using a wide range of formats and coding. XML would be ideal, but it is considerably more complex than

HTML, and few publishers capture their content in XML. Although XHTML is a great improvement on HTML, it remains a compromise, and not really suitable as a content capture format. Moreover, XHTML suffers from the same drawback as HTML in that it is open to copying. Although several techniques have been developed and some commercial software programs claim to prevent source code being copied, or the page printed, in practice these require no real skill to circumvent.

10.9 PDF

PDF (Portable Document Format) is one of the best-known formats for delivering digital documents. It is used because of its (relative) permanence; it is difficult to extract content from a PDF or to make changes to it, if the optional security features within the language have been enabled. Microsoft Word is ubiquitous as a format for creating content, but unsatisfactory as a publishing medium (it is difficult to ensure a Word file looks identical and remains unchanged on any platform where it appears), while PDF is able to represent complete published pages in a format that matches the printed page precisely. Hence, PDF is often used to disseminate digital versions of print magazines (see magazine licensing in section 4.3). PDF, created by Adobe, dates from 1993, so it pre-dates the World Wide Web; it became an ISO standard in 2008.[10]

PDF is platform-independent, so a file can be created on a PC and read on a UNIX system. It has the drawback of being slower to open than HTML, as can be seen from the delay users experience when downloading a large PDF document from the Web. PDF is based on PostScript, a page-description language, originally devised to describe layout and to drive printers. PDF and PostScript are descriptions of how material should appear (as essentially is HTML), whereas XML and SGML describe how they are structured (with no reference to how they should appear).

PDF can be viewed using a freely available viewer: Adobe Reader (formerly Acrobat Reader).[11] But creating PDF files requires some expensive software (although recent versions of Microsoft Office have a PDF creation facility – see section 10.19). Even though free programs are available, they often have minor inconsistencies and variations from corresponding print pages. Even using Adobe's own software, Acrobat, it was some years before near Web/print compatibility was attained:

early versions of Acrobat did not support the professional print colour standard CMYK (instead it used RGB, the standard system for screen displays).

There are two types of PDF: standard PDF comprises content that is ready for print publication. Enhanced or tagged PDF, by contrast, can include hyperlinks that enable on-screen navigation. Thus, for example, using enhanced PDF, a table of contents can become a list of links which, when clicked on, take the user directly to the start of the relevant chapter or heading.

PDF is probably the most commonly used format for publishing digital versions of printed books. For example, most titles in the Microsoft Press 'Step-by-Step' series contain a CD-ROM with the text in searchable PDF format.[12] Both versions are provided so that users can benefit from the full-text indexing of the digital version, and the ability to consult the entire text on screen.

In publishing houses, the majority of books are transferred from typesetter to printer in the form of PDF files. PDF is also used for just-in-time printing operations such as Lightning Source.[13] Services such as this enable a publisher to eliminate having a warehouse of printed titles, and simply to print individual copies of a title when a customer requires one; in this way, a printed book need never be out of print. The printer keeps a collection of PDFs of the title and uses a short-run digital printing machine.

10.10 Which format to use for data creation and capture

Choosing a company to capture data is described in section 6.3. A further question to resolve is which format to use for the capture of the content. For text, this is often a choice between PDF and XML. Broadly speaking:

- PDF is most appropriate if the original page layout needs to be preserved.

- XML is more appropriate if the content is accessed in sections rather than sequentially, as with dictionaries and encyclopedias.

When creating or capturing content using XML, simply choosing 'XML' is not sufficient, because there is a wide choice of DTDs or schemas (see section 10.4). Paradoxically, some of these are proprietary, in the sense that some data capture companies use their own variety of XML that is not used elsewhere in the industry, nor is it necessarily fully documented, and hence becomes a problem to convert to a more standard format. It is best to choose one of the widely adopted open standards; three of the best-known for publishing are DocBook,[14] the Text Encoding Initiative[15] and the NLM DTD (see below). All of these were originally developed as DTDs, but the first two are now provided in schema form.

DocBook is probably the most widely used format for text content capture. Originally designed for technical documentation, it has since been developed to manage a wide variety of content types. It is today managed by the standards organisation OASIS, but it was originally developed by the publishing company O'Reilly, and is used for many of their titles. Because of its wide use, DocBook covers many different kinds of publication, and many of its features are not needed for simpler projects; in fact some critics have claimed that it is unnecessarily complex. Today there are several versions of DocBook available; for straightforward short documents such as articles and papers, it is sufficient to use the Simplified DocBook standard, but this does not manage entire books.[16] All versions of DocBook use familiar tags such as <title>, <chapter> and <para> (for paragraph).

The Text Encoding Initiative (TEI) is a standard that is orientated towards academic use. It began as an attempt to standardise the format for representing and archiving texts as long ago as 1987, and is managed by a not-for-profit consortium. It too has a slimmed-down version, TEI Lite. TEI tends to be used more for research and archiving purposes than DocBook, for example the creation of scholarly editions of literary texts.

The NLM DTD,[17] first released in 2003, was originally used for academic journal creation and archiving, but now (since 2005) also exists in a version for books. In fact, the NLM journal DTD exists in two forms: a 'blue' form for article creation and a 'green' form for archiving. This latter is today the archiving standard used by the British Library and the Library of Congress. It is designed mainly for scholarly publishing, and is freely available for download.[18]

10.11 DITA

Although the licensing of images for use within other content has been practised for years, reuse of text content segments (as opposed to complete works) is rare. It is an indication of how exceptional is such reuse that

DITA,[19] an innovation in technical document structuring, was created for just that purpose only recently. DITA (Darwin Information Typing Architecture) was created by IBM, then handed to OASIS, the standards body, in 2004, and the DITA specification was published in 2005. DITA views content as a series of self-contained 'topics'. Each topic can be output in different formats, for example, publishing to print as well as to online help files. However, reuse of content in DITA is largely confined to different publishing platforms for the same content; it is not used as a means of creating a content-licensing platform for text.

10.12 DTDs for word processors

Both Microsoft Office (since Office 2007) and Open Office use XML DTDs in their current versions. Microsoft's Office 2007 format is called Office Open XML, while Open Office uses the OASIS OpenOffice.org XML format.

As both of these are XML, why are these word-processing programs not used more widely for data capture and content creation? The answer may be that the requirements of word processing and structured content creation for reuse are very different. The content creation formats described above, such as DocBook and NLM, are open to modification, but in practice they tend to be used exactly as specified. This is because any changes to the format reduce the interoperability of the content, which is the purpose of the exercise. Word-processing software, by contrast, is designed to be extremely flexible, to suit the varied preferences of many thousands of individual users. Although the underlying DTD of Word documents may be identical, it is very difficult to make content created by several different users genuinely interoperable, when each user has different and inconsistent ways of tagging and structuring content; few Word users make use of the program's inbuilt hierarchical heading functions, for example. Various commercial packages attempt to constrain Word to a set of standard tags, but these programs have had mixed results in anything but carefully controlled environments with highly trained users.

10.13 Other page make-up languages

The two most widely used commercial languages for coding print page layout are Quark Xpress,[20] introduced in 1987, and its competitor InDesign.[21] Adobe's InDesign, introduced in 1999, was a successor to the now obsolete PageMaker. In some respects, Quark and InDesign are similar. Both are proprietary, and both are design-based, rather than function-based. Both can output to PDF, but although it is possible to convert content from Quark or InDesign to XML, it is not easy, having made changes to the content, to convert it back again. Neither of these languages should be used to create digital content for licensing; they are best used as tools for the creation of output in a single format only, with no further reuse, and should not be used for the transfer of content to a different platform or format.

10.14 XML and publishing: ONIX

A good example of the successful use of XML in publishing is ONIX, a standard for transferring information about books from publishers to aggregators, distributors and booksellers.[22] ONIX (Online Information Exchange) was created in 1999, based on a European project called Indecs (see section 10.23). ONIX is a joint initiative of EDItEUR,[23] an umbrella body for e-commerce groups including the UK-based Book Industry Council[24] and the US-based Book Industry Study Group.[25]

ONIX is used, for example, to deliver information from publishers, via book industry data collection organisations such as Nielsen and Bowker, to Amazon, to keep Amazon's book information database updated. When a user browses book details on Amazon, it is likely that this information was transferred from the publisher using ONIX. ONIX was successful because without it, publishers had to provide information in a different format to each of the major book companies involved in distributing or selling titles. The existence of a standard has dramatically reduced the time and cost for publishers to deliver information about their content.

Currently, the ONIX DTD defines some 230 elements (types of data), such as title, language and edition. These elements are a mixture of mandatory (such as title) and optional (such as cover image).

Following this success, Onix has experimented with further developments, including ONIX-PL, for ONIX for publications[26] (originally called Onix for publisher licensing). ONIX-PL is based on the idea that contained within the digital text of the book can be information that states in a machine-readable way just what the permissions for that book are. So publishers will be able to specify to Google Book Search which of the permissions they grant for their book to be searched – full text, limited search or snippets only. For example, in the UK, the Onix-PL standard has also been used to show which titles have been licensed for use in higher education via JISC. Of course, adoption by one agency does not guarantee that it will become a standard solution, but nonetheless, with ONIX having been so successful at managing book data, there is a reasonable chance of this new initiative being adopted.

10.15 RSS feeds

Digital content has the advantage of rapid delivery, and users prefer short content to long content, so it is not surprising that there have been several innovations that link rapid dissemination with concise format. RSS is one of the most widely used types of feeds, electronic distribution of short extracts of text, taken from a longer source.

RSS,[27] which uses XML, stands for 'really simple syndication'. The extracts can be headlines, or brief information about new titles, or short reviews. Paradoxically, for a technique that most users would associate with speed and immediacy, RSS works like most email: it only arrives at a PC when the PC asks for it – in other words, it is a 'pull' technology. In practice, RSS 'feed readers', which are client-based (that is, based on a desktop PC), send out requests for new content every few minutes, so the user has the impression that the content is distributed as soon as it is published. RSS, which was first used on a large scale only as recently as 2002, is popular because it is straightforward for site managers to configure additional fields in an RSS feed, or to customise existing ones, for example all new articles by one journalist on a newspaper, or all news stories relating to one sports team.

There are different flavours of RSS, including versions 1.0 and 2.0, both currently in widespread use, and the former not entirely replaced by the latter. In fact, the RSS standard has a rather complicated history,[28] but despite this confusion, RSS is the most widely used feed system. As RSS is XML-based, if the content is already held in XML, it is very simple to produce an RSS output. RSS is based on the Resource Description Framework (RDF), a way of storing information about websites. RSS feeds can be managed by a dedicated feed reader; in addition, current browsers such as Firefox, Safari and Internet Explorer 7 include built-in support for RSS feeds.

RSS is used for content that is changing frequently, such as news, company information and events. There are many additional possibilities for feeds that are relevant to content licensing, such as alerting users when a new title in a specific subject or by a specific author has become available in a collection.

The benefits for content licensing are obvious: feeds such as RSS provide a quick method of syndication, and by delivering only the headlines or extracts, the content itself can be reserved for a paid service.

10.16 Atom

The other major XML-based format for feeds is Atom.[29] RSS and Atom are similar in concept, although Atom is more rigorous: for example, with Atom, the document title, author, creation date and address are all mandatory (it is surprising that they are not for some versions of RSS). However, Atom is less widely used than RSS, and if a website offers only one type of feed, it will almost certainly be RSS. Being a better and more open format is no guarantee that Atom will succeed against RSS.

10.17 Podcasting

A podcast is an audio or video file that is delivered via a feed such as RSS. Podcasts have the same advantage as other RSS feeds, in that the user can open or play them at a time they choose. Because of their convenience, therefore, podcasts create an additional market for content beyond an initial broadcast. The name 'podcasting' is derived from the Apple iPod, but podcasts can be heard or viewed via any feed reader that supports them. The audio or video file works in the same way as an e-mail attachment (called an 'enclosure' in RSS), opened when the file is delivered; this feature is included in current versions of RSS (since version 0.92). There are several programs that enable radio broadcasts to be converted to podcasts; one of the earliest was Replay Radio (now called Replay AV).[30]

Because podcasts are an additional market for audio and video content, rights organisations have set up podcast licensing terms for this new market, for example an MCPS-PRS podcast licence in 2008.[31]

10.18 E-book formats

There is a proliferation of formats in which content is delivered on e-book readers, many of them proprietary; they include the Microsoft e-book reader, Adobe Reader, Palm Reader and Amazon's Kindle format. Most online bookstores provide content in a range of e-book formats, although usually an incomplete range; see, for example, the comparative chart of e-book formats at *http://www.ebookmall.com/choose-format/*, which offers ten formats, or the overview of formats at Fictionwise,[32] which lists 13. Clearly the large number of incompatible formats for e-books must deter many potential users. However, some of these formats have already begun to be superseded, for example the Gemstar format. Currently, the most common formats are Kindle (from Amazon), Mobipocket (owned by Amazon), eReader (*www.ereader.com*) and Sony Reader.

Proprietary formats are a problem for end users, because if users have more than one device they may need to hold titles in multiple formats. In response to these proprietary formats, the International Digital Publishing Forum (IDPF) announced in 2008 the introduction of a new open standard, EPUB,[33] which has now also been adopted by the Sony Reader. EPUB is a version of XML, and can reformat book pages to suit the screen dimensions of the reader, rather than replicating the original page size of the print edition; the Mobipocket format has a similar capability. In this way a single file can be used to output to many difference screen sizes. For academic journals, this could be a problem if there are references to page numbers, but for mass-market fiction, it can greatly improve readability. EPUB has the additional benefit that it can be created directly from InDesign. One of the reasons for EPUB's rapid popularity is that it is the format used by Stanza,[34] a program that enables books to be downloaded to mobiles. Stanza does not support digital rights management (see below), but it can read a large number of formats, 21 in all, including Kindle, Word and PDF. Stanza provides tools that enable content owners to link their content automatically to the Stanza site, from where that content can be downloaded.

The Mobipocket format[35] was the first widely used format for text on smartphones such as the BlackBerry. Mobipocket is based on the Open eBook specification, also created by the IDPF, but with proprietary extensions that provide digital rights management (usually referred to as DRM), which is discussed below (section 10.19). The Mobipocket site includes some 70,000 titles, free and paid. The business model of the Mobipocket platform (owned by Amazon since 2005) is to provide the software for upload (Mobipocket Creator) and download (Mobipocket Reader) free of charge, but to charge commission to content owners from each sale, in return for hosting and delivering the content from the Mobipocket site. The publisher agreement is viewable at the Mobipocket site (*https://www.mobipocket.com/ebookbase/en/Homepage/pub_agreement. asp*). The DRM works by restricting viewing of the files to devices registered by the customer. One incidental advantage of the Mobipocket format is that, as would be expected from an XML-based format, users can search multiple dictionaries at the same time.

Amazon's Kindle uses a proprietary format called AZW, which is similar to the Mobipocket format, although files created on one format do not play on devices designed to use the other. eReader is a proprietary format used by ereader.com, an online bookstore. Its titles are either available in any of 12 formats, unencrypted (which it terms 'MultiFormat'), or in four encrypted formats: eReader (Palm Reader), Adobe Reader, Mobipocket or Microsoft Reader.

One response to the multiplicity of e-book formats is Feedbooks (Figure 10.4; *www.feedbooks.com*). This site provides free downloads, using mainly out-of-copyright content derived from sources such as Gutenberg and Wikisource, although some copyright books and magazines are included. The site provides each title in several e-book reader formats, so the user can simply select the format for their device.

Figure 10.4 Feedbook: e-books in multiple formats

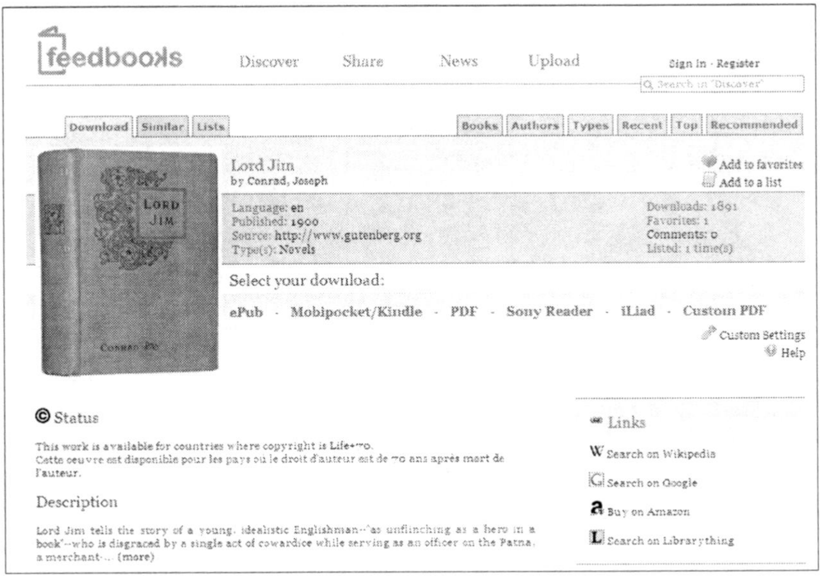

10.19 Controlling the use of content using DRM

Content owners are understandably wary of unauthorised copying of content, and several methods exist either to prevent copying or to enable copying to be monitored for rights purposes. DRM covers any technology used to protect the rights of copyright owners when content is replicated. This can include tracking of use, prevention of unauthorised access (such as use of area codes to prevent DVDs playing in certain territories) and setting up limitations on what users can do with the content (for example watermarking of images, to prevent them being reused in another context). DRM was initially used in music and video licensing. The best-known music DRM system is Apple's iTunes (see below). Other rival systems include Microsoft Windows Media DRM.

Copying of digital resources, whether text, audio or video, is very simple. In many ways text is easier to copy than other media: it takes up less space, and the major formats in which text is held, such as Microsoft Word format, or PDF, are widespread, unlike the many different formats in which video can be captured for digital dissemination (for example, Flash, wmv, mp4 and avi). As with audio and video, piracy of text content is rife; in a 2008 report the Association of American Publishers (AAP) reported hundreds of thousands of pirated textbooks available on the Web. In response to this threat, the major publishing associations have set up operations to attempt to counter piracy; for example, the AAP has set up an Online Piracy Working Group (OPWG).[36]

One strategy for avoiding piracy is to hold content in a proprietary format; for example, the Australian company eComPress[37] provides a highly compressed secure publishing format, used by the OECD (Organisation for Economic Co-operation and Development) and WHO (World Health Organization), among others. However, such a solution is often expensive and cumbersome (as purchasers have to have decryption tools on their local PC).

Another strategy is for hosts not to deliver the whole work but only small portions of it, perhaps a page at a time, and not allowing downloading of the entire title: if a user only has access to a single page at a time, it would be difficult to download an entire work. Nonetheless, there remains the possibility with websites of copying components within a page (such as images or multimedia). HTML is an inherently 'open' format, and it is very easy to copy text or images from most web pages. Of course, no content owner would publish an entire work in HTML or XHTML format unless they were happy for the content to be copied or downloaded.

PDF is a reasonably secure format, because with the optional security features in the software enabled, it is difficult to extract or alter the content. It is also possible to stop PDF files from being printed or saved to another format. Note that Office 2007 has no option to open PDF files for editing, although it includes a 'save as PDF' option – a feature that was not included in the initial release of Office 2007, due to lack of agreement between Microsoft and Adobe. Although PDF is in principle an open standard, Adobe was not happy for Microsoft to enable free saves from Word to PDF.[38] Several proprietary systems offer enhanced protection of PDF files, for example preventing printing, saving or copying the file.[39]

Another way of making content more secure is by 'watermarking', the practice of embedding an identifiable sign in an image or text file. This is often done with images to prevent their reuse without payment; the high-resolution version of the image, provided after payment, has no watermark. Often watermarking is used to identify individually every licence sale; any unauthorised copies will carry this unique ID and can be tracked back to the source of the leak. Watermarks (Figure 10.5) and 'dogs' ('digital online graphics', typically a logo in the corner of a moving image display) are commonly used by commercial agencies to trace cases where their content is being used unlawfully.

Figure 10.5 **Example of a watermarked image**

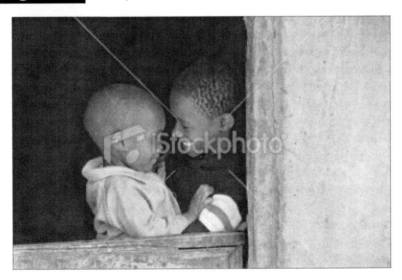

Security of digital content needs to be considered in the context of the intended market for that content, and the value of the content. Of course, any measure to prevent copying can be circumvented, given enough time, and content owners should never assume that any copy-protection system is fully secure. Perhaps the most imaginative solutions to issues of unauthorised copying have come not from creating additional security features, but from creating a new business model that creates a source of revenue both for the content owner and for the channel owner. Two of these initiatives, one with MySpace, the other with YouTube, are described in section 11.4.

Where content is divided into separate free and paid areas, a further check that content owners should carry out is to make sure paid-only content is fully secured. This can be checked by searching with the major search engines for content that appears behind the 'subscribers-only' wall. Despite the sophistication of many protection systems, content that is not intended for open access can sometimes be indexed unwittingly.

For more about controlling which pages Google should or should not index, see section 8.7.

10.19.1 Case study: iTunes

Apple's iTunes[40] is one of the great success stories of content licensing, with some six billion downloads. Since its launch for the Mac in 2001 (followed by a PC version in 2002), it has grown to a service that today provides over ten million tracks available for sale (initially at a standard price of 99 US cents per track, today at variable prices), together with freely available software that manages the downloads and cataloguing of the content. The service does not just include music tracks: spoken-word tracks, TV shows and films are available as well. In a 2004 interview, Apple VP Phil Schiller was quoted as saying 'The iPod makes money. The iTunes Music Store doesn't', but almost certainly iTunes is profitable for Apple today.[41] Yet there were definite question marks over the service when it was first launched. At first, iTunes only ran on the Macintosh; the iPod player could only connect to the PC using Firewire, rather than the more commonly used USB port. It was only in 2003 that a PC version of iTunes became available, and in the same year, the iTunes store was launched. In other words, iTunes became successful via several iterations of hardware and operating system, and in response to market requirements.

The service was immediately successful because of the single, low price and easy accessibility: users search an online catalogue of content licensed from the major record companies, and can continue to listen to songs even if they cease being a customer of the iTunes store.

Up to 2009, Apple used a DRM system called FairPlay for every track on iTunes. FairPlay is exclusive to Apple, and songs recorded in FairPlay format are not easily transferrable to other formats. FairPlay uses a system of keycodes, one of which includes a unique machine identifier. In this way, Apple can ensure that it controls the number of machines a downloaded track can play on. It does not restrict the copying itself. Currently, FairPlay is set to enable a downloaded track to be playable on any number of iPod players, but only to a maximum of five other computing devices. Users can change these devices, but only to a maximum of five at any time.[42] There is currently no restriction on copying to audio CDs. In response to moves from other music licensors, Apple began removing DRM from iTunes from January 2009.[43]

The iTunes store (Figure 10.6) is the best-known online music retail system, but it was not the first online downloadable music store – it was preceded by MP3.com's own music download centre, 'MyMP3.com' in 2000.[44] This site enabled users to access digital copies of their music that they had already purchased, for subsequent online access. However, this initiative was stopped by the recording industry, after MP3.com were sued

Figure 10.6 The iTunes music store

for 'making mechanical copies for commercial use without permission from the copyright owner'. In fact there is no technical difference between MyMP3.com and the iTunes service; in both cases, the provider holds a copy of the music that is then provided at a price to the purchaser. But iTunes gained industry support, while MyMP3.com did not.[45]

The success of iTunes has been enormous despite its limited availability at launch – it was then only available on the Mac. Most importantly, iTunes has demonstrated that a paid-for service that is convenient and cheap can be successful in the face of free but unreliable peer-to-peer sites. In addition, iTunes was a clear example of the strategy of a market leader in a channel, adopting proprietary, incompatible formats, while the other players grouped together to ensure interoperability.

10.20 Other personal ID systems

FairPlay is one example of a personal ID system (PID). Other PID systems for restricting content copying include the eReader system, which requires users to unlock titles after download by entering their credit card number, and Mobipocket, which requires users to enter a PID of the device on which the content is to be read. This PID must match that entered by the user when they registered as a member.

Although secure, PID systems are unpopular because they are annoying and cumbersome, requiring updating when a user changes their PC, for example.

10.21 Other DRM formats

Apart from iTunes, other examples of DRM-based secure formats are eBookBase,[46] used by Mobipocket, and Audible;[47] both these formats are used by the respective delivery platforms, but they are also offered to publishers for copy-protection using DRM on their own portals. Audible's format, called '.AA' (Audible Audio), is based on MP3 but with encryption. This also uses PID: files will only play on devices that have been enabled to read this format. Payment is by subscription, with one or two audio books downloadable per month, depending on the level of subscription. Audible, bought by Amazon in January 2008, provides most of the spoken-word content for the Apple iPod.

For mobiles, there is the Open Mobile Alliance DRM 1.0 standard, which is used by most of the European mobile operators.

10.22 ACAP

ACAP (Automated Content Access Protocol) is another DRM system, developed from 2006 by some of the largest media publishers. It is a would-be standard aimed largely at newspapers protecting intellectual property rights on the Web, providing a payment method for feed aggregation, as a response to the widespread practice of search engines indexing content from newspaper and magazine websites without payment. The standard was launched in December 2007, and has (not surprisingly) been adopted by an impressive roster of publishers, including News International, as well as academic journal and book publishers such as Elsevier. However, Google, the largest search engine company, has not yet adopted ACAP as a standard.

At the heart of the ACAP dispute is a simple file called robots.txt. This file specifies which parts of a website should not be crawled by search engines. ACAP is simply a version of this file with additional codes to denote the rights availability of the text. Its goal is to enable content owners to extract more revenue from their content, by sharing revenue with search engine companies:

> ACAP will make possible more sophisticated ways of collaborating in the sharing of revenues – not only advertising revenues, but (for example) revenues from search which result in content sales; there are many proposed 'micropayment', 'long tail' and 'micro-licensing' models for content commerce on the network that are only economically feasible with the development of much more sophisticated communication within the value chain. Search engines are well placed not only to direct users to content, but to facilitate further uses of that content.[48]

Thus, for content owners, some revenue may be gained using the automated ACAP system from reuse of content that could not be collected by hand.

Until recently, ACAP concentrated on licensing text. However, in June 2008 it adopted the PLUS image licensing standard, which will enable ACAP to manage image licensing as well.

Some critics have claimed that ACAP is more an attempt to prevent innovation than to cooperate with it;[49] however, the settlement of the Google Book Search dispute (see section 8.2.1) as well as recent agreements for posting of video clips on websites would seem to indicate that a settlement between Google and the newspaper publishers might be possible too.

In the meantime, some newspaper and magazine publishers give would-be purchasers admirably clear guidance about what content is available free and what is paid. For example, AMEInfo, publisher of the *Middle East Business Directory*, states on its websites that up to five headlines per day can be downloaded and posted on another website free of charge; this can be done via RSS. Beyond that, full news stories are sold on a monthly subscription basis.[50]

10.23 Indecs

The European Union has been very active in the area of DRM, with its eContent and eContent Plus programmes between 2001 and 2008. One of its projects, 'Indecs', was an ambitious project to create a single rights database for the buying and selling of electronic rights[51] across Europe. The goals of the programme were to make digital content more 'accessible, usable, and exploitable', using RDF, the Resource Description Framework. The project was launched in November 1998, and attracted a worldwide interest, with funding from the International DOI Foundation (IDF). More than one present-day rights system originated with Indecs: for example, DOIs (strictly speaking, the DOI data dictionary – see below) are based on the Indecs metadata framework, as is ONIX, the widely used system for exchanging book information (see section 10.14).

10.24 Persistent identifiers and DOIs

It is well known how unreliable URLs are. Web pages change their name and/or address frequently, so that there is little guarantee that a website that is available today will still be found in the same address in six months' time.

Moreover, Web pages are not the same thing as the content that appears in them: this may be a picture, a video or a painting, and HTML links are to a website, not to an object on a website. Digital Object

Identifiers (DOIs) solve this problem elegantly (Figure 10.7). First, they are associated with any type of object the content owner chooses, which could be a journal article, or an image or a poem; and secondly, they are 'resolved' via a 'handler', a redirection service that ensures the DOI link is always to a valid page. Even if the address of a website changes, the DOI does not; the only change is at the redirection service, which is managed behind the scenes and which need not concern the end user. The content owner or publisher is responsible for keeping the URL details up to date; the end user does not notice any change.

DOIs can be used to identify objects that are taking part in a transaction, e.g. buying, selling or accessing. DOIs have been described as the digital equivalent of the ISBN, used for print editions. However, unlike ISBNs, which identify only a complete book, a DOI can be assigned to a chapter of a book, or to a single image, or at any other level of granularity. Its widest use currently is to identify journal articles; this is managed by CrossRef, an association of journal publishers.[52]

DOIs are managed by the DOI Foundation, a not-for-profit organisation, and several registration agencies manage the assigning of DOI codes to information owners. The system is currently being processed as an ISO standard. The DOI system began in 2000, and today there are over 40 million DOIs in use.[53] Individual DOIs must be bought from a registration agency; there are a handful of these in each country, who in principle are in competition with each other. CrossRef is an example of a registration agency.

DOIs are the most widely used example of a persistent identifier, because of their use in retrieving journal articles, but there are several other systems of persistent identification, including Uniform Resource

Figure 10.7 Multiple DOIs in use

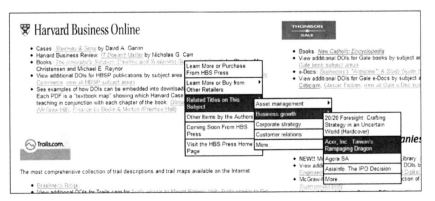

Names (URNs) and Open URLs. An article in 2008 by Emma Tomkin in *Ariadne* usefully compares several types of persistent identifier.[54] Whichever system is used, the advantages for content licensing are clear, as persistent identifiers enable content to be more precisely located, and hence more valuable.

It is also possible to use persistent identifiers to provide multiple resolutions from a single link, something not possible using HTML alone. This can either be to provide the user with a choice of destination, or, in the case of journals, to select only one option from a choice of several – that is to solve the 'appropriate copy' problem,[55] which is to direct a link to an article from a range of possible resolutions to the copy of that article that the library has subscription access to, rather than one for which an inter-library loan would be required for access.

10.25 Preventing video and audio piracy

Techniques for combating video and audio piracy include the use of watermarks and digital online graphics (see section 10.19), but a common method in use today is not to use a specific tool for copyright protection, but for content owners to target ISPs (Internet service providers) who have copyright content such as TV programmes and movies held on their system, and to persuade the ISP to reveal the IP addresses of customers who are infringing copyright. The content owner then sends a letter to these customers, warning them of their infringement and possible legal action, following which the majority of users stop their activity. This has happened in the USA, in the UK and in Australia. In cases where the ISP does not reveal user names or does not take any action, the copyright owners sue the ISP, for example the Australian Federation against Copyright Theft sued an ISP called iiNet in November 2008.[56] This technique has perhaps more chance of success than attempting to create ever more sophisticated copy-protection systems that are circumvented as soon as they are introduced.[57]

Another initiative that may provide a strategy to combat piracy of music downloading is Spotify (see section 11.4).

10.26 Tracking usage

Tracking usage may be helpful in identifying piracy, but it is perhaps even more useful in identifying how legitimate users retrieve and use content. Digital tools enable content usage to be tracked more precisely than was ever possible with print material. Some indication of the popularity of printed books can be measured in a library by the number of times the book has been borrowed; but how can the popularity of reference titles be measured, given that these are consulted without being loaned? Traditionally, libraries had to resort to cumbersome methods such as manually inserting a coloured slip of paper in every reference title, with instructions for users to comment on the title or to discard the slip when they consulted the book. With digital content, the problem can be solved far more simply.

By tracking the usage of licensed digital content, a powerful management information stream can be generated. Some of the early licensing deals provided no means by which a library or institution could track usage, but today any licensing agreement should provide feedback on usage, for example using the COUNTER standard (see below). Nonetheless, a surprising number of institutions still fail to monitor the extent to which licensed content is being used.

Tracking usage is a combination of assessing automatically generated information, together with qualitative research that must be carried out by talking directly to users. Surprisingly, much of the available automatically generated usage information is at present simply thrown away without any idea of its potential value. Ideally, any information professional in the content-licensing chain would want to know several strands of information about the content usage, for example:

- How often a content object has been accessed in a given period.
- For how much time the object was accessed.
- Where users came from before accessing the content.
- Where users went after accessing the content.

The best-known tool for measuring usage is the COUNTER standard.

10.27 Measuring usage with COUNTER

COUNTER[58] (Counting Online Usage of Networked Electronic Resources) is an automatically generated analysis of content usage, with a number of standard indicators that enable institutions and publishers to measure accurately how their content is used; it replaced several distinct small-scale tracking systems that measured usage in incompatible ways.

COUNTER was created for journal usage analysis; it rapidly gained acceptance, and has now become so widespread that many consortia refuse to license content unless it provides COUNTER statistics. Moreover, these statistics are considered sufficiently credible to be a measure of usage for audit purposes.

The COUNTER standard is based on a code of practice released in 2003, and has been implemented by many publishers and libraries. Among the information tracked by COUNTER is:

- Number of successful title requests
- Turnaways (if the maximum allowed number of users of the service is exceeded)
- Total searches
- Total sessions.

COUNTER has some limitations; for example, there are problems using citations as a basis for the importance of a scientific paper.[59] Moreover, as Philip Davis has pointed out, measuring an article's popularity by the number of times it has been downloaded is a dubious measure of its importance, as it is possible for unscrupulous publishers to automate the download process. Hence the concept of a 'Usage Factor' is of questionable value:

> Article downloads cease to be a measure of readership and become a goal in-and-of-themselves, as publishers become transfixed on maximizing the number of documents they send out into the ether.[60]

Despite these drawbacks, COUNTER forms an excellent starting point for measuring journal usage. Although a COUNTER standard for books and reference works now exists (since 2006),[61] it is currently nowhere near as widely used as the corresponding journal tool. COUNTER for books tracks invaluable additional information, such as the number of successful section requests (a section is a subdivision of a book or reference work). For reference books, the section requests will usually be considerably larger than the number of title requests.

The data obtained from tracking usage can be surprising: they do not necessarily reveal a steady uninterrupted trend away from print towards using digital resources. Most valuably, even simple usage statistics such as COUNTER can show clearly which parts of a collection are most accessed. One US research project using COUNTER found that of the

4,700 full-text articles in EBSCO's Academic Search Premier, just 178 of them (4% of the total) accounted for more than 50% of all the articles downloaded.[62]

10.28 Other usage that can be tracked

Identifying where users come from before using a site, and where they go after using it, are common Web analytics tools worth knowing for any website, and the same questions should be asked of any content-delivery service. In addition, if the website has a public-facing component, a check should be done of search engine optimisation (SEO), to make sure the site's web pages are easily found by the major search engines.

SEO got a poor reputation in the early days of the Web, when site managers found their site achieved a higher ranking in the browsers if they repeated the same words several times in the meta tags at the top of the HTML source. Today, the engines are more sophisticated, so it is all the more important that everyone involved in the licensing chain is aware of what tools are being used to make the content retrievable.

Aggregators will keep detailed statistics on usage of individual titles (obviously), but should also have comparative information on usage by site type. Aggregators may be unwilling to release specific comparisons between individual institutions, but any problems with sensitivity of the data can be eliminated by providing quartile figures, for example, that usage at one institution is in the top quartile of institutions of a similar size.

A further tool is for the end-user institution to obtain usage information through surveys of end users. These surveys are easily set up using software such as Survey Monkey (*http://www.surveymonkey. com/*). Surveys of this kind can reveal information that cannot be retrieved from tracking usage, such as user requests for additional content. Analysing aggregator statistics can only ever reveal how the existing content is accessed. That information is of course extremely valuable, particularly for content within a reference title. For print publishers, information that was more than simply anecdotal about what entries in a reference work were consulted has proved enormously valuable; this is tracked simply by keeping a log of user searches, successful or not.

A check of searches carried out on the data enabled *The Hutchinson Encyclopedia* editors to find that 'Hitler' was the encyclopedia article that US high school students accessed most frequently. Still more intriguing, the log of user searches revealed the unsuccessful searches carried out by students. One of these, in fact the most frequently misspelled search, was several different (and incorrect) versions of the name 'Shakespeare'. This information was then channelled back and used for product development, so that subsequent editions of the Encyclopedia included a drop-down menu of entries that appeared as soon as the user keyed the first few characters; in other words, the 'Did You Mean?' feature implemented by the major search engines, discussed in section 8.5.8.

Measuring the total number of unique visitors to a site is of course a contentious measure, because, among other things, it can be used by advertisers to estimate how much the site is worth in terms of selling advertising slots. Any self-regulated system, such as publishers measuring their own figures, as happens currently on most sites, will be treated with suspicion by advertisers. Attempts to create an independent measurement, via an organisation called JICIMS, the Joint Industry Committee for Internet Measurement Systems, collapsed in December 2008 following a failure to agree who was to fund it.[63] Although this might be a problem for the industry as a whole, it need not prevent anyone involved with an individual site producing comparative figures, that is, comparing this month's usage with last month's, or with the same month last year.

10.29 Tracking unauthorised usage: plagiarism

Sometimes content is reused without attribution, not in its entirety, but in segments.

There are services that have been set up to check for copied text, particularly in student essays, and in published content such as journal articles. Both services are web-based comparison services, taking samples of content and searching the Web for similar text. Plagiarism in student essays is the goal of a unit set up at Northumbria University in the UK, the JISC Plagiarism Advisory Service (*www.jiscpas.ac.uk*). This service provides (among other services) a software package from iParadigms called Turnitin; higher-education institutions within JISC can submit essays for checking via this service. A version for publishers and for corporate use is called iThenticate (*www.ithenticate.com*). The software is similar, and is in fact produced by the same company. The software is

Figure 10.8 Software to identify copying: iThenticate

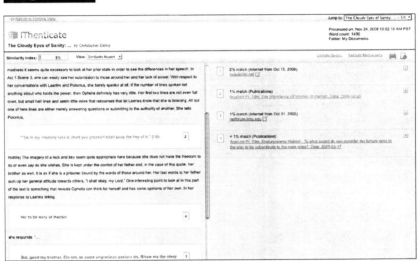

able to check not only Web-based content, but many password-protected sites such as academic journals. Similarly, CrossRef, the organisation founded by journal publishers in 1999 to manage linking across journals, has created a service called CrossCheck, which checks new journal articles for similarities with published material, based on DOIs (Digital Object Identifiers; see section 10.24).

Currently, such systems compare only text, not images or formulae, and display results in terms of percentage overlap. As iParadigms point out, such software checks for similarities, rather than plagiarism: plagiarism implies an intention to deceive, which software cannot determine. Hence, human intervention is required to establish if there is a motive behind the similarity. Nonetheless, services such as iThenticate (Figure 10.8) can be invaluable for content owners, as a means of detecting likely plagiarism of content.

Notes

1. *http://xml.coverpages.org/nitf.html*
2. SGML, the precursor of XML, insisted on a DTD, but in XML, the DTD is optional.
3. See, for example, 'Introduction to XML Schema', *http://www.w3schools.com/schema/schema_intro.asp*, for more about differences between a DTD and a schema.

4. *http://www.schematron.com/*
5. *http://unicode.org/*
6. *http://delicious.com/*
7. *http://dublincore.org/*
8. 'Raggett on HTML 4', Addison-Wesley 1998, *http://www.w3.org/People/ Raggett/book4/ch02.html*
9. To be precise, it was 'recommended', a term equivalent to 'published' for other standards organisations.
10. See *http://www.adobe.com/pdf/about/history/*
11. *http://www.adobe.com/products/acrobat/readstep2.html*
12. *http://www.microsoft.com/mspress/findabook/list/series_gy.aspx*
13. *http://www.lightningsource.com/*
14. *http://www.docbook.org*
15. *http://www.tei-c.org/*
16. There is more about DocBook at the Oasis site: *http://www.oasis-open. org/docbook/intro.shtml*
17. See 'NLM DTD Resources' at *http://www.inera.com/nlmresources.shtml*
18. At *http://dtd.nlm.nih.gov/*
19. See *http://xml.coverpages.org/dita.html/*
20. *http://www.quark.com/*
21. *http://www.adobe.com/products/indesign/*
22. *http://www.editeur.org/onix.html*
23. *http://www.editeur.org/*
24. *http://www.bic.org.uk*
25. *http://www.bisg.org/*
26. *http://www.editeur.org/onix_licensing.html*
27. See *http://www.w3schools.com/rss/rss_intro.asp*
28. See 'What is RSS?', *http://www.xml.com/pub/a/2002/12/18/dive-into-xml.html*
29. See *http://www.atomenabled.org/*
30. *http://www.applian.com/replay-av/*
31. See, for example, *http://www.mcps-prs-alliance.co.uk/playingbroadcastingonline/ online/Podcasting/Pages/podcasting.aspx*
32. *http://www.fictionwise.com/help/readingDevicesFAQ.htm*
33. 'International Adoption of EPUB e-book Standard to be Presented at Frankfurt Book Fair', *International Business Times*, 6 October 2008.
34. *http://www.lexcycle.com/*
35. *http://www.mobipocket.com/*
36. See *http://www.publishers.org/main/AboutAAP/DivisionsCommittees/about_ Comm_Roster_OnlinePiracy.htm*
37. See *http://www.eis.com.au/*
38. 'Microsoft, Adobe squabble over PDF', CNET News, 2 June 2006, *http://news.cnet.com/2100-1012_3-6079320.html*
39. For example, LockLizard (*http://www.locklizard.com*)
40. See 'iTunes: How Copyright, Contract and Technology Shape the Business of Digital Media – a Case Study', Harvard Law School, 2004 (*http://cyber. law.harvard.edu/media/uploads/81/iTunesWhitePaper0604.pdf*)
41. See 'Apple makes money on iTunes', *Macworld* 24 April 2007, *http://www.macworld.co.uk/ipod-itunes/news/index.cfm?newsid= 17845&pagtype=allchandate*

42. See *http://www.apple.com/support/itunes/store/authorization/*

43. 'Apple agrees to variable pricing on iTunes', *Financial Times*, 7 January 2009.

44. See speech by US Assistant Attorney General Thomas Barnett on the history of iTunes, George Mason University, September 2006, *http://techliberation. com/2006/09/14/barnett-butchers-itunes-history/*

45. See Sonia Katyal, 'A Legal malpractice claim by mp3.com', *FindLaw*, 7 February, 2002 (*http://writ.news.findlaw.com/commentary/20020207_ katyal.html*)

46. See *https://www.mobipocket.com/ebookbase/en/Homepage/pub_info.asp*

47. *www.audible.com*

48. From the ACAP website FAQ, *http://www.the-acap.org/FAQs.aspx#FAQ19*

49. For example, Ian Douglas, 'ACAP shoots back', Telegraph.co.uk, 23 January 2008 (*http://blogs.telegraph.co.uk/ian_douglas/blog/2008/01/23/ acap_shoots_back*)

50. See *http://www.ameinfo.com/content/*

51. For more about Indecs, see *http://www.doi.org/topics/indecs-rdd-white- paper-may02.pdf*

52. For more about CrossRef see Pentz, Ed (2004) 'CrossRef and DOIs: New Developments', *LIBER Quarterly* 14:1, *http://liber.library.uu.nl/publish/issues/ 2004-1/index.html?000063*

53. *http://www.doi.org/overview/080625DOI-ELIS-Paskin.pdf*

54. Tomkin, Emma (2008) 'Persistent Identifiers: Considering the Options', *Ariadne* 56 (*http://www.ariadne.ac.uk/issue56/tonkin/*)

55. Oren, Beit-Arie, *et al.* (2001) 'Linking to the Appropriate Copy', *D-Lib Magazine*, September (*http://www.dlib.org/dlib/september01/caplan/ 09caplan.html*)

56. 'Studios sue Australian ISP over video piracy', *cnet news*, 20 November 2008.

57. See, for example, 'Blu-ray DRM defeated', *The Register*, 23 January 2007 (*http://www.theregister.co.uk/2007/01/23/blu-ray_drm_cracked/*)

58. For more about COUNTER, see *http://www.projectcounter.org/about.html*

59. See, for example, Garfield, Eugene and Welljams-Dorof, Alfred (1992) 'Citation Data: their use as quantitive indicators for science and technology evaluation and policy-making', *Science & Public Policy*, 19:5, 321–327.

60. Davis, Philip (2008) 'The Article Download Game', *Society for Scholarly Publishing blog*, 27 October, *http://scholarlykitchen.sspnet.org/2008/10/27/ article-download-gaming/*

61. *http://www.projectcounter.org/cop_books_ref.html*

62. 'Aggregated Interdisciplinary Databases and the Needs of Undergraduate Researchers' (Barbara Fister, Julie Gilbert, Amy Fry) *portal: Libraries and the Academy* (July 2008) *http://homepages.gac.edu/~fister/aggregated databases.pdf*

63. 'Online Audience gauge fails', *Financial Times*, 6 December 2008.

11

Developments in content licensing: recommendations

This final chapter looks at some of the areas where the content licensing market is changing most rapidly. As the market develops, these are the areas where a different perspective or changed functionality will increasingly appear, or will be expected by users. By way of a conclusion, the chapter ends with recommendations summarising the main strands of the book for each of the agents involved in the licensing chain.

11.1 Changing attitudes to content: from reverence to disdain

Digital content licensing has played a share in the huge increase in the quantity of information available during the last 25 years or so. *Encyclopedia Britannica* was considered a large encyclopedia with 50,000 entries, yet today Wikipedia has over two million, and is still growing. One consequence of that explosion of information is a change in attitudes towards content, from reverence to (almost) disdain.

Consider, for example, the vast increase in the number of TV channels available in most homes, as a result of paid subscription services or free services in the UK such as Freeview. Paradoxically, users respond to a wider choice by becoming more discriminating – they may even watch less. The same attitude can be seen towards many different types of content – not just TV channels, leisure, but for business and for educational contexts as well. Users' expectations have grown as content has proliferated; they expect more from the content, they evaluate it more critically and they are increasingly dissatisfied if they cannot find content in a reasonable time.

One example of that difference is attitudes to content retrieval. The dramatic growth of scientific research in the twentieth century is well known. One of the abstracting journals mentioned in this book (see section 2.3) is *Chemical Abstracts*. In its first year of publication, it contained 12,000 abstracts of articles; in 2006, it contained one million.[1] Such a growth in scientific publishing was not initially matched by a corresponding development in information retrieval techniques. Literature searches, the technique of locating relevant research content, date back to the earliest abstract services; for example, *Chemical Abstracts* was founded in January 1907 as a series of handwritten entries by volunteers, but the majority of abstracting services started after 1945. By 1960, abstracting services were well established in all the major scientific disciplines. Nonetheless, when literature searches were carried out, they were cumbersome and slow; they had to be carried out by hand, using paper-based catalogues and indexes. Roger Summit, one of the founders of Dialog, recalls his experience of working at Lockheed in 1960:

> One of my first assignments was to investigate the use of the computer in information retrieval. A common statement around Lockheed at the time was that it is usually easier, cheaper, and faster to redo scientific research than to determine whether it has been done previously.[2]

Such a statement would be unthinkable today: the speed and quality of information retrieval has increased to match the explosive growth in content available.

A similar transformation has taken place in most areas of content retrieval. For example, finding general educational content would once have been done via a print-based library. Larger public libraries would contain a reference library. To resolve a question, a student would consult a number of encyclopedias (if the library was a reasonable size) or a single encyclopedia (if the library was small). Today there are more reference sources, and often higher-quality reference sources, available at the user's desktop. Even the smallest public library now typically has access to a range of online reference resources that it could never have afforded in print form.

Not only have secondary reference sources increased, but primary sources (journal articles, core texts and historical documents) have become increasingly available.

All students, even at school, now have access to, and can compare, primary sources in digital form. Information retrieval has developed from being a field exclusively for specialists to something we all do every day: we are all information specialists now. By providing content more readily, in a more accessible and searchable form, the content licensing industry has participated in a transformation of attitudes to content. The increased availability of content makes users more, not less, demanding when they access it and make use of it. Nonetheless, although people complain that Wikipedia is unreliable, they continue to use it because it is convenient.

One recommendation for anyone involved in content licensing is to provide the tools for comparison and for evaluation alongside the increased range of content that is available. The skill of evaluating information from a number of sources is one that is increasingly required today when dealing with content. It is far healthier to approach content with a critical eye than to unthinkingly assume that a resource is correct. This is partly a matter of teaching information skills, but can also be achieved by providing multiple sources, and means of navigating simply from one resource to another.

11.2 From paid to free content?

During the short history of digital licensing, opinions have shifted considerably about the best financial model: should content be free or paid? Most content-based sites tend to be either free or paid, but a few sites that have attempted to change their status from one to the other. More typically, content owners, even when they experiment with both models, attempt to keep them very clearly separate. Thus, in 2007, Elsevier launched a free portal for cancer doctors, *www.oncologystat.com*, funded entirely by advertising revenue, but this remains quite separate from its paid medical and scientific content sites.

One high-profile example of a paid service becoming freely accessible is the *New York Times*. Subscriptions were introduced for some of the columns on the online site in 2005, at a price of $49.95 per year. At that time, web-based advertising only contributed an insignificant proportion of the newspaper's revenue (2–3%).[3] By 2007, advertising revenues had grown dramatically, and the NYTimes.com site became free again. Nonetheless, it is by no means certain that the growth in online revenue from advertising can compensate for the loss in revenue from paid subscriptions. An article in the *Financial Times* Lex column estimated that the *New York Times* would need advertising revenue around four times higher than present levels to compensate for the loss of print revenues, if the paper were to switch to an online-only advert-funded model, even allowing for the substantial savings by not having to pay for printing, paper and distribution.[4] The issue with print-based newspapers is of course not simply free versus paid, but a paid print model versus a free online model; but in each case a business case has to be established.

The *Wall Street Journal* is one of the best-known case studies of how to make money from paid content: with around one million subscribers at $99 per annual web-only subscription, this looked like good business.[5] When Rupert Murdoch acquired the newspaper late in 2007, there was considerable speculation that the online site would become free of charge, although that has not happened. Nonetheless, the *WSJ* is enlarging its free site and attempting to attract more users via Google searching.

Finally, the *Financial Times* has, like the *Wall Street Journal*, extended its online content available free to users. After some years providing a tightly controlled subscription-only access to most of the articles, the *FT* switched in 2007 to making more articles free: the first 30 stories accessed in any month are free of charge, but beyond that subscriptions are available at £99 or £199 for enhanced content. Thus, occasional users have more free access to the content.

These examples show there is no single answer to the free versus paid debate, even within a single market, such as that of national newspapers. Several different models may coexist at the same time, with some paid services experimenting with free content, alongside entirely new services with no payment. In many markets, a new initiative such as Facebook may facilitate content creation without (currently) charging users to hold and to publish this content; again, there is no guarantee that this is a sustainable model in the long-term. The recommendation here is not to slavishly follow other players in the market and to assume their model is the only possible one.

An example of a different model using content licensing was described as 'reverse syndication'. In December 2008 the news agency Thomson Reuters began offering newswire content to newspapers free of charge, in return for a proportion of online advertising revenue.[6] The revenue-sharing initiative was an interesting response to many newspapers' difficulties in generating sufficient online revenue to pay for their news-gathering.

11.3 Changing business models in licensing: disintermediation

One trend in content licensing is towards disintermediation, the practice of eliminating links in the business chain, based on the belief that owning the delivery mechanism may be more beneficial than licensing via an aggregator. Traditionally, licensed content will have followed the path: author to publisher, to aggregator and finally to end user. But there is no reason why authors could not license content direct to end users, as is already happening with some audio and video sites (see section 4.6). Similarly, there is no reason why authors should not sell content direct to readers; there is, for example, EPIC, the Electronically Published Internet Collection,[7] a US-based group of self-published authors, with an online bookstore. Similarly, the site YouPublish[8] enables authors to publish their own content, sharing revenue from the sale on a 50:50 basis. The site also enables grouping chapters and other content items together. There is little difference between the business model for these self-publishing sites for text and a site like IstockPhoto (see section 4.8).

Another interesting example of publishing without any intermediary is enotes.[9] This service for students provides a mixture of licensed content from educational publishers such as Salem and Columbia University Press with content generated by enotes themselves; it comprises revision notes and sample question answers, for a one-time payment or by subscription. There is also a free question and answer site where users can post and respond to exam questions.

While sites such as these have a negligible significance in the wider market, there are examples of much bigger-scale paid sites moving to capture a larger share of total revenue. Thus, the *Financial Times*, around the same time as it increased its free content (see above), also started withdrawing its content from major online databases, requiring users to subscribe direct to the newspaper.[10] This corresponds to the practice of book publishers moving from licensing their content via third parties to creating their own portal (see section 6.8.1). Such a strategy may be perfectly sensible, as long as the content (as is the case with the *FT*) is of unique value – that is, not easily substitutable.

11.4 Rethinking business models for video and audio content

Having the legal right to content is not the same thing as being able to collect rights payments. Instead of attempting to stop the tide of illegal sharing, some recent deals for video and audio content have looked at the problem in a different way and come up with a win/win scenario for both aggregator and content owner.

Film and audio clips are copied in large numbers on the Web. Much of this takes place on peer-to-peer sharing sites, but illegal sharing of copyright content also takes place on many of the best-known social networking sites such as MySpace (*www.myspace.com*; owned by News Corporation) and YouTube (*www.youtube.com*; owned by Google). Both these sites contain huge numbers of copyright video and audio clips, posted by users. Not surprisingly, many TV and film companies have been unhappy with this infringement. YouTube was sued for $1bn by Viacom in March 2007, claiming that Google was guilty of 'massive intentional copyright infringement' by allowing Viacom video clips to be uploaded to YouTube.[11]

However, rather than try to remove the vast number of copyrighted TV shows from its service, MySpace agreed a deal with Viacom MTV Network in November 2008 to share revenue from such activity. Using software from a video technology provider, Auditude,[12] the content owners will be able to attach adverts alongside their own programmes when they appear on MySpace, with revenue shared between MySpace and the content owner. This represents a significant step forward for content licensing: end users can still post videos on social networking sites (which they would continue to do anyway), but the content owner now obtains a share of the reward.

A similar innovation, this time between YouTube and MGM, also in November 2008, has been to create a video-on-demand service by a partnership between the studio and YouTube, with a similar business model: videos will be free to download but will include advertising, with revenue shared between the partners.[13]

11.5 Web radio as a means of combating piracy

One great advantage of content licensing is the ability to create new market opportunities rapidly. For example, while collections of licensed audio along the lines of iPod are familiar, there are also opportunities for radio-style Internet broadcasting operations. Instead of downloading individual tracks, users subscribe to a service that plays a selection of music to the user. Naxos Web Radio has launched an operation of this kind for classical music, while Spotify, a Swedish-founded online radio service, offers a similar system for pop music.[14] The audio is streamed to the user, and downloading and copying music is not permitted. In addition to a paid service, Spotify offers a free, advertising-backed operation, which is an interesting attempt to provide an appealing alternative to downloading pirate tracks. However, it is revealing that it took Spotify two years to conclude deals with the major record labels to gain permission to use their tracks, before the service could be launched.

11.6 Moving into adjacent business territories

A further type of disintermediation is to take on additional roles in the content-delivery chain. The model described in this book of content owner, aggregator and institutional provider, all existing separately, is not carved in stone. There is no reason why an institution cannot provide a custom collection of resources, both free and paid – in other words, to act as its own aggregator. After all, this is already happening with most institutions licensing a range of content, and which can provide a range of content to suit more than one level.

Thus, for example, in 2007 the theology faculty at Oxford University provided for its students a range of content, from introductory to highly specialised, including:

- *Oxford Reference Online.*
- *The Bible in English* (ProQuest) – 21 different English translations.
- *Patrologia Latina* (ProQuest).
- *Thesaurus Linguae Graecae* (University of California at Irvine) – all the extant 89 million words of ancient Greek.

To create and manage such a subject-specific gateway is in effect a publishing role, and transforms the role of the information professional, because decisions of presentation, coverage and level are all publishing decisions. Creating and managing an institutional repository, which typically combines a wide range of content, is a similar task; in fact, an institution-based gateway and institutional repository could work well together, combining intellectual property from within the institution with third-party content (see open access, section 5.11).

11.7 Creating additional resources around the content

For many print publishers, the first step to digital delivery was to create a website to accompany the title or series. This is common in children's publishing, where pages from the Puffin website, for example, are devoted to individual writers such as Roald Dahl. In non-fiction and textbook publishing, the publisher may provide activities alongside the printed book, for example, a website providing activities for students using the Heinemann African Writers series (*http://www.africanwriters.com/*). Over time, the distinction between the ancillary material and the content itself can become blurred. For example, websites have none of the space restrictions that a printed book or magazine has, so they can contain additional content from the original resource. We saw (see section 7.6.6) how Safari Books Online is now creating additional content specifically for its portal, without any print original.

11.8 Finding additional markets for content

Once content has been licensed, it can be a simple matter to create further licensing deals in other markets. The limitations on licensing are often simply finding markets with self-contained segments (to ensure there is no leak from existing markets), so that content can be licensed into each market separately. One way of achieving such additional sales is to identify potential purchasers via an established trade show or other forum at which content can be bought and sold (see section 5.1).

Dictionaries provide exceptional opportunities for content licensing, given that collections of words, and word definitions, or equivalent words in other languages, can be used in so many different licensed outputs. Some places where dictionary content can be found are:

- Hand-held electronic devices such as crossword and word-game dictionaries (a well-known vendor is Franklin Electronic Publishers) that need a list of English words in all their morphological forms.
- Spell-checking tools for word-processing software.
- Dictionaries for Web search engine software that uses digital dictionaries for checking search terms.
- Dictionaries for e-book readers.

Whenever a new content delivery channel is created, there is usually an opportunity for a new licensing sale. For example, currently the BBC iPlayer (see section 4.12) shows only BBC content, but as the iPlayer has demonstrated so effectively that a strong market exists for delivering already broadcast content at a time of the user's choosing, there is a good opportunity to provide other licensed content on this or on an equivalent platform.

11.8.1 Case study: Licensing to new markets

Sometimes the markets for content can be completely unanticipated. In 1973, when CD-ROM was still in its infancy, Sun Microsystems, who manufactured high-performance workstations and servers, were keen to move all their system documentation and training manuals onto CD-ROM. As often happens when there is a change in technology, the manufacturer had some difficulty in persuading customers that the new technology provided an advantage over the existing print media: after all, these customers had already purchased print copies of the documentation, and had no knowledge of the power of full-text indexing for technical documentation. Sun were seeking some means of demonstrating the capacity and capability of CD-ROM players, and licensed a complete illustrated encyclopedia on CD-ROM, which they then gave away free of charge to every Sun customer who purchased a CD drive with their workstation. In this way, the customers saw the capability of CD-ROM – and the publisher made a sale that was completely unanticipated.

11.9 Regularly updated content: from product to service

Content licensing need not be a once and for all sale, and there are sound business advantages from a repeated sale rather than a single transaction. Journals, of course, are typically sold by subscription, but a series of books can be sold in the same way if they have a regular publication cycle; for example, a subscription to a book series could include every new title published in that series for the coming 12 months.

Content such as yearbooks, directories and subject dictionaries lends itself to subscription sale because it requires regular updating. Because digital publication has no plant costs associated with printing, it is very cost-effective to update the content and then to resupply the entire work, thereby transforming a product sale to a service sale. It is usually more cost-effective to resupply the entire content than to supply individual changes to be inserted into the existing content, as individual changes would require manual intervention, while the complete content delivery should be an entirely automatic process.

11.10 Enhanced linking

We have already seen content licensing opportunities enhanced by adding metadata (see section 4.5.1). In the future, better coded content, which provides more opportunities for interoperability, will be the most successful in the market. This additional metadata could be added by hand or by an automated process.

There are many examples of automatic linking applied to content. For example, a content-based website such as a repository of newspaper articles will often provide automatic links from one article to another, typically by using the terms from an article title as search terms to create a list of hits and display these as related articles.

However, it does not take long to discover the limitations of linking using current Web technology: take, for example, Google Scholar (described in section 8.2.2), which displays additional information for each book, by carrying out searches on the book contents. Unfortunately, much of this information proves to be incorrect. A search for Ronald Syme's *The Roman Revolution* (1939) (Figure 11.1) retrieves the book and provides a table of contents and what appears to be the bulk of the text, but the publication date is given as 2002; this is probably the date of the most recent printing. There is even a map of places mentioned in the book; but the locations shown on the map are unlikely to be the ones

Figure 11.1 Google Scholar: map of locations mentioned in Syme's *The Roman Revolution*

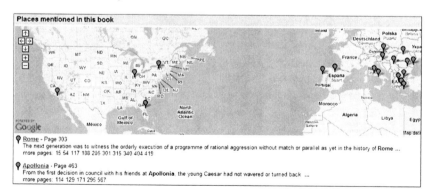

referred to by an author on Classical Rome – instead, they are places of the same name in the US, for example Placentia, CA, and Manlius, NY, caused by automatic (but erroneous) linking of proper names in the text to places of the same name in an atlas.

One of the reasons for Google Scholar's limited success is HTML itself. As a language, HTML is limited by its very poor metadata: it provides only one-way links, for example, and links to URLs are notorious for failing because URLs change so frequently. This is why such developments as DOIs and persistent identifiers were established (see section 10.24).

To understand what can be achieved by better linking of content requires some understanding of recent developments in how links are made, and in particular the move towards knowledge-based, or semantic, linking. Some examples of better linking are already visible, for example DBpedia (*http://dbpedia.org*), which is a reshaping of Wikipedia content into a series of machine-readable statements (e.g. that Paris is the capital of France); DBpedia tags all 200,000+ Wikipedia biographies and their dates, and converts them to machine-readable content objects that can be retrieved via a link and displayed in a web page. In this way, a reference to a famous person can have such background information as place of birth, and dates of birth and death, added automatically.

Microsoft attempted something similar with its Smart Tags initiative included in Office products since 2002[15] and in trial versions of Internet Explorer 6 (although withdrawn from IE before its final release[16]). Using Smart Tags, a document can be tagged so that text strings, such as people's names or a product title, can be associated with an action, for example a link to a website with information about that person or product. These tags (and links) are created using XML. Smart Tags were criticised because the links created could point users to sites of Microsoft's choosing. Nonetheless, many content sites would benefit from the provision of more powerful linking mechanisms to and from content.

11.11 Searching across resources

Another welcome development that enhances the value of licensed content is federated searching (see section 8.6) across the entire holdings of an institution, for example across both books and journals, or across both third-party databases and the institutional repository. By ensuring that content provides tools that enable such federated searching, its use can be considerably increased.

11.12 Better usage information

Usage tracking was described in section 10.25. This is an area where several additional items of information would be invaluable to determine not only what content is accessed, but the use made of that content. The types of questions that anyone in the licensing process would want to ask are:

- For what purpose specific items of content are being used.
- Whether the user market can be subdivided in any way. (For example, is it possible to distinguish school users from users in further education? Such knowledge is of enormous value to the licensor and to the aggregator.)
- Whether or not the information retrieved fulfilled the required purpose.
- If the user was not satisfied, where they subsequently obtained the information they wanted.

Armed with this kind of information, content licensing could become far more precise in meeting user needs.

11.13 Recommendations for content licensing

To conclude this book, here are a few recommendations for each of the players in the content-licensing market: the content owner or publisher, the aggregator and the information professional. Most of these recommendations summarise points from the earlier chapters, so if any of the points is not clear, the corresponding section of the main text should have more background details about the reasoning behind them.

11.14 Recommendations for publishers

For publishers who have not yet licensed their content, begin by licensing some content via an aggregator. Make use of the feedback to create new revenue streams by licensing content in digital form to a variety of aggregators. Having established the viability of the channel, the recommendations for next steps are:

1. Continue licensing with multiple aggregators. Aim to obtain short-term revenue and gain market knowledge to maximise longer-term revenue from understanding how to make electronic sales.

2. Always go for non-exclusive deals, unless there are exceptional conditions (such as working with the developer of a new delivery platform).

3. Ensure all new author contracts have a clear statement of electronic rights available for sale by the publisher.

4. Maximise exposure for titles by having them indexed via Google Print, and with selected contents available for preview both there and in Amazon.

5. After deals have been in place for a period, review online revenue by channel and by aggregator. Identify possible gaps where a known group of users is not reached. Compare profitability with other content owners in a similar market.

6. In the long term, consider the possibility of creating a publisher-based portal and/or bookstore, where content can be sold direct.

7. Avoid becoming locked into the proprietary coding of one aggregator – use widely implemented versions of XML such as DocBook. Try, if possible, to retain a digital copy of content captured by the aggregator.

8. Continue to review the online business models after a service has been launched. There is no guarantee the model will continue to be viable and may not be replaced by a different model entirely, such as a major shift from paid to free advertising-based content.

9. Test and ensure the security of licensed content. Does whatever delivery system is in use ensure the material is not accessed and retrieved without permission?

11.15 Recommendations for information professionals

Information professionals in libraries have a major challenge when licensing content. Libraries do not have a track record of promoting new books – they are discovered by the users. But many library users have little idea of the digital resources held by their library; this is true both of public and of academic libraries. So in addition to their other responsibilities, the information professional needs to become a marketing manager for the digital repository.

1. Success is not just signing a licensing agreement but ensuring that the licensed content meets user needs and serves a useful purpose.

Always monitor usage, by collection, and by title. Identify little-used titles that can be dropped from a collection when renegotiating a licence.

2. Try to get hold of other usage data such as searches made (successful and unsuccessful), use of indexes and types of content accessed. Combine these results with surveys of users.

3. Provide more integrated access to multiple collections: not just 'single-sign-on' but also federated searching across a wide range of content, assembled at the information repository.

4. Set up trials of new licensed content, if possible, before committing to a licence deal. Measure the results and then make a longer-term commitment if usage levels warrant it.

5. Make buying deals as part of a consortium wherever possible.

6. Look for aggregators that demonstrate some thinking behind the selection of titles, rather than simply selecting the aggregator with the biggest list.

7. Keep users informed about content updates and enhancements. An RSS feed, newsletter or blog can be a powerful incentive to encourage users to visit (or to return to) the site. For many collections, new titles are added without end users being aware that the content has changed at all.

8. Provide a feedback mechanism so that users can request additional titles or services. Both blogs and newsletters can also provide channels for user feedback.

9. Interaction between users, with moderation where appropriate, can be a valuable help for new users.

10. Look for collections with customisable contents, to ensure there is no duplication of titles from one aggregator to another.

11.16 Recommendations for aggregators and platform providers

1. Promote the service via email and/or news items on the home screen.

2. Survey users to find out how (and if) they use the service.

3. Rather than licensing the largest number of titles, use feedback and advisors to ensure that the most relevant content is being licensed.

4. Ensure differentiation from other aggregators by refining indexing and metadata tools, and linking to other titles, in response to user preferences.

5. Value can be added by combining more than one type of content. There is no need for an aggregated service to contain simply audio, or video, or book text. Some of the most innovative aggregation sites offer a combination of several types, for example Safari Books Online (see section 7.6.5).

6. Ensure your services provide interface tools so that libraries using metasearch engines can search your content.

7. Consider adding additional descriptive information, for example 'introductory', or 'advanced', to assist users in selecting content.

11.17 Recommendations for everyone involved in content licensing

1. Content licensing is a part of the Web publishing process, which is driven inexorably to simpler interfaces and faster retrieval. For content licensing to be successful, content has to be easily found, easy to open or to download and easy to use. The technical developments that made content licensing possible in the first place are at the same time its greatest risk, as hardware costs are inevitably driven downwards, and software capability – the performance of software for a given price – is inevitably driven up. This is not a market where it is possible to sit back and assume that nothing much is happening on the technical front. New formats, new platforms and new tools are continually developed, requiring a rapid response to prevent losing market share. Content licensing, in other words, is an area where it is vital to keep up to date with the market, whether by joining an email list, or subscribing to a blog or to an e-journal (see the Further Reading section for some suggestions).

2. Look at content licensing in several different markets; there is often a benefit in a cross-sector approach. Academic, commercial and educational licensing all demonstrate specific innovations that can often be deployed in a different sector. Are there innovations that could be successfully transferred from those markets? New developments may (and frequently do) appear from unexpected markets.

3. By a related process, whether content is accessed free or by paid access, the provision of content becomes progressively commoditised as more content becomes available. Content that had a safe sale with few competitors in print format suddenly becomes open to competition from other countries, other sectors and other industries, simply because the tools for retrieval are so powerful. This process cannot be avoided, but in future, the most successful content licensing will add value to the content. This could be done by providing enhanced linking, metadata and functionality that takes advantage of Web-based publishing.

4. Wherever possible, identify ways in which licensed content can be interoperable with freely available content; identify ways of working with the major search engines to index and to identify content.

5. Do not ignore the part that accident plays in business development. Mobile phone companies had no idea that text messaging would become so ubiquitous. Nobody has perfect insight into the future development of the content licensing business; this is not surprising, given that the development of the licensing industry has not been a steady one, but rather a story of peaks and troughs. Ensure your involvement in content licensing enables you to take advantage of the next development, accidental or intended, which impacts on the content licensing market.

Notes

1. 'CAS History Milestones', *http://www.cas.org/aboutcas/cas100/annivhistory.html*

2. 'Reflections on the Beginnings of Dialog', Roger Summit, *http://support.dialog.com/publications/chronolog/200206/1020628.shtml*

3. See 'NYTimes.com to offer subscription service', *New York Times*, 17 May 2005.

4. *Financial Times* Lex Column, 12 December 2008.

5. 'WSJ.com hits one million subscribers' Reuters, 4 November 2007 (*http://www.reuters.com/article/companyNewsAndPR/idUSN0420627120071104*)

6. 'Reuters, Politico to share political news coverage' Reuters.com, 14 December 2008.

7. *www.epicauthors.com*

8. *www.youpublish.com*

9. *http://www.enotes.com/*

10. 'FT.com Seeks Subs by Asking Factiva Users to buy new Licence', PaidContent.org.uk, 19 December 2007 (*http://www.paidcontent.co.uk/entry/419-ftcom-seeks-subs-by-asking-factiva-users-to-buy-new-license/*)

11. 'Our Case Against YouTube', *Washington Post*, 24 March 2007.
12. *http://www.auditude.com*
13. 'Full-length MGM films on YouTube', BBC News, 10 November 2008, *http://news.bbc.co.uk/1/hi/technology/7720918.stm*
14. See, for example, 'Spotify looks to scupper digital pirates', *Financial Times*, 2 March 2009.
15. See, for example, About Smart Tags, *http://office.microsoft.com/en-gb/word/HP030833041033.aspx*
16. 'Microsoft clips Windows XP Smart Tags', *cnet news*, 27 June 2001.

Glossary

Here is a list of some terms used in this book to describe content licensing.

ACAP (Automated Content Access Protocol) – a system by which intellectual property owners can disseminate a machine-readable version of information about the rights status of the information on a website to search engines.

aggregator – electronic equivalent of a distributor, a company that makes available content from a range of publishers.

'appropriate copy' problem – the task of directing a link to an article from a range of possible locations to the copy of that article to which the library has subscription access, rather than one for which an inter-library loan would be required.

archive copy – a permanent copy of a resource, which is not subject to expiry.

Athens – a UK-based authentication system providing access to protected services. Athens is used widely by higher- and further-education institutions. There is now a newer authentication system called Shibboleth (see below).

authentication – the process by which a user's identity is validated; for example, a student accessing a library online resource must first have his or her identity checked in some way.

boilerplate clause – a clause that is common to most contracts of a given type.

broadcast – the public dissemination of audio content, such as playing pre-recorded works in a concert hall, but also, less obviously, background music in a café.

click-through licence – the practice by which a user is deemed to have accepted the terms of use by the act of clicking to access the content, even if they have not explicitly read those terms.

codec – a software or hardware program that compresses or uncompresses moving images, typically to reduce the space required for storage. Codecs vary widely in their level of compression, interoperability and quality. Some codecs are 'lossy' (they throw away some of the original data), while others are 'lossless'.

collecting society – an organisation that collects royalty payments on behalf of copyright owners. Examples in the UK are ALCS and DACS; in the US, they include ASCAP and BMI.

content licensing – the practice of selling or buying the right to use intellectual property, today mainly in digital format.

copyright – the right to republish, replicate, distribute or perform content.

COUNTER – standards for the recording and reporting of online usage of content. A related project, SUSHI, is the initiative to enable the automatic harvesting of COUNTER usage statistics, without having to gather statistics from publishers individually.

CrossRef – organisation founded in 1999 by journal publishers to manage the technology of linking articles to each other. It uses DOIs (see below) to label the articles.

disintermediation – the practice of eliminating links in the business chain between content owners and end users.

DITA (Darwin Information Typing Architecture) – an XML-based standard for creating help and technical documentation content.

Digital online graphic (dog) or watermark – an icon or symbol in the corner of moving image screen that identifies the source of the clip, e.g. 'Sky'.

DOI (Digital Object Identifier) – a link to an object, such as a journal article, book or picture, using a unique unchanging identification code. This code points to a look-up table, which then points to the object's URL. In this way, DOIs solve the problem of links to URLs becoming out of date when the URL address changes, as the DOI remains the same at all times.

DRM (Digital Rights Management) – any access control mechanism that is used to monitor or to limit access to content.

Dublin Core – a set of metadata terms for describing content objects, designed to aid searching and retrieval.

e-book – a book in digital form, often the electronic version of a print publication. E-books may be read on a desktop PC, or on a handheld device such as an e-book reader.

EXIF (exchangeable image file format) – a metadata format for digital photographs.

faceted search – the organisation of content by multiple hierarchical categories, each of them searchable. Faceted searching is very suitable for web-based retrieval.

fair use – legal term describing the use made of a copyright work for purposes other than originally intended, e.g. for criticism or for review.

federated search – simultaneous search of several collections of content.

feed – electronic distribution of short sections of content, usually text or images.

feed reader – a software program on a user's PC that collects RSS and other feeds for viewing.

folksonomy – an informal user-generated collection of tags describing a collection of content.

grade-one content – content of such high value that it cannot easily be substituted.

HTML – the computer language used to describe web pages. It is not entirely browser-independent. Many websites today use XHTML, a more structured version of HTML.

Indecs – European-Commission-funded project from 1998 that created an industry-wide Rights Data Dictionary.

indemnity – in a contract, acceptance of financial responsibility as a result of an action or error by the other party.

information architecture – the technique of designing and managing classification to facilitate access.

intellectual property – content that has an owner (which is pretty much all content), and so that can be bought and sold.

interoperability – the capability for a software program to run on multiple platforms, hence used to describe any content or service that works on multiple formats or systems.

IP – abbreviation for intellectual property.

IP address – a unique number that identifies a computer. All computers have an IP address.

ISO (International Organization for Standardization) – a worldwide standards organisation based in Geneva. It is responsible for SGML and related standards.

JISC (Joint Information Systems Committee) – UK government-funded body that supports the use of IT in higher and further education.

JISC Collections – offshoot of JISC that licenses content for UK education.

JSTOR – US not-for-profit organisation that provides an online collection of journal articles for the education community.

keyword – any word in the content.

keywords in context – the practice of many search engines to show the full sentence or phrase in which a hit appears. This may be configurable by the user, or predetermined, e.g. five words either side of the hit.

licence (UK), license (US) – permission to read, perform or access a specific piece of content.

licensee – the person or company making use of the content (typically by passing it on to end users).

licensor – the person or company owning the rights to the content. An aggregator typically acts as a licensor, having in turn licensed rights to the content from the content owner, or from another licensor.

MARC (machine-readable cataloguing) – a system for labelling bibliographic records for machine-based handling.

market extension – creating new markets for content where none existed before. Examples include selling individual journal articles by download direct to end-users.

metadata – data about data, in other words a definition or description of data. For example, the data of a newspaper article comprise the headline and story, while the article metadata include the author, the publication date and the title of the newspaper in which the article appeared.

moderation – applying an editorial check to content before it is published.

moiré effect – distortion caused during scanning by one pattern being superimposed on another. It is often seen when a scanned image is rescanned, and the two patterns of dots interfere with each other to produce an unintended pattern.

namespace – a way of disambiguating elements and attributes that might have different meanings or functions in different contexts. Namespaces are defined using URIs (see below).

ONIX (Online Information Exchange) – an XML-based standard for communicating book metadata.

ontology – a classification of an area of knowledge, for example into classes, attributes and relationships.

Open Archive Initiative (OAI) – body that promotes free exchange of material in academic environments, including theses, pre-publication research articles and other content.

orphan work – material that may be in copyright, but for which the author cannot be identified or located.

optical character recognition (OCR) – a machine-based process for converting written (printed or handwritten) text to digital form using a scanner.

parse – to check that an XML document is well-formed, that is, that it complies with the rules of XML, for example that there is an end tag for every start tag. Compare validation.

PDF (Portable Document Format) – a platform-independent file format for exchange of documents, so that they appear on the recipient's screen or printer exactly as they were originally published in print or Web form.

performing rights organisation – an association that collects rights payments on behalf of rights owners.

perpetual licence or perpetual access – a licence that allows access to the content even after termination of a contract between licensee and licensor.

podcast – an audio file delivered via a feed such as RSS.

portal – a site with a single point of access to a collection of content.

Portico – not-for-profit electronic archiving service, launched in 2005, provided by (among others) The Library of Congress and JSTOR. Portico provides a permanent archive of electronic scholarly journals.

production music or library music – music for which composer rights have been bought by the agency, so no further author royalty is payable.

RDF (Resource Description Framework) – a language for storing information (metadata) about websites, such as the copyright information in a news article.

scraping or harvesting – acquiring data by mechanical means from a website for the purpose of republishing it. This is typically done without the agreement of the content owner.

semantic link – a link where the element itself contains some meaning-based information, such as <great soccer player>David Beckham</great soccer player>.

severability – a clause that is legally distinct from others in a contract, so that if it proves to be unenforceable, the rest of the contract remains valid.

Shibboleth – a federated authentication system for access to protected content, based on open standards. It is widely used internationally.

SERU Initiative – an attempt to do away with contracts for specific deals and to work instead within a shared framework of expectations.

SGML (Standardised General Mark-up Language) – a platform-independent standard for tagging and structuring content so it can be transferred from one medium to another. SGML has been largely superseded by XML (see below), which is technically a subset of SGML. Like XML, SGML does not control the formatting of a document.

site licence – a licence that extends only to one physical location, usually defined as a single IP address. This is usually distinct from a network licence, which enables a licensee to provide content to several locations.

smartphone – a mobile phone with additional capabilities such as Internet access, enabling it to download content such as e-books.

social networking – a group of individuals who interact for a common purpose. Social networking is a fundamental component of Web 2.0.

stemming – the practice of searching for words by their main part without the endings, for example a search for 'branching' also retrieves hits for 'branched' and 'branches'.

stop word – a word that is not indexed because it is such a commonly used term in the language, for example 'and' or 'not'.

sublicence – in a content licensing contract, a further licence granted to the licensee (e.g. the publisher), who may for example be granted the right to authorise publication of the work in electronic form.

subscription – access to content for a fixed period of time.

subscription agent – someone who sells subscriptions to journals on behalf of a publisher, typically receiving a percentage of the revenue as a result.

term – the period of time for which an agreed contract remains in force.

URI (Uniform Resource Identifier) – an address for a document anywhere on the Internet, whether a website or a private location. A URI can be, for example, a piece of text, a sound clip or a web page. Thus a picture (picture.jpg) may have a full URI of *http://www.nowhere. ac.uk/picture.jpg*. URLs (see below) are one specific type of URI.

URL (Uniform Resource Locator) – a unique address that identifies a resource on the Internet, such as *http://www.google.com/*. Every website has its own URL.

validation – checking that a document conforms to a particular schema or DTD. Hence validation is more rigorous than parsing (see above).

verbatim rights – the right to reproduce the work in its entirety without editing or altering the content.

W3C – the World Wide Web Consortium, a member-based organisation that sets standards for the Web, including XML and XHTML. It was founded in 1994. All its standards (which it calls 'Recommendations') are distributed free of charge.

walled garden – a closed collection of content kept clearly distinct from other content areas, and often with restrictions on how it is accessed. Most paid content is provided as a walled garden, that is, entirely separate from the world of free searching provided by Google and the major search engines.

warranty – statement by one party in a contract that makes an assertion about something that party has done; for example, the licensor warrants that all permissions have been properly cleared.

Web 2.0 – loose term describing recent Web developments, including greater personalisation and collaboration tools such as social networking (see above).

work for hire – copyright work where the copyright is held not by the author or composer but by the organisation that employs or commissions him or her.

XHTML – a language that attempts to close the gap between HTML and XML. It resembles HTML but uses a more precise syntax. XHTML can be handled by XML tools such as a DTD.

XML – a non-proprietary, platform-independent way of coding and structuring content, used when transferring content from one device or platform to another. Content is coded using matching start and end tags such as <title>this</title>. All XML documents have to be well-formed, that is, they must follow the rules of XML syntax. In addition, if the document has a DTD or schema (and most do), then the document can be validated, that is, checked for compliance with that DTD or schema.

XSL (eXtensible Stylesheet Language) – a tool for converting XML documents to other formats, for example into HTML to produce web pages. It comprises three languages, XSLT, XSL-FO and XPath; XSLT is the most widely used.

Further reading

This guide is a brief selection of resources relevant to content licensing. Works listed in citation footnotes are not repeated here, unless relevant to further reading. There are many other sources of information available, far too many to list here; although an interdisciplinary subject such as content licensing has relatively few resources dedicated wholly to it, there are a vast number of resources that relate to one or more aspects of the topic. Moreover, the world of content licensing changes very rapidly, so it is sensible to subscribe to some of the relevant newsletters, mailing lists and e-journals listed here to keep up to date.

Books

Durrant, Fiona (2006) *Negotiating Licences for Digital Resources*. London: Facet Publishing.

Harris, Lesley Ellen (2002) *Licensing Digital Content: a practical guide for librarians*. American Library Association.

Kasdorf, William (ed.) (2003) *Columbia Guide to Digital Publishing*. New York: Columbia University Press. True to its principles, this title was output from a single source to both a print and an online version.

Lessig, Lawrence (2006) *Code Version 2.0*. New York: Basic Books.

Megginson, David (2005) *Imperfect XML*. New York: Addison-Wesley.

Owen, Lynette (2006) *Selling Rights*, 5th edition. London: Routledge. First published 1991.

Owen, Lynette (ed.) (2007) *Clark's Publishing Agreements: A Book of Precedents*, 7th edition. Haywards Heath: Tottel.

Pedley, Paul (2007) *Digital Copyright*, 2nd edition. London: Facet Publishing.

Stim, Richard (2007) *Getting Permission: How to license and clear copyrighted materials online and off*, 3rd edition. Nolo Publishing.

Thompson, John B (2005) *Books in the Digital Age: The Transformation of Academic and Higher Education Publishing in Britain and the United States*. London: Polity.

Websites

The Copyright Clearance Center (*www.copyright.com*) provides managed services to publishers and to businesses in the US.

Current Cites (*http://lists.webjunction.org/currentcites/*) – a freely available digest of abstracts of articles relevant to digital information professionals. *http://www.publaw.com/erights2.html* – an introductory guide for electronic clauses in contracts.

Keeping within the Law (*www.KWtL.co.uk*) – website from Facet Publishing, the publisher of the Chartered Institute of Librarians (CILIP), which contains a collection of material about information law.

Keep your copyrights (*http://keepyourcopyrights.org*) is a useful site created by legal academics at Columbia University Law School. It is designed for content owners to make most effective use of their content when licensing it. It includes a range of contract clauses, with comments as 'creator-friendly', or 'creator-unfriendly', or even 'incredibly overreaching'.

Licensing Models (*www.licensingmodels.com*) is a free website that provides some standard journal licence agreements that can be freely used or adapted.

PaidContent.org (*www.contentnext.com*) – an online publication sustained by advertising that provides information and updates on the commercial content licensing scene.

The Fairuse site at Stanford University Libraries (*http://fairuse.stanford.edu/*) has excellent links and discussion of US copyright law, including relevant case law.

Yale University Library, Licensing Digital Information: a resource for librarians (*http://www.library.yale.edu/~llicense/index.shtml*) – a valuable site, with lots of relevant and up-to-date information. Mainly useful for libraries.

The SPARC Open Access Newsletter (*http://www.earlham.edu/~peters/fos/*) is a guide to what is happening in the world of open access scholarship.

The Open Access Directory (*http://oad.simmons.edu/oadwiki/*) is a collectively produced wiki that provides information about open access.

The Canadian Virtual Museum has a useful Canadian Museum's Guide to Developing a Licensing Strategy at *http://www.chin.gc.ca/English/Intellectual_Property/Guide_Developing/index.html*, most of which is valid for collections of intellectual property anywhere.

A good way to keep up to date with digital rights management is to read the DRM Watch newsletter at *www.drmwatch.com*.

For museums and institutions, there is a comprehensive guide to creating and managing a digital content collection at the Canadian Heritage Information Network (CHIN) *http://www.chin.gc.ca/English/Digital_Content/*, including an impressive section devoted to gathering and interpreting usage statistics.

Journals

D-Lib magazine (*www.dlib.org*) is a free e-magazine published every other month, with articles of relevance to digital licensing. It is a non-profit initiative funded by an alliance of academic libraries and commercial companies.

EContent magazine (*http://www.econtentmag.com/*), published in print and online form, covers many aspects of digital content relating to content licensing. The publication is owned by the publishers of *Information Today* (see below).

Searcher magazine (*http://www.infotoday.com/searcher/*), although focused on information retrieval, is highly relevant to the content licensing world.

Ariadne (*http://www.ariadne.ac.uk/*) is a quarterly UK-based free electronic publication for information professionals in archives and libraries.

Information World Review (*http://www.iwr.co.uk/*), the most established periodical for content dissemination, but its coverage of content licensing is patchy.

Information Today (*http://www.infotoday.com/IT/default.asp*), the leading US weekly magazine for information professionals.

Groups and associations

ALPSP (Association of Learned and Professional Society Publishers) (*www.alpsp.org*), a UK-based association for smaller not-for-profit book and journal publishers. They have an online journal, and organise conferences and training.

The Association of Subscription Agents and Intermediaries (ASA) (*http://www.subscription-agents.org/*) is a UK-based trade association for companies who carry out subscription agency work. They have an annual conference.

LITA (The Library and Information Technology Association) (*http://www.lita.org*) publishes a peer-reviewed journal, *ITAL*, a review publication called *Technology Electronic Reviews* (*TER*) and has a useful website.

SIIA (The Software & Information Industry Association) (*www.siia.net*), a US-based trade association for the software and digital content industries, with some 800 member companies. They have a weekly newsletter, and carry out lobbying and anti-piracy campaigns, as well as annual awards for software and services.

UKeiG (UK Electronic Information Group), a UK-based association for information professionals. It provides training and has an e-journal, *Elucidate*. It has some useful factsheets downloadable free, usually from the UKeiG blog (*http://www.ukeig.org.uk/blog/*).

UKSG (UK Serials Group), a not-for-profit association for the academic journals market. They have a useful e-book about dealing with e-content, the *E-Resources Management Handbook* (*http://uksg. metapress.com/link.asp?id=6tuu9n7wfl18*), which is regularly updated.

Index